D1602296

Spy Catchers
of the U. S. Army
in the
War with Japan

(The Unfinished Story of
the Counter Intelligence Corps)

by

DUVAL A. EDWARDS

FIRST EDITION

RED APPLE PUBLISHING
P. O. Box 101
Gig Harbor WA 98335

Printed by Gorham Printing
Rochester, Washington 98579

ISBN: 1-880222-14-0

Library of Congress Catalog Card Number: 93-87777

To
the Special Agents
and Dedicated Officers of the
Counter Intelligence Corps,
especially Ann Bray

Also by DUVAL A. EDWARDS:

The GREAT DEPRESSION
And a Teenager's Fight to Survive
(A Runaway Youth's Adventures in
the Great Depression)

TABLE OF CONTENTS

ACKNOWLEDGMENTS

This book would never have seen the light of day without the help of many CICers and other friends, and especially the manuscript Ann Bray left on her death to the NCICA. The list is too long to acknowledge the help of all, but to the following former CICers who contributed significantly to the final product go my everlasting thanks: Thomas R. Ackerman, William F. Aimone, Malcolm D. Aitken, Leland "Andy" Anderson, William Attwood, David B. Birt, Edward Boyles, Francis "Frank" T. Brown, James Calogero, James Chambers, George Charon, John "Jack" Christine, William B. Dallas, Robert Ebaugh, Frank Edwards, Albert M. Franco, Francis S. Furey, Jenis Roy Galloway, Fred Gloe, Marvin C. Goff, Jr., Richard L. Goodbar, Thornton R. Greene, John N. Irwin III, C. Reed Kennon, Harvey L. Kimball, Allan F. Hull, Arthur S. Hurlburt, Arthur Komori, Spady Koyama, W. David Krieger, Blair Labatt, David W. Lincoln, Robert MacDonald, David McCarthy, Ann McDonough, George T. Nakamura, LeRoy T. Newland, George S. Rea, Robert M. Reese, James Rubard, Stanley E. Rutkowski, Richard Sakakida, Carl F. Savino, Victor Shauklas, John M. Shuey, Edwin L. Simmons, George B. Spencer (Deceased, son Steve B. Spencer shared records), Dudley Skinker, Donald I. Suzuki, Bernard J. Sweeney, Delbert Westling, Joseph A. Whitlow, Isadore "Iz" Zack, Arthur J. Zinsmaster—and many more who were in CIC. Others not in CIC itself, but in allied services, or touched on counter-intelligence: Ralph Briggs, former ONI in WW2; Chris Hurd, Fort Huachuca Intelligence School Librarian; Ray S. Hurle, secretary of FSS veterans' Sub Rosa, Inc., New Zealand; Timothy J. Naftali, University of Hawaii professor and CIC researcher; Dr. Bruce Saunders, Army historian.

The non-CIC group who aided in the effort included but were not limited to: James Anderson, Val Dumond, Jack and Helen Dunn, Walter D. Edwards, Dr. J. P. Finnegan, Robert and Lynn Fulghum, Tommy and Theresa Kohara, Betty Joan Porter, Edgar Schrock, Sam Stinson, Wm. A. Owens Collection at Texas A & M Library, and Inez Heard Weatherly.

And special thanks to my wife Kay for her counsel, editing, and loving patience; Peggy J. Meyer of Red Apple Publishing for her expert help; Arthur S. Hurlburt, who was there in SWPA and Leyte, though our paths didn't cross until years later, and who contributed some of his personal, interesting incidents, along with editing most of the book; and to NCICA (National Counter Intelligence Corps Association) for permitting the use of material from *The Golden Sphinx*, its official newsletter.

FOREWORD

CIC is probably one of the least written about subjects to come out of WW2 and the cold war. Reluctance of people to write about it runs all the way from inertia to a real fear of divulging classified matter, no matter how ancient. There have been a handful of "I Was There" type of stories limited to the experiences of that one author. The first all-inclusive work was *America's Secret Army,* by British authors, Botting and Sayer, helped by 500 former CIC agents.

During the cold war Major Ann Bray and a special committee stationed at CIC HQ, Fort Holabird, in Baltimore, Maryland, began interviewing agents coming back from overseas or just passing through the "Bird." The committee amassed a wealth of material into some 30 volumes, some of it dry detachment reports about who was there and who went where, some of it personal stories of agents in the field. The committee was disbanded before it could correct its preliminary volumes, but Ann continued to condense the material into one manuscript, which she hoped to have published. But she died before revising her material or finding a publisher.

Bray left her unpublished, unedited condensed history to the National Counter Intelligence Corps Association, of which she was a proud member. The 30-volume history languished in files at Fort Meade until the British writers retrieved them for their book.

The second renaissance was when Duval A. Edwards, retired Texas lawyer, former CIC special agent who served in MacArthur's Pacific, got the bug. He got his hands on Ann Bray's condensation of the 30-volume history, and started to put it together into a more readable shape. Next he badgered and cajoled others to put down on paper their recollections to give some spark of life and make it more readable for the general public. This is Val's book, from page one.

Many of the best stories have not yet been written. They've been told over and over again at conventions and meetings. CIC was full of bigger than life people. All were pathfinders, facing a world of experts on the enemy side. Some were even magicians. It is a fond hope that this book can become the inspiration for others to pick up and write their challenging stories. Such as the story of the Manhattan Engineers—how the atom bomb secret was kept. And how CIC contributed to the war effort in other theaters—and how CIC stood as our only worldwide intelligence organization from the end of WW2 until CIA was formed and slowly became operational. Even if you were not in CIC, read this book, lean back and enjoy. Just imagine how it would have been for you if you had been there.

Arthur S. Hurlburt, LTC MI Ret.
Special Agent CIC 1942-45/51-52
Weekly Columnist, *Another View*

MISSION

of the Counter Intelligence Corps

"The mission of the Counter Intelligence Corps is to contribute to the operations of the Army Establishment through the detection of treason, sedition, subversive activity, and disaffection, and the detection, prevention, or neutralization of espionage and sabotage within or directed against the Army Establishment *and the areas of its jurisdiction.*" (Italics added)

Authority: AR 381-100

By order of Secretary of War, letter dated 13 November 1944 from War Department, AGO, to all Commands, including SWPA, clarified CIC duties and ordered distribution of same to *each* CIC detachment. Enumerated among them were:

CHANNELS OF COMMUNICATION

"In all cases where the time element is vital, direct communication between Counter Intelligence Corps detachments is authorized, such communication being reported promptly to the G-2, A-2, or S-2 involved."

POWER OF ARREST

"Subject to policies established by the appropriate overseas command, Counter Intelligence Corps personnel on duty overseas have full power and authority to arrest or detain any person who violates military security or whose detention is otherwise deemed necessary for the accomplishment of the counter-intelligence mission."

PUBLICITY

"When operating in civilian clothing or the civilian *uniform,* Counter Intelligence Corps personnel will be addressed as "Mister" and rank will not be revealed in orders .... identification cards issued .... will not bear a military title."

DISCLAIMER

I anticipate criticism from some who will feel left out of this account. They were not *deliberately* omitted. Many who have been asked for information for years have failed to respond in writing, so there may be a few significant gaps in the telling. I could not wait forever, so have proceeded with this "Unfinished Story." I invite them now to send me the facts as they recall them, so that in any reprint of this first edition, we can set the records straight.

The biggest problem with writing any history of the CIC, especially from the Pacific areas, has been the absence of any single source for checking records, and the paucity of those reports located. Had it not been for the efforts of the "Ann Bray" team in the fifties at Fort Holabird with the specific mission of writing CIC's history, much more data would have been lost forever. This team augmented scattered reports with live interviews with as many CIC veterans as possible. It is unfortunate the team was ordered to end its efforts before the 30-volume first draft, distributed throughout CIC centers worldwide, could be corrected and revised.

Especially helpful to the team were the lengthy, detailed interviews of those few who stayed in the service after WW2, and were thus more easily available. Included among this category were extended interviews with Arthur Komori and Richard Sakakida whose fantastic stories unfold as one reads this book.

University of Hawaii Professor Naftali was researching CIC in Europe, and finally located CIC records from that theater buried at National Archives under "OSS." Late in 1943 the Army's Adjutant General ordered CIC records burned! And as late as 1993, an eye witness stated that he overheard one of the generals under MacArthur give the order after the war to destroy CIC records from the Pacific.

Former agent William A. Owens, university professor and professional writer, reported he found some records at Carlisle Barracks in Pennsylvania, as he researched for his *Eye-Deep in Hell*. Those records were probably from the 30-volume first-draft history. I found them in the Owens Collection at Texas A & M. But when I went to Carlisle Barracks the records had been shipped to National Archives at Suitland; this was shortly after a big uproar in the press about the Klaus Barbie case.

Suitland refused to admit me until a call to Fort Meade authorized them to let me see CIC records. But they would show me only reports from CIC detachments after I provided the specific number of the specific detachment. Thus I was told there were no records on the 41st, 214th or 306th, the teams I had served with. There was one from the 441st, but detachments with any records were so limited I departed in despair at ever finding complete records of CIC's work in the Pacific. Was there an Army gremlin destroying any knowledge of even the existence of CIC?

In the early 1980s, the NCICA (National Counter Intelligence Corps Association) appointed me to a committee to try to revise the "short history" of CIC that Ann Bray had condensed from the 30-volume set and had planned to publish. She died after the first draft was completed, but left her manuscript to NCICA. She had attended many CIC reunions trying to enlarge the scope of her team's research by obtaining first-hand information from CIC survivors from every theater around the world.

With Victor Shauklas, Ann McDonough, John "Jack" Christine, all former CIC agents, plus Ralph Briggs, former ONI operative, our committee produced a first draft revision of the Bray manuscript, which we rearranged into two segments: one dealing with the war with Germany, the other with Japan. A preliminary search for an interested publisher proved negative; none was interested. Then Arthur Hurlburt discovered that two Britishers, Ian Sayer and Douglas Botting, were writing the history of CIC and had a British publisher and a deadline! NCICA authorized the delivery of our revised Ann Bray manuscript to the Britishers, who made effective use of the additional material and names therein in their America's Secret Army—The Untold Story of the Counter Intelligence Corps.

Reading America's Secret Army, those who served in the Pacific were disappointed that our part in the war seemed to lack much of the detail and events in which we were involved. I added a few first-hand stories to the Bray manuscript before turning it over to Sayer and Botting, but I knew there were many more awaiting a chance to be told. Hence this volume.

Even as I write, I know that somewhere another veteran of the war in the Pacific is breathing his last. In our advancing years there is a time pressure to complete this so that veterans may call attention to errors of spelling names, places, dates, and even events. I extend that invitation now, and thank you in advance for further information. My address for the foreseeable future is: Duval A. Edwards, 5666 E Hampton #153, Tucson AZ 85712.

Nota Bene: CIC had agents and special agents; for brevity, I call them all agents. Many argue with my spelling of Canon, insisting it was Cannon; his superior, Labatt, states it was carried on Sixth Army rolls as Canon. Officially the Air Corps until after WW2, in parts of WW2 it was the Air Force (e.g., 7th AF), so I don't worry what to call it; we all know what it was—and is.

1941

Japan modeled its espionage system on the Germans', which its military greatly admired. Before the end of the 19th century, Japanese agents in Honolulu were sending weekly reports to Tokyo on American defenses and activities there, right down to Pearl Harbor, and doing the same in the Philippines.

Japan's secret military police and counterespionage service was the Kempei Tai, the most powerful, hated and feared of all Japanese institutions, both by Japanese at home, and by people in occupied countries. It held a semi-independent position in the Army. It was a combat arm, commanded by a provost marshal general directly responsible only to the war minister.

Members were hand-picked volunteers, in peacetime required to have six years' military service before applying. Standards of intelligence, education, facility in foreign languages, health and physique were extraordinarily high. They were trained a full year at special schools, in law, languages, methods of espionage and counter-espionage, horsemanship, fencing and judo, invisible writing, shadowing—all the elements required for a good agent.

Kempei Tai had built up a membership approaching 75,000 by 1941, one third of whom were officers. They also recruited natives in occupied territories. They wore regular army uniforms as well as plain clothes. Counterespionage was a most important function, but unlike CIC, so was Army discipline: an agent could arrest a member of the army up to three ranks higher than himself; he could decide on and punish in the field; he could dress with a complete disregard of uniform regulations and refuse to salute; to emphasize his special standing he was released from all routine duties.

The extensive intelligence network, which included many civilian societies, blanketed the Pacific Rim and more. Embassies and consulates were used and recognized as such centers. Red-light houses and individual prostitutes were productive sources of information of interest to the military as well as to industrialists. This also followed the German model, whose originator, Wilhelm Stieber, as early as 1870 formed a network of German-owned and staffed luxury hotels in foreign countries, offering patrons every convenience, not all itemized on their bills.

Japan's spies had it easier in Asia and nations where facial features were not too different from Japanese. Natives were included in the network when they could be seduced, induced or blackmailed into cooperating. In Caucasian countries, such as Australia, Canada and the United States, success was difficult. Japanese nationals however were able to operate out of consulates and embassies with seeming impunity, until the war closed them down. To augment this source, Japan utilized Axis agents, enabling some to collect payment from two masters.

At first the U.S. relied primarily on the FBI (Federal Bureau of Investigation) and ONI (Office of Naval Intelligence) to combat foreign espionage at home. Other than information collected through our consulates and embassies, we had no organization devoted exclusively to foreign intelligence until OSS became operational after WW2 was well underway. When OSS was disbanded after WW2, CIC replaced it until the CIA was organized in 1946 and slowly took over CIC's efforts.

Our Army had organized the CIP (Corps of Intelligence Police) in WWI, to protect our forces in Europe from saboteurs and spies. Between the end of that conflict and up to 1941, the actual numbers in this specialized unit of Military Intelligence had shrunk to as low as fifteen agents in 1934. As the Axis danger began to be perceived more clearly by our military, a start was made to rebuild CIP. This continued at a slow but steady pace until December 7, 1941, when it accelerated into a gallop. On Pearl Harbor Day, the number of special agents in the CIP was still less than one thousand.

That is the picture of spy/counterspy "numbers" as war began in 1941: Japan's 75,000 contrasted to our fewer than 1,000. And that did not even include the tens of thousands the Axis had spread around the world—sharing their gleanings. When the Allies invaded Italy in 1943, for instance, almost 10,000 German secret agents were distributed throughout Italy. The body count of enemy collaborators and agents imprisoned by CIC in the Philippines alone by VJ Day was over 5,000.

But in this history you are about to read, the adversary that bothered CIC the most was not the spies of Germany, Italy and Japan—it was our own Army!

Many of the obstacles our CIC special agents had to confront and conquer were those posed by an army which knew little or nothing about its own Counter Intelligence Corps and apparently cared little for it, failing to understand CIC's capabilities. Only near the end of WW2 and in postwar years did CIC come somewhat into its own, with better ranks and grades denied during the war. Many brilliant corporal and sergeant CIC agents in WW2 eagerly departed the service at a time, especially in Europe, when their talents were desperately needed.

As this account opens in the Philippines, to get a broader grasp of the counter-intelligence situation in that great island nation, we invite you to read the special chapter titled "Japanese Fifth Column in the Philippines"—or if you prefer, after you have completed the section on 1945; or both before and after.

CHAPTER 1

Manila, Pearl of the Orient

Pearl of the Orient, Manila, in 1941 was a hotbed of espionage and intrigue, overflowing with expatriates, spies and agents, including many Japanese nationals. Add to that a small but significant minority of natives who hated Caucasians, and who collaborated with the Japanese going so far as betraying loyal Filipinos as well as Americans, and in the final months of the war spying and taking up arms alongside Japanese soldiers to shoot at Americans.

The Japanese barber who cut your hair could have been an undercover intelligence officer; so could the sidewalk photographer who snapped your photo. The clerk at your hotel, the waiter in its restaurant, the bellboy who carried your bags, could have been Kempei Tai (Japanese Army's intelligence and counter-intelligence unit). More certainly, the bartender serving you at the bar near the military post, or your companion in the "house of joy," may already have relayed some of your "loose" words to an interested listener.

Many could have been spies for the Japanese military—and were. Lt. Colonel Mori, commander of Cabanatuan Prison camp for some GIs who survived Bataan and Corregidor, was recognized by a prisoner as one who ran a bicycle shop in Manila who "couldn't be nice enough to us guys." Mori was not nearly as nice when commanding the prison. Mr.. Niimura, interpreter at Cabanatuan, was identified as the former operator of an electrical shop in Baguio, the "summer capitol" and most fashionable pre-war resort in the Philippines. Captain Gidoka, who tortured an American guerrilla, had been a clerk for an American company in Manila before the war.

Warlords of Japan, aided and abetted by loyal secret societies, had embedded tens of thousands of agents and moles into the fabric of nations around the Pacific Rim. Not the least of these were red-light houses near the military, and the native anti-American minority.

Largest city in the Philippine Islands, Manila was not neglected by the military then ruling Japan. A growing portion of its population was Japanese, expanding into businesses—with a steady flow of Japanese travelers coming and going. It was an ideal situation for espionage—and reporting safely to Japanese military headquarters.

The Philippines were still under U.S. protection, with a small

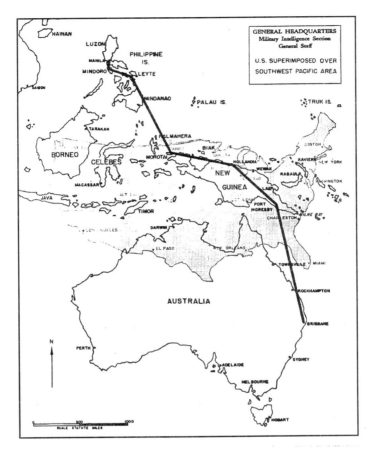

military presence there. General Douglas MacArthur had undertaken
to whip into shape a Filipino army looking to the day the Philippines
could protect itself as a free and independent nation. In our token
force was a Military Intelligence section. A part of it was a unit of the
Corps of Intelligence Police composed of a mere handful of specially
trained soldiers, known as CIP Special Agents. Their job: identify and
pinpoint potential enemy agents operating in the area.

Someone in that Military Intelligence section clearly had strong
suspicions about what was going on, what it portended, and tried to
do something about it. Unfortunately, no one in this Manila CIP Detachment spoke fluent Japanese. Some were Filipinos who spoke the
various languages and dialects of their native land, but had no ability
to go undercover to ferret out suspected Japanese agents and nullify
their activities. That unknown person on the Military Intelligence staff
evidently recognized the need for Japanese-speaking CIP agents. So

the call for them went out to the most logical place: Hawaii.

March 13, 1941, two Hawaiians of Japanese ancestry were inducted into the U.S. Army in Honolulu. Both could handle the Japanese language. One was twenty-five-year-old Arthur Komori, a bespectacled part-time real estate salesman and part-time bartender at the Kapaakea Grill in Moiliili. Born at Haiku, on the island of Maui, Hawaii, of Christian parents, an Issei (Japan-born) father, Yoshitaro Komori, and a Nisei (second generation) mother, Arthur was educated at McKinley High School and University of Hawaii, graduating from the Manoa school in 1940 with a BA degree. He was an ROTC graduate, and was the 1933 Hawaii champion backstroker and former UH swim team captain. In 1935 he had an AAU championship in the 220-yard backstroke. To ten years of Japanese language school training, he added his father's native tongue as his foreign language at the University of Hawaii. He also was a licensed private plane pilot.

The second inductee was Richard Sakakida, son of Japanese parents who had emigrated from Hiroshima, Japan. Educated at an American high school in Honolulu, Richard Sakakida at twenty-one had not yet attained the accomplishments of Komori. But this soft-spoken, highly regarded Japanese-American had already turned down an opportunity to go to West Point, as well as a chance to become a Buddhist priest—either one of which would have been a history-making event for Japanese-Americans.

The course the two new recruits took was equally historical, though few Americans today know about it. They volunteered for the Army, out of loyalty to their native U.S. and love for their parents.

Army officer Gilbert personally approved Komori and Sakakida. Then the Hawaiian CIP exposed these two special young men to a brief basic training course in counter-espionage. They told the new agents to prepare for a secret mission, the nature of which would be revealed later; their destination was Manila, to reveal the destination but nothing else about it—only to their immediate families.

Manila called for haste. Handwriting on the wall became more obvious—at least to that prescient person or persons who requested two Japanese linguists, if not to our Pentagon top brass.

7 April 1941, the new Army recruits, now sergeants and civilian clothed CIP agents, boarded the U.S. Army transport Republic bound for Manila. To conceal their Army connection, they signed on and worked as crew members until April 21, when the ship was about three miles from Manila. The ship's purser then told them to report to the captain on the bridge. There for the first time they met U.S. Army Captain Nelson Raymond, who revealed he was the commanding of-

ficer of the CIP Detachment in the Philippines, their boss from now on. Emphasizing the need for them to remain undercover, he arranged for a later meeting ashore to brief them on their specific mission.

Once on shore at the appointed time they rendezvoused with Captain Raymond, a long time CIP agent. Special Agent Grenfell D. Drisko, who would be working with them, was with him. Komori and Sakakida were then driven on a short tour of the city during which they learned their specific mission. The magnitude of the task began to dawn on them: investigate the entire Japanese community of Manila, identify Japanese spies and potential saboteurs, many long suspected but never proven. A tremendous challenge for new agents, but those involved in the selection of these two Nisei agents had done their job well. It was up to Komori and Sakakida, now provided with a suitable "cover" story by the fortuitous arrival and departure of the SS Cleveland on the same day they arrived. They would tell anyone asking that they had jumped that ship.

To maintain surreptitious contact with the local detachment, they were given keys to a mailbox at the Central Post Office in Manila under the name of "Sixto Borja"—Sixto, as Sakakida had been assigned an identification code of B-16, and Borja, a common Filipino name. They were to check the box twice daily for instructions on rendezvous places. Raymond or Drisko would pick them up at least once a week at some obscure spot and take them by a roundabout route to the Military Intelligence (G-2) office in Fort Santiago, where they could submit their reports and receive new briefings while safe from blowing their cover. And once a month collect their Army pay.

Some valuable information the two provided U.S. included 1) when Japanese nationals began shipping their families home and 2) when those remaining in the Philippines began collecting survival kits.

Ferreting out and neutralizing Japanese espionage agents and potential saboteurs was not the sole task of the CIP. They were aware of Spanish Falangists as well as Nazi and Italian activities. Like any competent investigators they had a network of informants to keep track of potential subversive activities from these Axis agents as well. One such informant was Luigi Zavattero, an Italian radio operator in Manila. Detected illegally handling commercial messages, his license was suspended and radio sealed by FCC (Federal Communications Commission). He offered his services thereafter to agencies in the Philippine government, reporting on activities of pro-Franco, Nazis, Falangists and his Italian countrymen. His services, even though questioned by users as to their value, came to the attention of CIP.

The initiation of case investigations more often comes about through tips, rumors and data from informants. It can be tricky, depending on the reliability of the informant. Though Luigi was not given a high rating, he nevertheless reported to CIP's Raymond and Keeler not only on his Nazi and Italian sources, but also on Japanese poultrymen, Japanese-Filipinos (mestizos), and people who employed Japanese. He reported to Raymond usually at the latter's home.

Now Komori and Sakakida, the imported expert "informants," received their first detailed instructions: go undercover in the Japanese community with a good cover story, secure employment, get acquainted with the Japanese community, target those who posed a threat to the security of the U.S. Army and Philippine Constabulary, and report their findings and suspicions without revealing their identities to anyone. Raymond and Drisko were the only two who knew who they were, what they were doing and why. We might call them "moles"—but their mission was still counter-intelligence, well in keeping with the duties of the CIP.

In subsequent secret meetings Raymond had with the two, he gave implicit instructions and encouragement. Their introductory course in Hawaii had been very short, but as Komori recalled, Raymond "gradually instilled in us the techniques of subtle investigations and subterfuges in the best traditions of the CIP." They developed a great admiration and affection for this man who extended to them also an affection and openly deep appreciation for the important, dangerous work they were doing; he knew perhaps better than they that an untimely mistake while undercover could cost them their lives.

* * *

The two split up to look for a role in keeping with their assumed identities. They told anyone curious enough that they had been crew members on a freighter, but had tired of their sea duties so they jumped ship. The SS Cleveland freighter that had also put into port that day made their story more credible. Komori went further to enhance his cover by adding he was a draft dodger, which "was favorably received by the pro-Emperor sons of Japan."

Sakakida registered at a small Japanese-operated hotel, the Nishikawa, while Komori checked into the Toyo Hotel. Operating from these centers, they sought jobs that would least betray them, as well as permit the best observation posts for performing their mission.

Komori secured a job that filled the bill—teaching English at the Manila Japanese Cultural Hall, where leading Japanese residents were improving their command of the language. In the months preceding the Pearl Harbor attack, he won the confidence and friendship of the Japanese Consul General, the Chief of the Japan Tourist Bureau, the

Chief of the Japan Cultural Hall, the Chief of the Domei News Agency—known espionage centers—and other leading residents of Manila. He found many to be "arrogant and expansionist-minded," increasingly impatient with "weak-kneed" policies of the Konoye Cabinet (Japan's governing cabinet not sympathetic to the hawks in the Japanese Army). But the cards were stacked against them. Warlords were taking over, sure of their future role in the Orient; so much so that a student in Komori's English class wrote an article for a newspaper in Osaka, Japan, pointing out the probable route for the Japanese army in an invasion of Singapore. To maintain his cover, Komori played along with the thinking of his students and contacts.

Sakakida also was successful in penetrating the Japanese community. The operators of the Nishikawa Hotel were a childless couple named Fujii. They took an instant liking to him, so much that they even wrote his mother in Hawaii asking permission to adopt him!

During his initial days at the hotel, Sakakida was deluged by questions from the Fujiis, as well as the hotel's permanent residents and guests, all curious about this Japanese who spoke excellent English. He told them he was born and reared in Hawaii, but had grown tired of life there, and wanted to see more of the world; this led to his going to sea. When his freighter stopped in Manila, what he saw of the city appealed to him as a nice place to live for a while.

To enable Sakakida to continue gathering information, Raymond arranged with the Marsman Trading Company, sole agents for Sears-Roebuck in the Philippines, to list him as a part-time employee. To keep up this pretense, he wandered into the Trading Company every morning at eight o'clock, loitered a while doing routine tasks and ran a few errands, and then spent the rest of the morning at the Lyric Theater.

"It's just a part-time sales job," Sakakida explained to his Japanese acquaintances who wondered how he had time to visit them and move around the city the rest of the day. This setup enabled him to spend most evenings in the Japanese Club, where in time he made friends with Japanese businessmen who frequented the club. Having memorized Sears' sales brochures, he carried out his role safely.

The friendship of the Fujii's resulted in his becoming a clerk in exchange for room and board. This opened up yet another source for information, as it gave him the opportunity to inspect passports, and also assist many people in making out their requests for passport entries required by the Philippine Commonwealth Government.

Another source of information came from a friendly Japanese-American. Shortly after Sakakida's arrival in Manila, Captain Raymond suggested he make friends with Clarence Yamagata, a Hawaiian-born Nisei practicing law and a part-time legal advisor to the Japanese Consulate. Yamagata introduced him to key people in the Consulate, from whom he obtained information of interest.

Sakakida received another break when the U.S. froze all Japanese assets in the Philippines. Japanese nationals had to file declarations of all bank accounts and assets. Many needed help in filling out the numerous forms, so Sakakida interviewed a good portion of the Japanese community, and subtly obtained information that did not go on the forms. The most pertinent concerned prior military service. Often the Japanese would ask if they should admit their military service; sometimes he advised against it but reported the information through channels. This enabled him to provide G-2 with the complete military backgrounds of a large number of the Japanese in Manila.

Late in November 1941, his friend Yamagata told Sakakida he had arranged for him to work for the Japanese Vice Consulate at Davao, Mindanao, the large southern island. As an active Japanese colony was located in that strategic area, Captain Raymond gave his approval for Sakakida to accept. Before it could come to pass, the outbreak of the war canceled these plans.

Thus it went, until the sneak attack on Pearl Harbor on 7 December 1941, which was 8 December 1941 in Manila.

CHAPTER II

This Side of the Pacific

While Komori and Sakakida were warming up to their new role of special agents, in 1941 I was warming up in Georgia to a life as a $21 a month trainee in Uncle Sam's Army. Like many others in 1941, I waived any exemptions I might have, to get my one year in the army over with and return to a lawyer's life back in San Antonio, Texas. Draft board orders were forwarded to Columbus, Georgia, where I was visiting a lifetime friend. Rather than return to Texas, I opted to be inducted in nearby Fort McPherson, Atlanta, erecting another barrier to the past. June 26, 1941, I became a buck private in Uncle Sam's Army.

"Any openings in the Judge Advocates' office? "

"No way, too many lawyers already in the Army," the induction center advised.

I was soon on my way to Camp Wheeler, Macon, Georgia, for thirteen weeks' basic training in the infantry. Far from being a lone lawyer, my training platoon had one preacher and forty-eight lawyers from Tennessee. An experiment, we were told. The army planned to train this platoon of lawyers and one preacher into the most effective-ever, intelligent, knowledgeable Intelligence and Reconnaissance (I&R) squads, which in war penetrate enemy lines and bring back combat intelligence information and prisoners of war better than ever before. A delightful prospect for lawyers. "The preacher would be needed," I thought. An ingenious scheme to get rid of an excess of lawyers?

For thirteen weeks we drilled and marched and studied, and studied and drilled and marched, over the red hills of central Georgia, simulating wartime situations and games, never thinking we'd ever have to use what we learned. After all, our President Roosevelt had publicly said he would never send us overseas in combat, and we believed him—and we were to be in the army for one year only.

Midway through training, our I&R platoon was given a Morse code test. Signal Corps was shorthanded. My grade was high enough that I was transferred to the future Signal Corps dot-dit-dot program, graduating with a Morse-tapping speed of twenty words a minute, a skill I've never used. What was planned for me I had no idea.

Training tedium was relieved by off-duty encounters with the more interesting of our officers. For instance, the popular young chaplain assigned to the battalion lectured us at least once on venereal diseases. His entire talk reveals the reason for his popularity:

"All I have to say to you men about venereal diseases is this story of my favorite dog, Fido, who loved to race trains over crossings. One day he was just a tad too slow—the engine's wheels clipped off the tip of his tail. Fido looked back to see what had happened—whereupon the train clipped off his head." Pause. "In other words, gentlemen, don't lose your head over a little piece of tail!"

With basic training over almost everybody shipped out to places unknown. A few were kept behind; our officers planned to send us to Officers Training School (OCS) at Fort Benning, Georgia, or elsewhere when openings occurred. To qualify as an officer, I was told I had to have a minimum number of teeth. And I was on the borderline! An increasing demand for officers eventually did away with this archaic rule. Pressure from false teeth manufacturers? So, to meet the minimum dental standards for officership, while awaiting orders to OCS I endured many painful hours at the camp dentists' offices while they bored holes in my teeth without the use of pain killers. Was that part of a test also to see if I was qualified to be an officer?

To avoid the inevitable waiting in the army, I obliged the assistant to the commanding officer of the battalion who wanted my skills as a secretary-typist. It kept me out of long hours of KP (kitchen police); my friends will recall my problem with washing dishes: I washed them "too" clean. More importantly, there was a shortage of instructors at a voluntary Spanish class in the evenings. I was surprised to be accepted as the "Tex-Mex" instructor from Texas. Spending late hours many nights reviewing a Berlitz conversation book, I tried to keep up with my classes—and I'm not sure I did.

But bragging on Spanish came in handy. Somewhere I heard of a search for something called the Corps of Intelligence Police. Without thinking seriously, I filled a form and forgot about it, other than to recall one needed a working knowledge of one foreign language, an officer's IQ (actually, 10 points higher), and be at least 25 years old—as well as pass an intensive investigation into loyalty and character.

Thus it went in the States, until 8 December 1941 in Manila when CIP agents Komori and Sakakida had already completed eight months of a shadow war with Japan, which was 7 December 1941 where I was, and where the Pearl of Hawaii was.

* * *

CHAPTER III

Pearl Harbor—7 December 1941

At 7:55 a.m., Hawaiian time (1:55 PM EST), Sunday, 7 December 1941 (8 December 1941 in the Philippines west of the International Dateline), Japanese bombs began falling on our fleet anchored in Pearl Harbor. Within minutes, agents and officers of the Hawaiian CIP detachment were racing to their contact headquarters in the Dillingham Building, downtown Honolulu. In Hawaii, CIP agents identified themselves to the public as MI (Military Intelligence) Special Agents, which indeed they were; they found that term more effective in doing their job.

Two of these MI Special Agents hit the jackpot on the way to headquarters. They noticed something not seen on the same route in preceding days: lights blinking from a window in a cottage on Kalama. They would have thought nothing of it during peacetime, but now enemy planes were overhead: this was war. The dot-dash signals aroused their suspicion further, so they detoured, and burst into an attic catching German Otto Kuehn (aka Kuhn) and his stepdaughter Ruth in *flagrante delicto,* flashing messages about the ongoing results of the bombing to the Japanese Consulate which had a clear view of their window. About the same time, Honolulu police entered the Japanese Consulate and seized Consul General Kita in the act of burning official, incriminating papers.

The consulate staff was interned and later exchanged for American diplomats. But their spies, the Kuehns, were tried and convicted. Kuehn saved his life by revealing the entire operation, being sentenced to fifty years, later reduced after the war ended. Ruth got away with only a few years in prison.

It is obvious why a "Japanese" spy in a Caucasian-dominated society was not Japanese: facial characteristics made it impossible for them to infiltrate Occidental communities, so an alternative had to be found. Because of close ties with Germany, Japan sought help from General Haushofer, head of the geopolitical department of Berlin University, in recruiting Europeans to spy for them.

15 August 1935, Otto Kuehn with wife Friedel, Ruth, and 6-year-old-son Hans arrived in Honolulu. Their cover was Kuehn's supposed-interest in the Japanese language and the history of ancient

Hawaii. He traveled with Ruth throughout the islands, writing articles for German publishers, especially about German settlers. Income from this did not pay for the family lifestyle. But the $100,000 deposited into their Honolulu bank account did, which they explained to the curious was family inheritances and profitable investments.

Frau Kuehn made secret trips to Tokyo with her husband's report on naval and military installations in the Islands. But 18-year-old Ruth was the top spy of the three; her date book was filled with young naval officers at Pearl Harbor, eager to brag about jobs and tours of duty, which Ruth carefully recorded for the reports. The Japanese were pleased with this trio, who supplied much useful data.

Before 7 December 1941 they moved to the Kalama cottage with its excellent view of the naval base. With 11-year-old Hans now on the team, all were working every angle. Most productive was Ruth with her beauty parlor in Pearl Harbor that was a favorite with navy wives and her continuing partying at night. Information was delivered to the Japanese Consulate on a daily basis, finding its way to its final destination in Japan through secure, diplomatic pouches.

Nota bene: These were not Issei, Japanese immigrants, nor Nisei, the first born away from the homeland. There has never been proof that either Issei or Nisei in Hawaii or the U.S. spied for Japan before or during the war. Japanese nationals did, but the warlords were forced to rely on this German family, plus their regular Japan nationals working through the Consulate in Hawaii. All these were well-known to the FBI, ONI and CIP, even the Kuehns, who undoubtedly would have been picked up possibly within hours—except that two "MI Officers" caught them red-handed and halted the further flashing of messages to the still open Japanese Consulate.

* * *

Following a prearranged plan, CIP agents arriving at their Dillingham Building office held a ten minute huddle, then dispersed in teams to apprehend all pro-Japanese sympathizers. For months leading up to this historic day, they had been quietly investigating and compiling names and addresses on potentially dangerous individuals. Those believed strongly pro-Japanese were on a list classified as "1-A," the first to be picked up under code name "Operation Pickup."

Those on the suspect list, classified as "1-B," were placed temporarily under careful watch until further investigation could determine their future.

The bulk of information in confidential files about the Japanese population in the Islands came from U.S. citizens of Japanese ancestry, commonly called "Nisei" though that term in Japanese applies only to the first generation born away from Japan. Although the vast majority living in Hawaii, especially the Nisei, were believed to be loyal to America—and time and events did not disprove this—precautions nevertheless had to be taken, as no one at the time knew exactly what to expect. The FBI alone counted 700 Nisei informants working with it; CIP also had a very large number reporting to it.

CIP along with FBI, ONI and the Honolulu Police Department worked untiringly through that fateful Sunday. By day's end, 200 strongly pro-Japanese people were in temporary detention compounds—with the Kuehn family incarcerated and held for prosecution as spies. Operation Pickup continued for 72 hours following the attack; by 10 December more than 400 were confined at the Honolulu Immigration station. Some of those 400 could conceivably have committed sabotage or espionage if not behind bars. CIP's job was to *prevent* such subversive activity, not necessarily "make a case that would stand up in court" as the FBI was usually compelled to do.

The only recorded instance of *potential* disloyalty by a Hawaiian of Japanese descent took place on Niihau, westernmost island of the chain. It was owned by the Robinson family, isolated by choice; only weekly did a boat come over from Kauai, 20 miles away, to leave supplies. There was no other communication with the outside world.

In Puuwai, only village on the island, workers were about to enter the church when two planes with red circles under the wings flew overhead. Many sensed trouble on recognizing the insignia, and guessed an attack on Pearl harbor. About two o'clock one plane reappeared, crash-landing near the house of Hawila Kaleohano. Hawila ran up and took a pistol away from the pilot who could not answer their questions in English; so Harada, one of two ethnic Japanese on Niihau, was summoned. A 30-year old Nisei, he was assistant to the other Japanese named Sintani. He questioned the pilot who would only say he was from Honolulu, denied any raid, and was vague as to the bullet holes in the plane. The islanders decided to hold him until the boss arrived on the next boat from Kauai. But the boat did not come at the scheduled time. Four days passed.

Harada took the pilot to his house. There the pilot got through to Harada who then apparently joined him in an effort to capture the whole island. They tried to convert Sintani, to join them, but he flatly refused. Meanwhile, as six islanders slipped away for help in a boat to Kauai, Beni Kanahali overcame the pilot. Harada immediately committed suicide, cleansing the slate of any known disloyal Nisei until after the war (a few caught in Japan by the war may have been compelled to commit certain acts considered disloyal).

Elliott R. Thorpe, the man MacArthur put in overall charge of his counter-intelligence, relates that before the war he was visiting in Hawaii and was invited to the home of an Issei, who gave a farewell party for his son and two other Nisei drafted into our army. Thorpe wrote that the oldest man there made the principal speech after the meal, in which with great solemnity he addressed the three draftees, "You are Americans and your country has honored you with a call to its service. This is fitting. You must be good soldiers and thus reflect honor on all of us. We hope you will never be called to fight against the land of our ancestors, for that will bring us sorrow. But if you are called upon to fight against the land of our fathers, then you must fight harder than anyone else, for you must prove that you honor both your family and the nation of which you are a member."

Too bad some of our other military leaders were apparently unaware of this attitude that permeated Japanese immigrant families.

Between the outbreak of war and a formal declaration of martial law, by mutual understanding among the three agencies, CIP was responsible for the internal security of Hawaii. This initial understanding, soon followed by a declaration of martial law for the entire Territory, meant more responsibilities than normal in CIP's sphere of jurisdiction. CIP was recognized as the one army organization that could best serve as an agency between civilians and army in a multitude of matters related to internal security. The major part of CIP investigations was to determine if a subject was considered dangerous to our internal security; if so determined, he was interned. During the first year, CIP interned about one thousand.

Under martial law, the Military Governor took over control of the Islands, and issued through his Office a series of General Orders published in newspapers, including two Japanese bilingual ones. CIP was the dominant investigative body which, along with other governmental agencies, assisted the Provost Marshal in enforcing those General Orders. To strengthen security, initial orders to civilians covered weapons, blackout, curfew, short wave radios, subversive activity, enemy uniforms and flags, changing addresses, and meetings. Any person of "enemy extraction" was required to get permission for any of these from the Provost Marshal; this was intended to prohibit people already on the black list from moving without violating the order. CIP was consulted regarding the issuance of these orders, and on one occasion drew up the initial draft.

The Military Governor established a Civilian Internee Hearing Board to consider the cases of those interned. Some internees were in fact released who were later reinterned after a more complete investigation. To process investigations CIP set up a Preliminary Hearing Board composed of one agent each from the FBI, ONI, and the CIP. The FBI and ONI agents were solely in an advisory capacity. When a CIP agent considered a person potentially dangerous to internal security and recommended internment, the subject was brought before this board and the investigation reviewed. William T. Hiraoka, a Japanese-American, was the CIP agent on this board in the Honolulu office before being transferred to SWPA.

If the board agreed with the agent, his report, together with the Preliminary Board's finding, was forwarded to the Civilian Internee Hearing Board. If subject desired, he could be represented by attorney at this second hearing. If the latter board concurred, it sent the reports and its own to the Military Governor's Office for a final review.

Families of internees presented a special problem. In some cases family heads were sent to be interned on mainland U.S., leaving those left behind without means of support. The American Red Cross helped until these could join the internees. But some balked at being sent stateside and had to be handled on an individual case basis.

An important phase of martial law was the suspension of the writ of habeas corpus, enabling the internment of American citizens. An error was made early in the war when some American citizens of Japanese ancestry were interned and sent to the mainland. On arrival they would retain an attorney and be released under a writ of habeas corpus. It was necessary to return them to the Hawaiian Islands for the duration of the martial law phase.

What a far cry from how Japanese and Japanese-Americans on our West Coast fared in 1942! No boards or hearings of any kind, even for American citizens; they were routed out of homes and businesses, hauled in groups under guard and taken to "Relocation Camps" where weapons of guards were pointed inward, not outward. (Years later, some CIC agents who worked in the Western States felt strongly that this incarceration protected many from the violence of former neighbors, directed against them on racial grounds only.)

Although rounding up persons who conceivably presented a threat was CIP's principal duty during the first frantic days, some agents were delegated to trace the origin of innumerable wild rumors rampant on Oahu. Most of these typically turned out to be hot air with no substance in fact. FBI agent Robert L Shivers later stated that "Japanese spies and saboteurs who, at the signal of attack were supposed to rise up and aid their racial brothers, simply did not exist."

Not one of the flamboyant stories of road blocking, disguised machine gun nests, and other penny-thriller paraphernalia was true.

There was no fifth column in Hawaii! At least, none was proven to exist. IF there was one, it was most certainly contained and totally nullified by CIP's Operation Pickup and continuing efforts.

And all the confusion about what was happening in Hawaii that was rumored, gossiped about, and even printed by some newspapers on mainland U.S., simply did not exist in Hawaii because its civilian population was *not* confused.

"Nowhere under the sun," FBI agent Shivers declared, "could there have been a more intelligent response to the needs of the hour than was given by the entire population of the Islands ... As a matter of fact, had it not been for the lack of hysteria in the civilian community and the orderly manner in which it responded as a result of preparations previously made for war, especially by doctors, law enforcement agents and Office of Civilian Defense, there would have been confusion with which the community could not have coped."

Shivers' view was supported by the Honolulu Chief of Police and Lt General Delos Emmons who replaced Lt General Walter Short as CG of the Army's Hawaiian Department. Yet many mainland Americans continued to believe for years that there had been sabotage at Pearl Harbor. In February 1943 Colliers printed as fact a story about a milk wagon dropping its sides and machine gunning personnel at Hickam Field—a wild tale entirely without basis.

* * *

Officer-agent Malcolm D Aitken[1] describes a couple of these incidents, thusly: "We operated around the clock for many days after the attack rounding up Japanese aliens ... and investigating innumerable reports of alleged espionage and sabotage. One of the last attack-related investigations I participated in was into persistent rumors that an arrow had been cut into the cane fields which pointed directly at Pearl Harbor. Special Agent Everett Afook and I were sent to run (this) down. Based on aerial photos of the site we located the plantation and drove through the fields until we located the 'arrow.' After taking pictures we talked it over with the plantation manager.

"Several acres of cane that had been cut were in a roughly diamond-shaped experimental section used to grow different cane varieties and had been used for this purpose for many years. It stood out from the air only because the experimental cane had been harvested a few weeks before the 7th and had not yet been re-planted."

Pure coincidence, Aitken's report concluded. Quoting from Gordon Prange's *At Dawn We Slept*, " Missing Pearl Harbor from the air over Oahu would be like overlooking a bass drum in a telephone booth." Enemy pilots had aerial photos of their objectives and had no

---

[1] *From May 1994 issue of Gram, Pearl Harbor Survivors' Association.*

need of help from a directional arrow.

Investigating a report of "Japanese radio transmission emanating from a point just west of Keahi Point, near the entrance to Pearl Harbor" combined the efforts of the FBI, CIP, Army Signal Corps, FCC and the Military Police. Aitken states "the location had been fixed by triangulation with the assistance of the FCC; and all agents, MPs, and other members of the investigation force converged on the area. We ... thoroughly combed the area. Several days later we learned the signal was actually a 'bounce' resulting from the transmission from a Japanese submarine off French Frigate Shoals (about 600 miles ENE of Oahu). Through unusual atmospheric conditions, the signal had bounced back to earth at the Keahi Point area and then back up into the atmosphere appearing as an original signal from that point."

* * *

Until 1941 the Hawaiian CIP unit consisted of only a meager four-man staff, with no definite mission to perform. The agents simply went about the Islands observing people and events of intelligence interest, and filing reports for future use. On 5 April 1941, seven agents arrived from the mainland, and until Pearl Harbor succeeding shipments increased the unit to a total of only 30 agents! After Pearl Harbor the unit was temporarily augmented by agents from the West Coast to question suspects rounded up in Operation Pickup and later.

In the first months of the war, one event which greatly enhanced effectiveness of counter-intelligence operations in Hawaii throughout the war was the declaration of martial law by the Civil Governor after the attack. Martial law lasted until October 1944, giving CIP-CIC broad powers nowhere else delegated to the Corps in American territory for so long a time.

For many years Japan had maintained an active Consulate in Honolulu admittedly for the purpose of reminding Japanese in Hawaii that they still owed devotion to the Emperor. This made the Consulate suspect as a clearing house for espionage data, as in fact it was. The Consulate had sponsored numerous Japanese activities, including 1) religious sects; 2) schools to teach children the language and ideologies and 3) maintenance of Japanese societies and commercial concerns. It registered all births of Japanese, as all children of Japanese parentage were considered to be citizens of Japan regardless of where born or living. Moreover, all Japanese were encouraged to spend vacations in Japan, and particularly to send their children there for schooling.

* * *

To insure fairness in the treatment of suspect alien Japanese interned at the beginning of the war, all such cases were brought before the hearing boards. A treatment quite different from that accorded over 110,000 Issei and Nisei from our western states, and from Central and South America brought into U.S. internment camps *without a hearing of any kind*. But the final decision in each case in Hawaii, on whether to release or to continue holding, was made by the military governor's Review Board.

CHAPTER IV

Double Peril:
Face Value in Manila

As Japanese bombs fell on Pearl Harbor, it was 8 December 1941 in the Philippines. The fact that only Raymond and Drisko in the CIP Detachment knew the true loyalties of agents Komori and Sakakida put the latter in grave danger when news of the attack was flashed to Manila. The outbreak of hostilities changed the climate. Now they would be spying on a declared enemy people, and yet their own Americans and Filipinos would consider them *at face value* to be the enemy. It was double peril for Komori and Sakakida.

Within hours many in the Japanese community were indulging in euphoric celebration, drinking toasts to the Emperor even as America went through the process of declaring war on Japan. To keep up their undercover roles, which they had not as yet been ordered to abandon, the two CIP ostensibly played along with their Japanese contacts, joining in the celebrations while secretly wondering "what's next?"

Komori found the answer in the Japanese News Agency in Manila as he downed another toast to the Emperor in keeping with his undercover role. The door suddenly burst open and Filipino Constabulary troops grimly confronted him and his companions thrusting rifles with fixed bayonets in their faces. They herded him along with officials of the News Agency down the stairs into a waiting bus. They were driven to and deposited in "the hell hole of Manila," the fabled, stinking old Bilibid Prison, not too distant from the old Spanish Walled City. "As bad as the Black Hole of Calcutta," Komori was quoted in later years. Still silent about his real identity, which he regarded his duty to protect until told otherwise, he consoled himself with the hope and trust that Raymond would learn about the situation in time to pull him out before anything dire happened.

Anti-Japanese feelings and actions in the city followed swiftly on the heels of the declared war. Armed Filipino constabulary and policemen ran along the streets, closing Japanese stores. Some businesses voluntarily shut down. Guests at the famous Manila Hotel who went to cash travelers checks were told by a bank clerk, "We just stopped cashing them."

When enemy planes appeared in the skies over Manila, 54 Japanese bombers in formation, people stopped what they were doing to look up. Streetcars stopped in their tracks, autos and *carretelas* drew up and stopped against the curbs. There was yet no panic, just wonder, about when American planes would show up to gun down the bombers. But our planes never appeared.

One American newspaper woman was heard to cry in rage, "Why don't we fight them? Where are our planes?"

Unknown to her and others, our fighter planes lined up on Clark Field, north of Manila, had already been bombed into scrap in broad daylight. On 8 December 1941 our planes had circled in the air all morning until noon, guarding against the expected enemy; then *all* came down to refuel and for the pilots to have lunch. The enemy had advance intelligence on exactly when to strike—at noon—and it worked perfectly for them. Their spy network paid off with this victory alone.

* * *

Meanwhile, Sakakida was having his troubles. He had not revealed to any of his contacts that he was actually an American citizen. And, like Komori, to all outward appearances he looked like a Japanese among hostile people. He was now aware he could be in actual physical danger. When a radio station announced that aliens should report to the local police for internment, Sakakida decided to comply for protection from overzealous Filipinos. Police at the station threw him and three Japanese nationals in the back of an open vehicle and drove them to the Japanese Club House on Taft Boulevard, an evacuation center for Japanese, Italians and Germans. Along the way through Manila's narrow streets, angry crowds threw missiles and aimed blows at them; when they arrived at the Japanese Club sanctuary, they were bloodied, battered and thoroughly exhausted.

At the center Sakakida was quizzed by a Paul Marinas. He did not know at the time that Marinas was also an agent of the Philippine CIP Detachment. In routine follow-up after the questioning, Marinas searched the premises of the people he had interviewed. In Sakakida's quarters he found Richard's passport; although fictitious, it did reveal he was an American citizen. Marinas returned to the evacuation center, and pulled Sakakida aside for further questioning.

"You are a citizen of the United States. You don't belong here, in fact you're not even *eligible* to be here," Marinas stated.

"Look at my Japanese face. Do you think I'd be safe from the Filipinos if I left here now?" Sakakida responded.

Marinas thought this was reasonable and consented to Sakakida's staying, saying, "You're free to leave when you feel it's safe to do so."

Unaware of Marinas' position as a CIP agent, Sakakida made no attempt to volunteer any information about himself. He was faithfully keeping up his cover, not yet knowing what the future held.

One development satisfying the entire CIP Detachment, especially Komori and Sakakida, was that all the suspects on their list had probably already done what damage they could do. When word of the bombing of Pearl Harbor reached Manila, all agents immediately fanned out with their pick-up lists; many enemy aliens were taken to local prisons and other holding facilities. However a number of the key Japanese aliens, apparently alerted, had already disappeared. The detachment was besieged with reports of suspected Japanese agents transmitting radio signals, flashing mirror signals to their bombers already appearing over Manila. Until they left for Bataan all agents worked at full speed, 24 hours a day, investigating reports of enemy activity. They had been busy like their Hawaiian counterparts in rounding up all names on their list of aliens and suspects, who were now at least where they could no longer do harm: behind bars at Bilibid and other prisons, or in guarded custody at a center like Sakakida's refuge. Included with these were all enemy aliens, Germans, Japanese and Italians—with the probable exception of someone like CIP's informant, Luigi Zavattero. Zavattero's safety was assured for December as he continued working for a Mr.. Wilkinson, who ran an asbestos factory owned by English-Australian interests.

After a few days, food supplies in the center became critically short, especially for the children. Sakakida volunteered with another internee to venture into the city to replenish their supplies. After dispatching the other internee back to the center with the food, he went back to the Nishikawa Hotel to pick up his belongings. As he started packing his bags, three Filipino Secret Service agents entered his room and put him under arrest on suspicion of being a Japanese spy. Thus he joined Komori in the "hell hole" of Bilibid Prison. It took another few days before Agent Drisko was able to rescue them and introduce them for the first time to the remainder of the Philippine CIP Detachment—including a surprised agent Paul Marinas.

Meanwhile, the position of the American and Filipino troops fighting invading Japanese infantry was worsening at an accelerating rate. As invading Japanese marched on Manila in December 1941, a fifth column helped them along the way. Filipinos guided them, gave information about our troop movements and installations, and told of waiting ambushes. When Bataan and Corregidor was history, these fifth columnists worked with the Japanese occupation forces to prevent us from ever setting foot on their shores again. These anti-American Filipinos were among the targets of CIP-CIC in 1945 when the liberating forces returned.

Vainly trying to blunt the advance of the enemy until help arrived from Hawaii and mainland USA, the outnumbered defenders were compelled to retreat steadily toward partially prepared positions on the Bataan peninsula and the small island of Corregidor. The Japanese Air Force had badly crippled America's bombers and fighter planes at Clark Field on Luzon and elsewhere; our Cavite Naval Base near Manila was effectively demolished. The loss of these important, modern components of a full-fledged Army gave General MacArthur no hope of holding Manila after the enemy landed additional ground troops in force on Luzon beginning 20 December, less than two weeks after the initial fighting.

As his troops continued withdrawing to Bataan and Corregidor, on 26 December MacArthur declared Manila an "open city." This meant to the civilized world that the enemy would avoid bombing the open city. It took a while for Japanese military to recognize its noncombatant status. Bombing attacks continued more intensively, even as the citizens of the Philippine Islands' capital began to realize that Japanese troops were on the march into the city.

In a particularly heavy air raid, the noise of planes overhead was deafening. The people of Manila were finally thrown into a panic. People hailing taxicabs were told by the drivers, "The government has taken over all the taxis." Knowing that the approaching Japanese troops would confiscate all their supplies, Chinese grocers and other storekeepers opened their doors and invited their customers to help themselves, no charge for this "clearance" event. Even warehouses were opened and people allowed to take what they wished. And they did. They were grabbing anything they saw that might help them survive.

Some men spotted a large unopened box in the street. With considerable effort they carried it to a convenient place and opened it in anticipation of finding something useful. And then disappointment: it only contained a dead body shipped to Manila for burial!

A couple of days before the declaration of the open city, the CIP Detachment and the G-2 section with which they were working had packed up all documents and files. On Christmas Eve, while bombs fell on Manila and the sky was a lurid red from burning buildings and oil tanks, the entire detachment boarded a tiny steamer bound for

Bataan and Corregidor. On Bataan near little Baguio they set up head-quarters built of bamboo sticks and banana leaves in a spot concealed by jungle growth and tall trees.

Sakakida and some others of the team went on to Corregidor, The Rock, a natural island fortress guarding the entrance to Manila Bay, where MacArthur had set up his headquarters in hopes of holding out until relief arrived. And he desperately needed a personal interpreter and translator during the difficult days ahead. The CIP agents were ready to do their duty for their commander and country, a duty far removed from what CIP agents were trained and expected to do. But they did not hesitate.

Informant Luigi's last contact with CIP was just after Christmas 1941 when Raymond told him to remain in Manila and infiltrate the enemy, even though Luigi complained he would be in danger from the Fascists and other Axis agents. CIP agent Ralph W Montgomery had already changed from civilian to army garb as he asked Luigi to "see my wife and tell her not to worry."

When by the end of December the American forces had finally withdrawn from Manila, Luigi realized the terrible truth as he saw the Italians displaying their fascist flags, the Germans their swastikas, the Spaniards their Franco banners—all along with the Rising Sun of the Japanese. Some civilians were already ridiculing the Americans on Bataan and Corregidor, and even some high Filipinos were pleading for "cooperation" with the Japanese.

* * *

Thus it was in the Philippines, on 31 December 1941 on the Far Side of the Pacific. As the year ended, two CIP agents of Japanese descent had been shadow-boxing the enemy for many months—while the rest of the U.S. Army had only been in action a mere 24 days. More Americans should be aware of these two loyal Japanese-Americans confronting the enemy eight months before most of us even knew we'd have a war.

CHAPTER V

Java, NEI
(Netherlands East Indies)

On 8 December 1941, two Americans who were to play an important CIC role in the war with Japan were in Java, in the far southwest corner of the Pacific in what was then called NEI, the Dutch East Indies. One was Colonel Elliott R. Thorpe who was assigned to Dutch GHQ as liaison officer and military attaché; the other was 27-year old Jennis Roy Galloway who managed a factory near Batavia for the National Carbon Company, and was preparing to return to his Maryland home when the Japanese struck Pearl Harbor.

No one there knew the extent of the damage at Pearl. The general feeling was that the U.S. Navy would soon come steaming across the Pacific to deal quickly with the Japanese upstarts. With impregnable Singapore guarding the left flank, and Corregidor the right, Java seemed to be a logical base from which to mount a counterattack.

Galloway was a graduate of Johns Hopkins Engineering School in Baltimore in 1937 where he also acquired a reserve army commission in the ROTC. Thorpe knew this, and knew Galloway's knowledge of the NEI country and the languages would make Roy more valuable in Java than with some engineering outfit back in the USA. Though initially there was doubt the Japanese would reach Java, concern shifted to apprehension when on 10 December the British suffered the loss of two of their most powerful ships off the Malay peninsula: battleship *Prince of Wales*, and cruiser *Repulse*. Hong Kong fell on the 25th. Manila, though earlier declared an open city, was bombed on 28 December as U.S. troops were vacating for their valiant stand on Bataan and Corregidor. Whereupon, Thorpe persuaded Galloway to resume his commission and join him in Java—which Roy did on 28 December 1941.

Galloway was attached to Dutch General HQ in Bandoeng, Java—his first assignment being to secure English translations of all Dutch intelligence reports, encode them by hand (no code machines there), and dispatch them to the War Department in DC, and to receive and decode incoming messages from DC, taking such action as was appropriate.

A few miles away in Lembang, Java, an allied combined headquarters, ABDACOM, was established under British General Sir Archibald Wavell, hero of Tobruk. U.S. General Brett commanded the American ground forces, and U.S. Admiral Hart commanded the remnants of the U.S. Navy Pacific Squadron with Dutch Admiral Helfrich in overall command of the combined Allied Naval Forces.

* * *

As 1941 drew to a close, neither Thorpe nor Galloway could foresee the perils ahead.

CHAPTER VI

Stateside Shock

7 December 1941 was a beautiful Georgia Sunday. I was enjoying an early afternoon movie at Camp Wheeler, outside of Macon, when the show was interrupted by the announcement of the attack on Pearl Harbor. We were ordered to return instantly to our barracks and prepare to defend ourselves!

After the initial shock of the sneak attack, life settled into a somewhat more reasonable pace. But activities in certain directions increased: to better prepare those waiting for the call to an OCS, the powers that be initiated a series of refresher courses in basic infantry training and tactics. I had just received orders sending me to one of these when 7 December 1941 rolled around. News from Pearl Harbor only sharpened the need for such a course and its aftermath—new 90-day wonders, second lieutenants by the scores. Would I make it?

I didn't have time for elaborate conjecture. I was hurried into the special pre-OCS training school that brought back all the valuable information we had thrown at us in basic training, plus a lot more added stuff that second lieutenants definitely could not do without—for instance, how to give an order that would be obeyed promptly and efficiently. Could I fit in?

After the two-week course was over and the officer in charge personally congratulated me—sympathy for a fellow lawyer?—I found myself back in my old training battalion, waiting for the next step in my fate. It was not long in coming.

23 December 1941, I received a call from PIO (Post Intelligence Officer) Captain Carl Flom, in civilian life a Madison, Wisconsin, lawyer, to come to his office at camp headquarters. Wondering at this unusual summons, I hastened there. In his outer office were his two clerks, Frank Edwards and Jack Gautier. I had met Frank and his twin brother Charles at USO dances in nearby Macon. Frank motioned me on in to the PIO, to whom I gave my best salute.

"How did you learn about the CIP?" he curtly demanded.

Taken aback at this unexpected question, I stammered a little before stating I heard of it from Rene Mittelbronn, a friend in my training platoon. Rene had long gone elsewhere at the end of training.

"Well," the PIO stated slowly, looking me straight in the eye, "you've put me in a dilemma. This has never happened before to my knowledge. Here I have orders transferring you to infantry and OCS at Fort Benning." He held up one hand with papers in it, then held up the other also with papers and continued, "Here I have orders transferring you to the CIP in Atlanta. There would be no problem EXCEPT they are both dated the same day!"

If he was stunned, I was more so. If he had said nothing further but "take your pick" I would have instantly selected OCS. I knew what OCS was all about but CIP was an unknown, strange animal at this point. But his tactic had a little more finesse. He handed me both orders and said, a little more quietly, "Go out into my outer office, look these over—and think carefully which one you want to choose. Then let me have your decision."

Did he anticipate what would happen? I sat down and stared at the two orders dated the same day. Having met me socially, it seemed only natural when Frank opened a conversation in which he described his feelings about the CIP.

"I have applied for CIP," Frank informed me, "but have not been accepted. Right now the CIP is desperate for lawyers and people with training in investigations. You fit the bill. Not only are you a lawyer but also you have had collection experience, were a credit manager at one time, and know how to get information."

He continued: "Besides, anybody can go to OCS. And CIP will be able to make you a warrant officer within the next six months, if not a commissioned officer. Besides, we are in a war, and your country needs your talents in the CIP, Duval."

* * *

What could I say? Frank's last sentence was most likely all I needed to hear. In any event, I returned to the PIO, handed him the OCS orders, and told him I'd go to Atlanta. I don't know what he did with my OCS orders. I should have kept a copy and shown it to CIP in Atlanta, but didn't. I was naive enough to think Atlanta knew everything about me, and would know I had been selected for OCS.

(Frank entered the Corps within three months, twin Charles within a year; they both did a great job—Frank retiring as a LTC, MI; Charles as a Major, AF Intelligence. Moreover, through the Camp Wheeler PIO came a number of excellent agents into the Corps: William Aimone, David McCarthy, William Humphrey, Flewellyn Murphy, and Jack Gautier, among others.)

I now was a part of the same outfit as Komori and Sakakida, who were on this date involved in a real wartime situation in Manila.

The next morning, Christmas Eve, 24 December 1941, with orders in hand, I packed my few possessions, borrowed $5 from Donald Slack,[2] another soldier, for bus fare to Atlanta and headed for four years as a Special Agent in the CIP-CIC. Through no fault of the CIP-CIC, nor mine, it was three-and-a-half years before I became a second lieutenant, though in order to perform my job I would assume, on occasion, ranks as high as colonel.

Reporting to Colonel Stacey Knopf, G-2, in Atlanta, I met Asa Candler III, the assistant to Willis Everett who was in charge of the agents in the Fourth Service Command. A lawyer and former FBI agent, Asa Candler was closer to the daily activities of the agents, assisting in their training and problem cases. He quickly indoctrinated me by advising me not to breathe, speak or write of my being in the CIP, especially not even to my own family; he stated also that whatever happened, there would be no medals, let alone publicity, for doing our jobs. All orders affecting us, other than undercover assignments, were classified "Confidential." Even our interoffice correspondence required special handling, to-wit: my daily report to Headquarters after I was in a field office was placed in an envelope and then sealed, with the addressee on it and "Confidential" written boldly across the front; this was then placed *inside* another envelope which was addressed and mailed as regular mail.

After I was thus inducted into the Corps, Candler directed me to a men's clothing store, where I was provided the civilian clothes I would do most of my investigating in, with the bill going to the G-2.

The day after Christmas I received my CIP credentials, my gold badge, and my first case to investigate. It was a routine background check on an officer slated for a highly confidential position. I needed no special training for this. I checked the police, court and credit records in the nearby town where he had lived most of his life, checked with his former employer, asked his former neighbors all about him, his clubs and organizations, his discretion and loyalty, found nothing adverse, and turned in my completed report the following morning.

Until 31 December 1941, I was given plenty of routine work to do in and around Atlanta, where I encountered diners drinking Coke with their breakfasts. It was a pleasure working in civilian clothes again, though I could foresee the time when wearing them around GIs would probably evoke jeers, "Why aren't you in the Army, draft-dodger?" But a few months would pass before that stage was reached.

* * *

Thus it was in Atlanta, Georgia, on 31 December 1941, on This

---

[2]   *My letter repaying him was returned "transferred." I still owe him!*

Side of the Pacific from Manila, Bataan and Corregidor, where now CIP agents Sakakida and Komori probably had no inkling that on the following day they would no longer be CIP agents.

1942

1 January 1942, the Corps of Intelligence, CIP, was no more—at least by that name. From then on and into the early 1960s it was the Counter Intelligence Corps, CIC for short.

There were two training sessions in 1941 for CIP special agents, one at the War College in the District of Columbia area, the second later in the Chicago area. The first one held under its new name was in January 1942, in what was called the Town Tower Club. Later that year, the school moved to the Women's Club, 66 E 11th Street, Chicago.

The January '42 class was also the first following Pearl Harbor, and much larger than those that followed, with well over a hundred students from the Service Commands. The assigned quarters overflowed, with excess students lodged in nearby hotels, including the Blackstone/Knickerbocker.

* * *

1942 was the year CIC operated on an equal footing in the continental U.S. with ONI and FBI in combating subversive activities. Immediately following Pearl Harbor, aroused Americans became extremely suspicious of anything or anybody that appeared to pose a threat of espionage or sabotage to the U.S. Consequently agencies were flooded with complaints of all kinds, which in keeping with good investigative techniques required adequate checking out even though most proved inconsequential. There were so many of these, agents often crossed lines and investigated a case or incident that rightly belonged to another agency.

In February 1942, a Delimitations Agreement was signed by the three, clearly setting out the boundaries of the jurisdiction of each. CIC in general was not limited to investigating only army and air corps personnel, but also covered any and all civilians working for any army and air corps base and installation. It also took in employees and incidents in those industries with contracts to supply equipment and goods to the army.

On occasion two agencies had joint jurisdiction. For instance, if army personnel were suspected of involvement with a civilian spy, FBI and CIC were jointly responsible for resolving the case. There were a number of such instances. But at times it was necessary to investigate far enough to clarify to which agency it properly belonged.

* * *

Under the Agreement reached by CIC, FBI, and ONI in Hawaii, CIC was provided even wider jurisdiction: it became responsible for all espionage, treason, sabotage and subversive cases in the Territory of Hawaii until the repeal of martial law as the war wound down. Only CIC units outside the continental U.S. came near to such a wide authority.

CHAPTER VII

Hawaii: Martial Law!

Its new name of Counter Intelligence Corps (CIC) did not affect operations in Hawaii, nor elsewhere, for that matter. CIP agents automatically became agents in the new CIC which was issued a Table of Organization and was still under the Army G-2. The Hawaiian unit had a succession of commanding officers: Colonel Joseph Twitty, Colonel Joseph Bicknell, Lt Colonel Frank Blake, and Lt Colonel Byron Meurlott who remained CO until 18 August 1945 when Lt Colonel Kirby Gillette replaced him.

Aliens and citizens alike objected more strenuously to martial law under which the Military Governor's hearing boards were authorized, as it became evident after their stunning defeat at the battle of Midway in 1942 the Japanese could not launch any sizable attack against the Islands. However, Lt General Emmons, CG of the Hawaiian Dept., and Lt General Richardson, Jr. who followed him in June 1943, continued martial law until the President abolished it by proclamation 25 October 1944.

As Hawaii grew into a huge supply base and staging area for troops, a special security section was created to survey all vital installations, a job so vast that at one time or another a CIC agent took a turn in continuous inspection of the various installations.

As the military situation changed during the war, a number of administrative changes occurred which should be mentioned. At the time of the Pearl Harbor attack, CIP was an agency of Army's Hawaiian Department, superseded 14 August 1943 by the newly activated U.S. Army Forces, Central Pacific area (USAFCPA).

Office of the Military Governor added an important security control when it created a Central Identification Bureau. It was organized under supervision from CIC, FBI, and ONI, and was composed of civilians assisted by the Office of Civilian Defense. Over several months the entire population of the islands of the Hawaiian Department were fingerprinted and identified by a card carrying the name, address, physical description, citizenship status and thumb print of the individual. A General Order required each person to have this card at all times.

Civilian employees of various defense projects were also required to have an identification badge issued by Central Identification Bureau, with a photo, badge number and the individual's organization. To qualify for this badge, the applicant completed a personal history statement, was finger-printed and photographed, with the picture placed on the statement. Falsifying any part of the form was a violation. A liaison CIC agent checked this Bureau for questionable information which could open a new case, or add to a pending one.

A seldom-mentioned but very important counter-intelligence function consisted of censoring mail and other outgoing communications. The Army took over mail censorship, while the Navy handled wire and cable censorship. This provided CIC with another source of leads to any violations, and the immediate initiation of investigating the more suspicious ones involving a potential threat.

In order for CIC to maintain complete liaison with local police, it arranged for a captain of detectives to be assigned to a desk in the CIC office. To assure the adequate performance of the wide range of its responsibilities, CIC had to make certain that local police and army MPs were diligently enforcing General Orders.

* * *

Inter-island traffic by air and water was another area that needed security surveillance. To control this movement and deter any subversive actors and activity from spreading, CIC stationed an agent in ticket offices to check and approve these passenger lists.

Another agent served as liaison with the Civilian Internee Hearing Board and presented all internment cases. ONI placed a liaison officer in the CIC office, as did an agent from OSS (Office of Strategic Services) after it came into existence in 1942. FBI maintained a close relationship as its offices were on the same floor as CIC. In addition, the FCC operated with its equipment from two rooms inside the CIC office.

Due to their type of work, CIC agents operated in Hawaii like most did on the mainland, in a civilian capacity—in civilian clothes. Because of the huge caseload, CIC officers in civvies also conducted investigations as did special civilian employees. Officers performing administrative functions wore uniforms. It was found that an enlisted or officer agent in civvies did a better job and had more prestige than lower grade uniformed officers—very important in investigations.

As in all areas where CIC units were stationed, Hawaii had a constant shortage of agents, requiring in many cases local recruitment and training. Counter Intelligence Division, at first called the Contact Office, expanded rapidly after the outbreak of hostilities so that by 27 January 1942 there were 27 agents; a year later there were 81; two years later, 97 agents, the greatest total reached, although the Table of Organization provided for 36 officers and 107 enlisted agents. Besides Honolulu, CIC had branches on the islands of Hawaii, Maui, and Kauai, with two to four agents in each.

Honolulu Headquarters was divided into an administration section, plus many investigative sections established by the category of the case investigation. The principal ones were Japanese, Chinese, Korean, and Filipino, plus Germans and Italians. General investigations were made of subjects of the designated racial extraction:

• sabotage and espionage, wherein agents specialized in all cases of such character

• technical section was charged with the technical equipment and rendered assistance to other agents with photographing, finger-printing, arranging telephone taps, etc.

• personnel section, agents took care of personnel clearance checks, including reserve officers to determine their suitability for active duty

• and a final section for agents charged with general investigations of subjects in a specific geographical area plus setting up reliable informant networks. If an investigation was started that required an agent from another section, the area agent advised and assisted the agent-in-charge assigned to conduct the investigation, such as what informants to use and what further leads to pursue.

* * *

For example, George B. Spencer and another agent were assigned to an area surrounding Pearl Harbor, Schofield Barracks, Wheeler Field and nearby towns. At least two days a week were spent in contacting their network informants.

The Japanese section was quite large, as it initiated several projects that concentrated on specific typed subjects. Example: the Kibei project. Kibei was Japanese for Japanese-Americans who spent their formative years in Japan, where they received all their education, had most of their families, and were more indoctrinated with Japanese mode of thought and action. Actually this knowledge made them valuable as interpreters when inducted into our army as time went by.

Another project dealt with the "dual citizen" problem. Japan expected its emigrants, the *Issei*, to register each child, the *Nisei*, born in America, with the nearest Japanese consulate. Japan considered each one registered to be its citizen. Agent Richard Sakakida's parents had registered him, but his mother had the foresight after he was inducted into the U.S. Army to withdraw that registration, saving Sakakida from execution as a traitor to Japan.

Still another project involved the *Issei* who were ex-soldiers of the Imperial Japanese Army who had come to Hawaii in pursuit of a better life, and were caught there by the Pearl Harbor attack. It was considered highly important to determine if they retained a loyalty to Japan that would constitute a threat to our security.

* * *

In each of these special projects, the project agent in charge developed a set of factors used in determining if a subject was potentially dangerous. Several hundred investigations of a specific category were concluded more expeditiously.

In the early days, CIC agents experienced difficulty in moving about and gaining entry to certain installations. CIC badges and credentials were not recognized and accepted without a loss of valuable time and effort. This had unforeseen dimension: when interviewing a policeman, an agent would show his credentials, and badge if necessary, get his interview and go on his way. A few days later a message from an irate J Edgar Hoover (chief of FBI) would notify CIC that agent So-and-so was passing himself off as FBI, and he wanted something done about it. This happened also on the mainland. Hawaiian CIC HQ arranged with installations most often visited by sending them a master list of CIC badges and credentials. That solved this irritant to the FBI chief, at least in Hawaii.

This was not the fault of CIC but a natural reaction by even a policeman being interviewed, who automatically associated the flashing of the badge and credentials with our FBI. This was often true of our soldiers and officers, who simply could not accept that the man interviewing them, even though in uniform, was actually in the Army! Had they known their interviewer's actual rank, many (especially officers) would not have cooperated fully, or at all.

The Treasury Department's Office of Foreign Funds Control (FFC) was another government agency that greatly assisted CIC. Where a certain percentage of a business was owned or controlled by aliens, the FFC had to issue a license. To qualify for that license, the business would submit reports that included a list of stockholders. Many foreign interests were thus uncovered, leading to subsequent investigations. When an agent arrested or interned the owner of a store, he would notify the FFC which would often arrange for its agent to accompany the CIC in order to assume control of the business in the interest of the U.S. If operating the business contributed to our war effort, FFC saw to its continuation. But if it did not help our war effort, FFC held the assets for liquidation with proceeds placed to the credit of the internee and interested owners.

FCC monitored Radio Tokyo, and informed CIC regarding the enemy propaganda line. The CID (Counter Intelligence Division) of G-2 placed its public relations branch next to CIC offices to inform CIC on our propaganda line. This information was helpful to a CIC agent's judgment of the effectiveness of either line while conducting an interview.

* * *

Houses of prostitution in Honolulu were permitted to operate with Army and Navy supervision. The girls were inspected periodically by medical officers from both services, which also periodically patrolled the houses with their respective police force. Prostitutes were an excellent source of information on perpetrators of dangerous loose talk, of disaffection by a soldier or sailor, and so on. Two CIC agents with vice squad experience handled this assignment. As a disloyal prostitute with connections to an espionage ring could be advantageous to the enemy, CIC continuously checked on this as well.

After the 72-hour Operation Pickup following the Pearl Harbor catastrophe was over, the Military Governor ordered CIC to use search warrants. The forms were prepared and approved by the Military Governor, who then directed that no search could be conducted by *any* agency without the warrant issued by CIC. Only the head CIC officer was empowered to sign such warrants. Thus neither the Provost Marshal personnel nor local police could conduct a search without one of these warrants. Usually when conducting a search the agent in charge would present the duplicate of the warrant to the inhabitant of the searched place with a list on the back of any confiscated articles. The original was then filed with the report.

Many search sweeps were made around vital military installations. The size of the area to be searched determined the number of CIC teams used. In some instances FBI, ONI, and Honolulu Police assisted CIC. During a search translators circulated to aid as many teams as possible. Each house was searched and inhabitants interviewed for routine information. When questionable information was developed, a full-blown investigation began.

It is a matter of record: there was not one known, legally proven act of Axis-inspired sabotage committed in Hawaii, and only ONE conviction for espionage—the Kuehns mentioned earlier, who were Germans, not Japanese; and certainly not *Japanese-Americans*! The Kuehns were taken into custody by the CIC while the bombs were still falling, and sentenced to terms in a Federal pen.

Agents Donald Fenton and Albert Turner made numerous surveys of vital installations and public utilities following suspected sabotage incidents, but found every one was the result of carelessness or negligence.

An especially busy agent was Andrew S. Wong who headed the administrative section for most of the war, and had to keep well informed as to everything that transpired in the entire Detachment.

CIC in Hawaii was so successful in holding in check the Communist Party's attempts to gain membership among the military and civilian populace that the communists were forced to channel their efforts into labor organizations and concerns. Of 116 alien-owned corporations surveyed, 53 were wholly or in part owned by residents of Axis nations. Members of the German Bund were found working in key defense factories. They were soon weeded out and sent to mainland U.S. internment camps.

* * *

Another CIC unit in Hawaii, the 607th, originally the 7th AF CIC Detachment, was activated by Chief of CIC in Baltimore at the request of the Commanding General of the Air Forces. Crashes of airplanes newly delivered had become frequent. CIC's talents were called on, but its agents could only find carelessness by civilian employees, as well as defects in materials from the mainland. Though no cases of actual sabotage were uncovered, largely through preventive measures taken and recommended by CIC, much carelessness and poor workmanship was eliminated.

* * *

Thus it was in Hawaii in 1942, with CIC responsible for internal security. There, as elsewhere, the first year of CIP under its new name of CIC was an outstanding one—though unknown to most Americans.

CHAPTER VIII

Bataan: CIC's
"Lost Detachment" in Combat

After the Manila Detachment set up its bamboo headquarters on Bataan, with little precedent to guide them, the CIP—now CIC— agents plunged into a frenzy of activity, performing a variety of tasks foreign to their specialized training simply because there was no one else to do them, and because they knew they had to keep busy.

Much of this "variety of tasks" they performed is now standard in a competent modern army. It consisted of collecting enemy information, interrogating prisoners of war, checking the security of communications and documents, going on patrols and scouting expeditions through the lines, interning collaborators, and translating captured enemy documents and inscriptions on captured enemy materials. So great was the quantity and variety of the latter that one day in a pile of equipment dumped in the headquarters they found a live land mine and a Molotov cocktail!

Komori was attached to General Wainwright's (in charge for MacArthur) headquarters on the Bataan peninsula specifically to help identify Japanese, as there were some Japanese *Kempei Tai* who penetrated our lines posing as Filipino tribesmen. Such a security loophole had to be closed, definitely a CIC job. Several members of the Detachment, Sakakida among them, were on Corregidor deciphering the code then in use by the Japanese. (Our Intelligence had cracked one code before Pearl Harbor, but there were others.)

* * *

The desperate need for linguists to interrogate the few captured enemy soldiers caused Komori and Sakakida to alternate shifts. When Sakakida was on Bataan, Komori was on Corregidor. On occasion, Sakakida accompanied patrols to search abandoned headquarters of enemy units for documents, as well as bodies of the dead enemy for highly prized diaries that sometimes contained tactical information of value. When an enemy unit succeeded in penetrating as far as some cliff caves, then were surrounded, Sakakida came to the front lines and broadcast a surrender appeal which was totally ignored.

The presence of Sakakida on our front lines was usually dreaded by our troops. When he had set up his microphone and loudspeaker in a fox hole, and finished broadcasting an appeal to the enemy, inevitably it was answered by a barrage of artillery and grenades. Early in April he was joined by Komori and civilian Yamagata, whom Captain Raymond had brought out of Manila with the Detachment to assist in translating documents. Yamagata of course had severed his Japanese connections in Manila, since he was known to them as a Nisei and likely loyal to the U.S. (which he proved time and again).

* * *

Other agents of the detachment often found themselves heavily involved in the fighting. Agent Lorenzo Alvarado was attached to a unit which lost all its officers, whereupon he took over as commander during a fire fight. For his courage and initiative, he won an award; though there is no record of it in the scant CIC records from SWPA, it was probably at least the Bronze Star. Harry Glass made CIC history as the first agent to be injured in action. Hit in the neck by sniper fire, which luckily did no serious damage, he was back on duty in two days with only patches at the entry and exit points of the bullet.

When pressure was not too great on Bataan, both Komori and Sakakida were back on Corregidor working up to 20 hours daily to monitor all Japanese Air Force communications now coming through in the clear; this gave advance warning to all the places enemy pilots planned to bomb, permitting soldiers to find whatever safe spots remained on the Rock. Yamagata joined in this effort.

* * *

As the days and weeks passed, it was apparent capture by the enemy was imminent. Hope faded for any aid from Hawaii or the mainland. With no prospect of escape except for a handful, General MacArthur in Australia (ordered there by the Pentagon) and General Wainwright on Corregidor both expressed deep concern for the safety of Komori and Sakakida. These two CIC agents would no doubt fare worse under captivity than Caucasians since Japan refused to recognize the right of any one of Japanese blood to bear loyalty to another country. There was also danger that their months of undercover activity among the Japanese population in Manila would be revealed, which could seal their death warrants.

The commanding general of our forces on Bataan surrendered the troops under his direct command on 9 April. General Wainwright, who had replaced MacArthur on Corregidor, continued the fight from the embattled Rock into May. Approximately 75,000 surviving Filipinos and Americans were in the infamous Bataan death march during which their numbers were further diminished by a combination of starvation, lack of medical attention, and outright barbaric treatment by a high percentage of their captors, some bent on personal revenge for previous defeats by our forces.

Many agents from the Manila CIC were in this march of defeat, though one, Grenfell D. Drisko, managed to escape to the hills where he later joined a guerrilla group. Drisko maintained sporadic contact with Angelita Sobral, a former secretary in the office of the G-2, and a member of a wealthy Manila Spanish family. She was able to get supplies and money to Drisko and his guerrillas. Unconfirmed reports were that before we liberated the Philippines he was betrayed by one of his own, captured and killed by the Japanese, who had a bounty on his head—likely another first in the annals of CIC's history!

* * *

Early April, Komori and Sakakida were informed by Lt. Colonel Stuart Wood, former Commander of the Detachment who became G-2 after General Willoughby's departure, that General MacArthur ordered them to leave via the mosquito or "bamboo fleet" and join him in Australia where there was plenty of work for their talents, as well as a need for the practical experience they had picked up in combat.

Sakakida made a most difficult decision, a historic self-sacrificing one. He realized that his friend Carl Yamagata's situation under capture would be even worse than his own, since Yamagata had worked openly for the Japanese in a position of trust and had willingly come over to the Americans. Besides, his wife and two children were then in Japan, and Sakakida realized, as did Yamagata, that the Japanese would bring every kind of pressure against him under threat of what could happen to them. Sakakida persuaded Colonel Wood that Yamagata should replace him. Colonel Wood obtained General Wainwright's reluctant permission, who in turn obtained permission from MacArthur. During a postwar interview, Sakakida refused to recognize his action as heroic but only something he "had to do."

On 13 April, Komori and Yamagata bid Sakakida good-bye and along with an emissary from Chiang Kai-shek and a correspondent named Hewlett, they left the Rock in a "50-50 attempt" to get out in two Army training planes. With previous CAA flight training in Hawaii, Komori rode as copilot in one to Iloilo, Panay. There a legendary daredevil pilot known as "Pappy" Gunn took them the next leg of their flight with Japanese planes breathing down their necks. According to Komori, "Captain 'P. I.' Gunn rescued us from Panay with his B-25 in a flight in broad daylight through enemy territory in a hedge-hopping, canyon-shooting, wave-skipping trip, which were Gunn's specialties. He kept telling us enemy planes could not see us since we were flying only a few feet above our shadow."

They were picked up on Mindanao Island by "General Boyce's raiding squadron" and flown on to Melbourne, Australia, where Komori joined a little handful of CIC agents who had arrived on 9 April from the United States.

* * *

On Corregidor, Sakakida joined other detachment members preparing for the inevitable. Other than destroying all detachment records, there was little to do but wait. For his protection, he was listed as a civilian on remaining records, and all those who had been in contact with him were instructed not to reveal he was in any way connected with the army except as a conscripted civilian interpreter.

On 6 May, superior enemy forces succeeded in landing on the Rock, and General Wainwright and aides left the tunnels under a white flag to surrender. When Wainwright failed to return, Sakakida accompanied Beebe, Wainwright's deputy, to Bataan as interpreter to find out about Wainwright. Agent James Rubard was also along and recalls that on landing at Bataan, an enemy NCO addressed Sakakida in Japanese; hearing the reply in the same language, he struck Sakakida repeatedly, breaking his glasses, cutting his face and knocking him down. Rubard feared Sakakida would be killed on the spot. Instead the Japanese said they had their own interpreters and retained Beebe and aides, returning the agents and others to the Rock.

* * *

In what was probably another first in the history of CIC, agent Rubard participated in dispatching Filipino natives in small boats to gather positive intelligence about the enemy wherever they could. Fearful that under intense torture he might unwittingly reveal the identities of his collection agents, he intended concealing his identity and work as long as possible. But a traitor from our own army foiled Rubard's plan, imperiling his life as well as Sakakida's.

This traitor at one time had been considered a potential recruit for the Manila CIC, but the extensive background investigation CIC made of all its applicants in those days revealed adverse information. He had spent several years in Japan learning the language and studying to become a Buddhist monk. Thus he was a suspected Japan sympathizer. Also, in those days when homosexuality was a closet matter, the investigation indicated this proclivity which definitely made him a security risk in those days when blackmail, the threatened exposure of being a homosexual, could turn one into an unwilling informant. In today's enlightened world, with homosexuals not worried about being so tabbed, the blackmail threat seems to have disappeared, so that alone would no longer seem a factor in a background check.

Shortly after the surrender of Corregidor, this traitor voluntarily began interpreting for the captors. He relayed orders to sick and wounded Americans and Filipinos in the hospital wing in a tunnel, saying they must move out so Japanese wounded could replace them. Captain Thompson of the Medical Service replied, "Tell them to go to hell; the men are too sick to be moved." On the traitor's interpreting this answer, the Japanese dragged Thompson away and killed him.

The traitor next led enemy soldiers to where the prisoners were kept, and pointed out Rubard and other headquarters' staff. Rubard was interrogated for three days with ceaseless questions about his information on American codes, and especially about Filipino agents. By the third day they were slapping him and swinging swords as if to behead him for not coming through with answers. He maintained a consistent story that his only duty had been to update the G-2 situation map, that the codes were kept by Signal Corps, and that Filipino agents had been handled by G-2 officers who left by submarine for Australia just before the surrender. The next day he was returned to the other prisoners and departed for a prison camp on Luzon. He was never questioned again, probably because his interrogators were not among the expert Kempei Tai, and even Japanese records must have gotten lost in the shuffle at times.

* * *

Sakakida was the one in whom the Kempei Tai was most interested, intrigued by his ancestry. At least the record was not lost of him going to Bataan to act as an interpreter for the Americans. So, unlike the other Americans, he was kept on Corregidor for another six months! He told his captors the Americans had taken him from Bilibid where other Japanese had been jailed after Pearl Harbor, which fact they could easily confirm. He said they took him and made him work for them under duress as an interpreter.

But his interrogators confronted him with liberated Japanese POWs who testified he worked for the U.S. Army voluntarily. In the face of this contrary testimony, he was kept in a side tunnel and questioned over a period of several months, with an increasing degree of severe torture. Sometimes they beat him, sometimes burned him all over his body with lighted cigarettes. Water was pumped into his stomach which was jumped on by his guards. He never knew if this torture was because he was a Nisei, or whether they were still trying to make him talk, or both.

The Kempei Tai couldn't believe that a Japanese appearing with an American high officer didn't have *some* information of interest to them. For the next several months he was under constant interrogation by either the Japanese Military Police or officers of the Judge Advocate General's Section of Japan's Fourteenth Army HQ, interrogation that eventually repeated the painful torture, mainly burns with lighted cigarettes. They never brought him into court, but informed him he was on trial for treason, since anyone of Japanese ancestry was automatically a Japanese citizen.

Through it all Sakakida was able to stick to his original story convincingly. He claimed he was a victim of circumstances and that the Americans had taken him to Bataan and Corregidor as an interpreter; he was an American citizen (true) and a civilian (not true). Never once during torture did he so much as hint he was in the U.S. Army and an agent of its intelligence apparatus.

In December he was sent to Bilibid Prison, where he shared the same cells as Japanese soldiers serving life sentences for surrendering to the U.S. on Bataan. Some he had probably interrogated himself after their surrender, and he did not relish the thought of sharing their cell. He was now informed that he would definitely be tried for treason, as he was of Japanese ancestry and had served his country's enemy, the Americans. For this offense, he faced the death penalty.

Timely, however, Fourteenth Army Headquarters received word from the Japanese Ministry in Tokyo that, although Sakakida had been registered with the Japanese Consul in Hawaii at birth as was the custom of many Japanese residents there, his citizenship had been officially voided in August 1941 by his mother. She had the forethought to take this step after Sakakida had left for the Philippines, an action which even the Japanese recognized made the charge of treason illegal. They changed the charge to disturbing the peace and order of the Japanese Imperial Forces in the Philippines, and the interrogation continued, although not quite as severely.

He was still in the "hell hole" of Bilibid Prison at the end of 1942.

* * *

Elsewhere on Luzon, soldiers who refused to surrender and managed to escape to the hills gradually began to gather in guerrilla bands and start the process of unifying their actions into what in time became a worrisome thorn in the side of the enemy, tying down more and more of their troops that could have been utilized on other fronts.

The Japanese authorities did not wait for the fall of Bataan and Corregidor before initiating their plans to transform the Philippines and its people into an asset in their Co-prosperity Sphere. Nine leading political leaders sent telegrams to Roosevelt and Quezon, pleading for the end of hostilities and for cooperation with the Japanese who promised immediate independence for the Philippines.

President Quezon and family had been previously rescued by submarine and were on the way to safety in the U.S. He broadcast again that the U.S. would return to restore the freedom of the Filipinos. The nine, who had called for stopping the battle and cooperating with the Japanese, simply shrugged their shoulders and stated they had been personally ordered by Quezon in private to "play ball with the invader" for the good of the people.

Among those holding steadfast in their loyalty to the U.S. and the Philippines was Jose Abad Santos, Chief Justice of the Philippine Supreme Court. He had been given the choice of going with Quezon on the latter's escape to Australia, or staying in the Philippines. Santos preferred to stay, whereupon President Quezon appointed him acting head of the commonwealth government in the Philippines.

He and his son were captured in Cebu, and he was ordered to turn over his papers and instructions from Quezon as the price for his life. He refused. "I would be a traitor to my country if I did that," he is quoted by his son as saying. He was then taken to Malabang in Mindanao, where his captors said he would be shot for refusing to collaborate. In the cell with him, his son, Jr., broke down in tears; the jurist calmed him smiling: "This is a rare chance, Pepito. Not everyone is given the opportunity to die for his country."

Jose Abad Santos, appointed by Quezon to run the government in the unoccupied areas in 1942, paid with his life for refusing to collaborate with the invader. He was shot on 7 May 1942. His son survived to tell CIC agents in 1945 about his father's last days.

Zavattero Survives

Luigi was arrested by the Japanese and then released to the *Kempei Tai* which had him in a dungeon for four months, torturing and questioning him as to his activities for the American G-2. When Manila was liberated in 1945, Zavattero finally wound up at the 493rd CIC Detachment where he was questioned in great detail by agent Del Westling. His story was so rambling and confusing that Westling sat him down at a typewriter and had him try to put his story into some kind of logical order.

Unfortunately, what came out of the typewriter is still chaotic, but depicts a story of Luigi walking a tightrope after the Japanese released him on his promise he would help them. Helping them was a real test of his skill to keep from betraying those he knew to be loyal Filipinos and Americans, while giving his captors just enough radio matériel and data to prevent being returned to prison or worse.

While supposedly aiding the Japanese, beginning in 1942 he claims he was able to contact the guerrillas and get information to them. Unfortunately, those who could verify this part of his story appear to have died. He also claims he collaborated only under duress, as he had a wife and two children who depended on him.

* * *

Agent Westling concluded that Luigi appeared at the CIC office at an appropriate time: about the time that the Philippine government offered a general amnesty to those with no complete case of collaboration against them. He did not have to go to jail again.

CHAPTER IX

South Pacific Greets CIC

United States Armed Forces in the South Pacific (USAFISPA), later called South Pacific Base Command (SOPACBACOM), became an immense marshaling yard for millions of tons of equipment and thousands of troops bound for the South Pacific combat zone (Navy Theater), a separate Theater of Operations from MacArthur's Southwest Pacific (Army Theater). It had only a few strategically important military actions—Guadalcanal, Munda, and Bougainville campaign—but extremely important naval battles.

As in most of the Pacific, USAFISPA was slow to obtain CIC agents to protect this mass of men and matériel. It was not until June 1942 that the first six agents arrived in the Fiji Islands with the 37th Division. This was one month after the naval battle of the Coral Sea, which marked the end of Japan's southward thrust and the beginning of a lull in which both sides prepared for further conflict.

Fifteen agents had been allocated to the Task Force led by the 37th Infantry Division, six to join at the port of embarkation, the other nine after its arrival in the Theater. But the other nine never made it, in spite of an urgent appeal from Major General Beightler, 37th's Commanding General (CG).

Few records of the work of this Detachment are available, but it appears to have been directed by John Burden as the CIC Section Chief, G-2. The main duties were security checks and surveys of military installations throughout the Fiji Islands.

In September 1942, Marvin C. Goff, Jr. (Tennessee lawyer) and six agents arrived with the newly organized USAFISPA headquarters, landing first at Noumea, the capital of New Caledonia, then being directed to Auckland, New Zealand, with the rest of the Task Force. Six weeks later, when it was apparent offensive power had been wrested from the enemy, CIC returned to Noumea. Faced with the overwhelming task of maintaining counter-intelligence coverage of an area thousands of miles square, Goff spread his agents as carefully as possible, while continuing to request more manpower.

In October 1942, a globe-trotting Australian female school teacher became a CIC target. She had traveled extensively in the Orient and Europe just before the war. Examining her personal effects and diaries revealed an unusually detailed account of military and semi-military matters garnered from acquaintances with American Army and Navy officers. Any intent on her part to pass this information on to the enemy was never established, but her reputed freedom with her favors raised such a question mark as to military security that the Fiji governor deported her to Australia, along with the dossier, so she could be closely watched there.

The New Hebrides Island Group consisted of 11 major and numerous minor islands lying 250 miles northwest of New Caledonia, and 500 miles west of the Fijis. When U.S. troops arrived in the fall of 1942, the inhabitants numbered 40,000 natives, 600 French and 200 British subjects, jointly administered by High Commissioners of Great Britain and France. The natives were mostly Melanesians, with a small number of Polynesians and some 1,000 indentured Tonkinese.

* * *

Commanding the CIC detachment was George Crow, followed later by William Wallace. CIC constantly received reports of Japanese submarines being sighted but were never able to verify same. 1942 was a comparatively peaceful year for CIC, though things began to pick up as more and more troops and supplies arrived.

CHAPTER X

NEI Joins SWPA

As 1941 ended, the Allies had hoped to mount an offense against Japan from their base in Indonesia. Early in 1942, this hope quickly dissipated as Japanese seized Bali and South Sumatra, closing the only deep water navigable straits in the Western Indonesian archipelago, trapping Allied naval forces in the Java Sea. Most of this fleet was later destroyed in the Battle of the Java Sea.

All major ports along Java's north coast were rendered useless. Few military supplies reached Java: some British Hurricane fighters without armament diverted from Singapore; a half dozen old B-17s that escaped from the Philippines; remnants of a Texas National Guard artillery unit with only 10 rounds of ammo per gun (enemy planes had sunk the rest of this unit in Darwin, Australia). One of our older aircraft carriers, the *US Langley*, en route to Java was torpedoed and sunk, losing its load of valuable fighter planes.

In this utter confusion, ABDACOM, the Allied command, quickly dissolved, with some of its top brass escaping to Ceylon, others to Australia. Thorpe and Galloway were ordered to get to Melbourne by any means possible. On March 6, Batavia, capital of NEI, fell; the defending Allies, including American troops still there, surrendered unconditionally to the invaders.

How Galloway managed to escape by one of the last two Quantas plane flights out of Java to Broome, Australia, seemed a miracle. He arrived safely in one of the two; the other was never heard from, obviously intercepted and shot down.

Senior officer Thorpe beat Galloway to Melbourne to find all intelligence activities being handled by the Military Attaché at the U.S. Embassy. Thorpe took over as G-2, responsible for mail censorship and counter intelligence activities.

* * *

March 17th General MacArthur arrived from the Philippines to take command and lead the troops back to his beloved Philippines. With him was Major General Charles Willoughby who was put in charge of all combat intelligence under MacArthur; he also worked unceasingly throughout the war and even afterwards to wrest control of CIC from Thorpe. At one time he tried to use the early arriving CIC

Western Pacific, showing SWPA section

agents as additions to the excellent coast-watching network the Australians had in place long before the war began. He failed, due to Thorpe's adamant opposition. These coast watchers, and the outstanding performance they turned in, undeniably turned the tide in fighting later that year on Guadalcanal, Bougainville, and elsewhere. They, together with the network of guerrillas evolving in the Philippines, were an excellent reason for MacArthur to refuse General Donovan's famous OSS; Mac simply did not need them.

Australia then became the hub from which MacArthur—and CIC—began operating from a base almost nonexistent at first, changing into a relatively small but highly effective force that would eventually defeat the enemy. Following closely on the heels of MacArthur, former CIP special agent Arthur Komori reached this hub haven, and was quickly shunted into a new organization established under MacArthur to translate and interpret, and later interrogate, everything in the Japanese language and any prisoners taken.

* * *

It was called ATIS, for Allied Translator and Interpreter Service. It became the organization to which more than 2,000 Nisei were to devote their talents and loyalty throughout the war,[3] and ATIS formed a pool from which many valuable CIC agents were drawn to serve in the occupation of postwar Japan. Colonel Sidney F Mashbir who headed this vital unit declared of these Nisei: the U.S. "owes a debt to these men and to their families it can never fully repay. Thousands of American lives and millions of dollars in matériel were saved by their contribution. This group had more to lose than others—if captured, their torture would have been indescribable; any relatives in Japan, if identified, would have been subjected to brutal cruelties."

Komori's first task was based on his and Sakakida's recent, first-hand experiences on Bataan: a guideline for ATIS personnel on how best to interrogate Japanese POWs who lived long enough to be questioned. Give him a drink of water, an American cigarette, any immediate medical attention, and thus demonstrate he was not about to be executed as he had been taught. Such treatment always resulted in an outpouring of everything the captive knew. This approach more than paid off on the long island hopping that General MacArthur was able to initiate within a year after Corregidor fell.

Komori remained with ATIS and participated in its growing success in translating enemy documents and questioning captured Japanese. When it reached a certain peak in strength of numbers and capability, he was reassigned to the headquarters of General Elliott Thorpe, chief of counter intelligence under MacArthur in SWPA (South West Pacific Area) and then still later, into active duty as a CIC agent in time to see action in the Philippines. One of the first CIC agents to enter Japan after its surrender, he went on to a career in CIC, retiring as a colonel to practice law in his Hawaiian homeland.

Most of these Americans had to complete a tough language school to perfect their knowledge of their parents' native tongue before they were accepted into ATIS. Many were doing this for their country despite the fact that their families were interned behind guarded barbed wire back in the States. Mashbir was only one of many quoted as stating the work they performed was credited with shortening the war if not by years at least by many months—which also meant saving thousands of Japanese lives as well as American.

* * *

When Galloway arrived in Australia from NEI, the CIC presence was nonexistent. Neither were there any American fighting units, though the 32nd Division, Wisconsin National Guard, was en route to Adelaide, Australia. Its advance party to organize logistics had al-

---

[3]   *Despite what happened to their families in the U.S.*

ready arrived in Melbourne. As Japanese forces rampaged toward all their objectives, it was rumor time, and a time when the Japanese were reputed to know about most Allied troop movements through spies and loose talk. Tokyo Rose taunted our troops by reporting this information over radio broadcasts from Tokyo. Hence there was considerable concern for the security of this convoy. A major effort was mounted to prevent leakage of its whereabouts and destination.

Galloway was at the time attached to the Australian Army, Southern Command. To protect the arrival of the 32nd Division, his first counter-intelligence experience was right in line with what many other CIC agents were doing back in the States: listening to conversations at bars for loose talk that could reach the enemy and imperil our operations and the lives of our troops.

With the cooperation of the Australian Southern Command and the Melbourne Police's CID, two attractive young ladies of the night were assigned to Galloway. He guided them to the night spots known to be frequented by members of the advance party, bought them a drink, then left. Next morning he met them at a designated place and heard any information they had obtained during the night.

It wasn't long before this type of broad (in both senses of the word) surveillance paid off. They came to the meeting with the whole story on the convoy, the port of arrival and estimated time of arrival! Whose loose lips spilled the beans? Surprisingly, none other than the commanding officer of the advance party! This was reported to Thorpe and in turn to the Chief of Staff, General Sutherland. The loose-talking officer was relieved immediately of his command and sent on a return trip to the USA.

Galloway's success at this first CI (counter-intelligence) operation caused Thorpe to assign him to organize a security show for the 32nd Division troops on their arrival. Again with the help of the Australian authorities, about 20 of the prettiest young ladies of Adelaide (this time from socially prominent families, not street walkers) were each given a poster with an appropriate security message, and paraded on the dock as the transports pulled in. The reception the girls received from these troops so long at sea was overwhelming: whistles, catcalls, cigarettes and money poured from the ship. But despite all the hoopla associated with this welcome arrival, it was believed to have heightened awareness of the need for security, e.g., tight lips.

* * *

Until April 1942, there were no formally trained counter intelligence personnel around SWPA. Then the first CIC agents began to trickle in. Realizing the growing need for trained personnel, and aware that a trickle was not enough, an aggressive recruitment of promising candidates began among the troops now there. Around May 1942, the first CIC training school was opened in the Melbourne Grammar School. Among its first instructors were Blair Labatt and John Irwin. These two and Galloway and Harold Gelwicks, Thorpe praised in his personal account of the war, *East Wind, Rain.*

Still hampered with a lack of enough trained CIC agents, officers such as Galloway were called on to do special agents' jobs. It was excellent training ground for them. Galloway was not a novice on ships, as he had had recreational sailing back home in Maryland; he was assigned to an undercover job on the *SS Stagen* which was carrying vitally important equipment from Australia to New Guinea. His cover was an Engineering Officer; his mission was to see that the ship reached its destination safely with its badly needed cargo intact.

While nothing suspicious occurred on this voyage, later that year Galloway was stationed at Port Moresby when the *Stagen* suffered a fire of suspicious origin in its forward hold while unloading cargo.

At this time the enemy occupied almost all of New Guinea, the second largest island in the world, with no roads or other means of communication other than by water. With American planes being shot down over this vastness, there were genuine fears of what New Guinea native fuzzie-wuzzies might do to the pilots: would they turn them over to nearby Japanese? Or, would those natives who were cannibals actually welcome a downed airman for, and as, dinner?

To gain a better knowledge of these natives and how to deal with them, Galloway was assigned to one of the ANGAU (Australia New Guinea Administrative Unit) field teams. ANGAU was responsible for native affairs, and made routine two-week trips into the jungles. These jaunts through the bush were to persuade the natives to return any downed flyer, for which they would be rewarded appropriately. Usually a pig or two was considered appropriate

Two chiefs of the Chimbu Tribe from the Mt Hagen area of Papua, a head-hunting people with a stone-age culture, after a lot of persuasion and the help of ANGAU were put on a plane and flown to Port Moresby. There Galloway was able to provide a Cook's tour of our installations to impress them they should cooperate with the Allies and not with the Japanese—quite a bite for such a swift passage from the Stone Age into the Twentieth Century!

This bush assignment must have been successful, for William McCauley of Baltimore, Maryland, one of the CIC agents who reached SWPA early, also journeyed with ANGAU on similar missions.

* * *

Theater Headquarters for CIC was located first in Melbourne, then in Sydney. In October 1942, Galloway was promoted to captain and transferred to Port Moresby to set up the first Advance Base Intelligence Office in New Guinea. The first group of CIC agents assigned there were Leland "Andy" Anderson, Walt Wagner, Don Winterbourne and Ted Steinway. One of the most important duties at this time was "port security" that required every ship coming into Moresby to have its cargo and crew checked out for potential sabotage and espionage. It was a time-consuming but necessary part of the routine of counter-intelligence, as was censorship. CIC agents took care of the ships; others took care of the censorship though, turning anything that warranted investigation over to CIC to pursue.

The Australian forces, which up to now had born the brunt of the fighting, began to push the enemy back over the Owen Stanley mountains from its advance to within a few miles of Moresby. What later became in 1943 I Corps (known as "I," pronounced "Eye," Corps) of General Krueger's Sixth Army, was supervising the Theater's only two American divisions, the 32nd and 41st. As the end of 1942 approached, MacArthur ordered I Corps to take Buna on the north coast of New Guinea, over the mountains. It was done with considerable damage to the 41st, which was more deeply involved.

As U.S. ground operations expanded, it became necessary to set up sub-base CIC units in the far-flung areas where our army bases were being established. Each base was known by code. There were at least three sub-base CIC detachments, all reporting through the Advance base CIC at Moresby. Sub-base "A" was commanded by James Broz, "B" by William B. Clark, "D" was probably at Milne Bay, under Robert Hollings (brother of U.S. Senator Ernest Hollings).

* * *

CIC was almost in place, though sparse in numbers of agents. CIC detachments formed a very tenuous ring around the Pacific rim, from Hawaii to the South Pacific, and then by 1943 over to action in India, Burma and on into the vast expanses of China.

The neck of this ring was the south, Australia, where MacArthur began congregating in driblets and spurts an ever-growing armada that would thrust like a spear right up the middle, straight into the underbelly of Japan, while ever-mounting pressure would continue from the Central Pacific in the east, and from CBI in the west.

From the south under MacArthur would come the greatest mass of Allied forces fighting its way into Japan itself. So, we have reserved this section to depict the activities of the Counter Intelligence Corps doing its share in this final, famous island-hopping dash of an ever accelerating Army hell-bent for Japan's heartland.

As researchers freely admit, CIC data from MacArthur's Theater did not all reach the repositories in the War Department, certainly not in the same quantity and details as from the other theaters. In fact, many strongly believe a certain general in Theater HQ ordered CIC files destroyed after VJ day. Therefore, much of this material comes from the years of searching records and interviewing agents such as Komori and Sakakida, by the committee set up at Fort Holabird in Maryland in the 1950s, through the belated contributions from others, including Roy Galloway who was eventually to head the CIC under MacArthur for the duration and beyond.

As noted elsewhere, only in MacArthur's Theater was CIC required to openly carry its special agents attached to *combat* troops on all records showing the actual rank of the agents. In other theaters, agents wore shoulder patches like war correspondents did; and as such pseudo-civilians, the agents could and did mingle with army officers on an equal footing, making their job easier in more ways than one; this also permitted them to approach enlisted personnel in a similar equal fashion, since their patches indicated they were civilians.

It turns out that agents in CBI were likewise protected in their ranks, and for the same reason, also in Hawaii. When an agent needed to identify himself and his mission, he presented a gold-plated badge carrying the words "Military Intelligence - War Department," and if necessary supplemented this with credentials stating he was a Special Agent of the War Department Military Intelligence. While some credentials may have differed somewhat in some areas forced to come up with their own supply, essentially none of them revealed the *rank* of the agent.

Not so in SWPA. Agents there still had their numbered badges, and their written credentials, which they brought with them to SWPA, but in addition their rank was not concealed when ordered to a detachment serving with a combat unit or command.

How then did SWPA CIC agents handle this problem? In a number of ways. An experienced agent usually could put on a front that convinced officers that just maybe he was not really a sergeant, but was in actuality the FBI, temporarily attached to the Army.

Practically all agents were college graduates, some even college professors, and many of them were lawyers and other professional men, or had years of experience in some field of investigation. Investigators are trained to overcome obstacles of all kinds. Take the instructors at the CIC Training School in Chicago, who asked the question: "What do you do if you are tailing a suspect and he suddenly turns on you and demands to know why you are following him?" The clever agent immediately throws up his arms and cries, "Oh, YOU are not the one I thought was fooling around with my wife! I apologize for mistaking you for him." (We never know about the cases in which THAT doesn't work, do we?)

The main area of the problem, when it was one, occurred in combat zones. In SWPA there was one definite peculiarity among army officers: most did NOT wear their insignia of rank openly on their shoulders. They learned early, in the Buna-Gona, New Guinea, campaign, the first major fight won by the Allies (the Aussies and the Yanks): DON'T show you are an officer because an enemy sniper could end your life and is watching for such insignia in order to make his kill more valuable! It actually happened often enough that precautions began to be taken voluntarily.

Enter the CIC experienced agent in this atmosphere. Where did he carry his official agent's badge? Why, right on the UNDERSIDE of his fatigues' lapel, the same place a major, a captain, a lieutenant pinned his rank, with the bottom of the pin barely visible just a few feet away. How easy it became for the trained, intelligent special agent to casually flip his lapel, just enough so that the officer being interviewed caught a quick glimpse of a flash of gold—a second lieutenant's bar, or a major's leaf!

Of course this did not work everywhere, especially in the headquarters of the combat unit to which the agent was attached. But here it was not as important; it was elsewhere in the command that agents were conducting investigations—and it was effective in stress situations.

* * *

There are literally thousands of stories of ingenuity, of daring, of success—and of failure—about CIC that will never see the light of day. The factual collection of the Fort Holabird researchers just touches the surface. And this is particularly true of the Southwest Pacific, so much so that one wonders what happened to the monthly reports of CIC activities that should have reached the War Department. Some got there, but where are the rest of them?

For instance, there isn't a single word about the weeks and months that special agent William McCauley tramped through New Guinea jungles in 1943 with fellows of the Australian Field Security forces, the Aussie's equivalent of the CIC. Their mission was to make certain of the loyalty of Papuan natives, to locate any sign of enemy penetration not revealed by air observers and Australian coast watchers, and to counteract any rumors planted with the natives that would cause interference with the Allies' prosecution of the war. His experiences could rival that of some of the agents in CBI, yet not a word appears to have reached Washington, at least where it could be available to researchers.

We do find one other group and mission in the account, which deserves telling over and over again—until the value of its services is more widely recognized: the approximately two thousand Nisei soldiers in our uniform, in our army, fighting the enemy from the homeland of their ancestors.

Following his ordered rescue from Corregidor, Agent Arthur Komori was extremely valuable in working with Colonel Sidney Mashbir in ATIS, which among other duties controlled the activities of the language teams operating often down to the front lines. A major mission of ATIS was the translation of captured enemy documents, made very difficult because of the complexity of the Japanese written characters. As Dr. John Patrick Finnegan, a postwar CI agent who later became a historian with the U.S. Army Intelligence and Security Command at Arlington Hall, Virginia., points out in his *Military Intelligence: A Pictorial History,* on ATIS language teams: three document translators were needed for every interrogator of captured soldiers. This was the exact opposite of the ratio in ETO.

ATIS was able to transcribe 350,000 documents captured during the war. These documents for the most part were collected by CIC agents, often from the macerated remains of the enemy bodies; or from stinking billets full of the dead; from hurriedly abandoned enemy headquarters; and even some from our own troops who failed to recognize their value and were taking them home as souvenirs!

* * *

While most wartime CIC agents could not translate the Japanese language, they could and did recover every scrap of Japanese writing they could lay their hands on. And in lectures to troops they explained the importance of doing so. In this 350,000 collection, there were priceless Japanese Navy and Army code books, orders of battle, plans, etc. In tons of paper, which ones were to be read first? Often the ATIS interpreter on or near the front-lines had time only to scan though piles of these documents for their value, speeding the invaluable strategic ones back to Theater HQ, translating the ones of immediate tactical value, and shipping the bulk back to HQ for a more thorough examination.

One important fact should be emphasized for the record: our loyal Nisei soldiers happened to look like Japanese soldiers in our uniform. The *unwritten* mission of CIC, adopted in the jungles, was to accompany the ATIS Nisei when they were required to go to forward elements to translate a suspected tactically valuable document, or question a dying Japanese soldier. The reason: concern that our own troops might in a moment of panic on spotting an "enemy" in our uniform pull the trigger, and end of life of a loyal fellow American. It was a mission that the CIC agents were proud to perform. And in one known incident, a Nisei returning with a patrol from an important mission actually was shot and killed in error by one of our soldiers; no CIC agent was accompanying him at the time.

* * *

CIC operations in the Southwest Pacific Theater (SWPA) varied widely for a number of reasons. Most important were the geographical distances, which kept detachments widely separated. Among others was the shortage of manpower—the SWPA Theater was not built for strength until after the ETO campaign was well under way and victory there believed secured.

There also were constant personnel changes, attributed to General MacArthur's burning desire to find the right combination of staff and field officers who would hurry him with all possible speed back to the Philippines. For example, the G-2 of the theater, in whom counter-intelligence responsibilities were vested, was changed SEVEN times between December 1941 and April 1942; there were nine changes in Commanding Generals between December 1941 and July 1942.

There were so many changes in the designations of headquarters and subordinate units that records of unit numbers and initials appear in bewildering confusion.

* * *

For the purposes of this history, suffice to say that SWPA Headquarters and various of its echelons shuttled back and forth between Sidney, Brisbane and Melbourne. And that USAFIA, although technically the United States Army command in the Southwest Pacific, was responsible for administration, procurement, training and supply, while the strategic and tactical operations were under the direction of GHQ, SWPA.

To researchers, however, some confusion continued, resulting in some aspects of CIC's operations in this theater never being fully clarified. It is believed that the confusion stems in part from the fact that two histories of CIC's participation in SWPA events were written shortly after the end of hostilities with Japan: one by the Chief Counter Intelligence Officer, General HQ, Army Forces, Pacific, in 1946, Brigadier General Elliot E. Thorpe, USAFIA G-2; the other by Major General C. A. Willoughby, G-2, Far East Command (FEC), and of an account of his life; and no doubt some errors have crept in, for which there has been no way of correcting.

For example, the only complete CIC Headquarters' rosters that have been found were dated 28 February 1945. By that time however there had been much shifting of personnel; when the names of certain agents are mentioned in the text as having come into an area with certain combat units, the roster often does not list those agents with that particular unit on that date.

Amusingly, much space is given in General Willoughby's history to criticizing General Thorpe's rendition of the history. For instance, in General Thorpe's version, the assignment of all CIC agents to Headquarters in May 1943 was hailed as a "corrective move," whereas General Willoughby bitterly criticized the move. This division of intelligence responsibility "ultimately led to friction, overlap, duplication and general inefficiency," according to General Willoughby, while General Thorpe stated: "There was to be close cooperation in the G-2 Section USAFIA and G-2 GHQ, SWPA."

With the documents now available, it is impossible to assess objectively the relative validity of these widely divergent views. There are sufficient documents however to reveal that CIC agents operating in detachments and as individuals were generally able to overcome whatever handicaps the peculiar command structure of the theater may have imposed. The question remains: *why* should it have been necessary in the first place?

* * *

Counter-intelligence operations got off to a slow start. It was not until the United States Forces surrendered on Bataan that the first trained CIC officers arrived in Australia, 7 April 1942, to join the Allied troops preparing to start the long island-hopping journey to Tokyo. Working under Thorpe, USAFIA G-2, these first CIC men concentrated on what they knew needed doing: tightening security measures in general; imposing censorship on Allied troops; and keeping a situation map of Japan's rapid thrust in the Pacific. Would you believe for the situation map they used one from an old copy of National Geographic? Yes!

The early-bird CIC men were John N. Irwin II, who became the assistant executive officer of the G-2 Section, with responsibility for establishing CIC operations; Leo J. Nielson, Jr., appointed assistant military censor; Harold G. Gelwicks, assigned to Base 4 at Melbourne as intelligence and investigative officer; and Blair P. Labatt, assigned as a G-2 investigative officer. These men, with Jennis Roy Galloway, formed the nucleus of the theater's counter-intelligence agency that eventually was to become widely known as the 441st CIC Detachment.

Lars Skattebol, a U.S. citizen who operated a credit investigative system in Australia before the war, volunteered for the Army. Because of his investigative background, he was placed on duty with CIC, the first enlisted CIC agent in the theater.

By April 1942, the USAFIA G-2 was operating primarily as a counter-intelligence agency, despite a dearth of trained agents. At that time, Allied prospects were desperate as Japanese forces were jumping from island to island; an actual Japanese foothold on the mainland of Australia seemed quite possible.

However, the 41st Infantry Division arrived in Australia; a month later the 32nd made it. These new divisions immediately began an intense jungle-warfare training program. U.S. Forces in SWPA came to the grand total of 85,500 by 10 June 1942. CIC numbers had expanded somewhat from the original nucleus of 14 officers and men, but were still woefully understaffed.

* * *

Thorpe, then a colonel, realized that the acute shortage of personnel made adequate counter-intelligence coverage of the base sections impossible. He requested the War Department to send him 40 additional agents, plus a CIC table of organization. His request was relegated to a back burner, as immediate attention in the States was devoted to channeling most of the CIC Training School graduates into ETO, the European Theater—or else into still undermanned stateside assignments. The role of CIC agents in a combat zone was not clear until reports came in from North Africa in 1943.

Thorpe utilized his first batch of CIC agents to indoctrinate American troops. In May 1942 CIC agents checked out the possibility of sabotage in connection with a series of mysterious accidents along the important Australian transportation lines at Adelaide, Alice Springs, Brisbane, Darwin and Sydney. Cooperation with Australian Intelligence authorities, and its Field Security activities, became more pronounced; arrangements were made with the Australian Military Intelligence to send Americans, including CIC agents, through Australian Intelligence Schools. Americans continued to attend similar schools there throughout the war.

Under direction of Lt. William Shelton, a Naval Intelligence officer serving with G-2, an intensive security indoctrination program was launched, one feature of which was a "Biweekly Intelligence Summary," containing information designed to make troops more security conscious, including tabulation of the latest rumors seeming always to be circulating in military units.

On 16 July 1942, the *SS Matsonia* pulled up the Yara River to dock in Melbourne, Australia, to unload some 10,000 troops that included two CIC agents, James Bradford and Bill Latham, both black. This "force" of two new agents was assigned to the Quartermaster Division, where considerable pilfering of supplies had occurred. All other troops entrained to Camp Darley. When no more agents had arrived from the States by the end of July 1942, Thorpe received permission to recruit a group of agents from the First Replacement Depot at Camp Darley, Australia. He set the usual high standards in vogue for CIC, refusing to consider any who scored less than the minimum requirement for Officer Candidates on the Army General Classification Test. He preferred men who had been lawyers, investigators, or newspaper men, with emphasis on "mature youth."

* * *

Of 1,500 men screened for CIC, only 15 survived the process far enough for personal interviews by Thorpe and other G-2 Section officers. But even 15 additional agents helped relieve the shortage of CIC personnel somewhat. These new men were Leland R. Anderson, Ted Beck, Hugo Cecarelli, John Choate, William Geiger, David Henninger, Arthur Jackson, Norman Jacques, Clint Johnson, Frank Leahy, William Moddemeyer, Willard Wurtz, Duane Williford, Walter Wagner, and Arthur Zeigler. Their varied civilian occupations ranged from lawyer, civil engineer, newspapermen, insurance investigator, biologist, to the less prestigious salesmen, bartender, student. But they all had the basic minimum qualifications sought by CIC—minimum standards for an officer in the Army.

This group was the only class to attend the Melbourne school. Among the instructors were Captain Suave, Lt. Jack Irwin, Lt. Jennis R Galloway, and an ONI officer named Richardson, plus 13 others. The staff outnumbered the students! This three-week course was described as the grass roots of the CIC in SWPA, which was officially attached at that time to the U.S. Army Services of Supply. This one and only school graduated on August 22, receiving their credentials from Thorpe, in the presence of visiting General Marshall. Their immediate assignments took Anderson, Ceccarelli, Jackson and Williford to Townsville; Zeigler and Jacques to Berduin; Johnson and Geiger to Brisbane; Beck and Choate to Sydney; Wurtz to Melbourne; Henninger to Mt. Isa; Wagner and Leahy to Port Moresby; and Moddemeyer to the Air Corps.

While this modest effort put agents where most needed, a few new agents were beginning to arrive from the States. Compared to the size of our forces in ETO, MacArthur's army could only be described as anemic in numbers—and CIC was in no better shape, with only a very thin spread of agents covering an immense territory.

By 12 September 1942, the Allies, primarily Australian troops aided by our Air Corps, had halted the Japanese in the Owen Stanley mountains in New Guinea, a mere 20 airline miles from Port Moresby—which itself was the last step away from the shores of north Australia. To Port Moresby near this battle line, a month later went CIC agents Walter C. Wagner and Frank J. Leahy; in December 1942, the arrival of new agents allowed the assignment of James Broz, Dean H. Caziarc and Arthur W. Linde to Milne Bay, a strategic spot on the easternmost tip of New Guinea, where a sub-advance base had been created after the Japanese troops there had been expelled in a key turning point of the war.

* * *

From then on, agents were assigned as quickly as they arrived, or could be trained and made available, to the various bases where the proximity of the enemy imposed a definite threat of espionage and subversive activities. In December 1942, three cases of sabotage were investigated at the Jackson airdrome at Port Moresby.

CHAPTER XI

CBI Theater: No CIC Yet

One of the three nations in this enormous, far-away theater was Burma, a country of rugged mountains, dense jungles and disease-laden swamps, known to most Americans through Kipling's stories.

United States Army Forces, China-Burma-India (USAF CBI) had been activated on 4 March 1942 with headquarters in Chungking, China. It later transferred to New Delhi, India, where British headquarters were located, with Chungking becoming the forward echelon. Its original mission was to "increase the effectiveness of United States' assistance to the Chinese Government for the prosecution of the war and to assist in improving the combat efficiency of the Chinese Army"; this now was enlarged to include the "exploitation of the development of overland communications to China."

As yet, CIC had made no significant appearance by the end of 1942 in this huge theater.

* * *

That was the picture from the western Pacific Rim by the end of 1942.

CHAPTER XII

Stateside CIP Reborn as CIC

The first training school for CIC (as opposed to CIP) agents was held in Chicago in January 1942. I was one of the 100-plus students. I have found no roster and can only recall a few others in attendance: William F. Aimone, Theodore Black, Keirn C. Brown (my roommate), George Lubovich, Arthur Newton, Jack Staley. Many of us had to be quartered in nearby hotels. And leave it to army tradition, even those in the hotel rooms still had to endure Saturday morning inspection: we stood by our beds freshly made up for us by our maid service, as an army major wearing a Russian-style hat and another officer trooped in, looked around quickly and left! And on days when the temperature plunged to minus 15 degrees, we were doing our daily exercises on top of the school building in our shorts, with the wind whipping off of Lake Michigan.

Month after month other classes, not as large, followed in 1942 and 1943, with the curriculum about the same, though sharpening and changing as reports came back from wherever the graduates were doing their bit. After this first class came others with outstanding agents like Arthur S. Hurlburt (who has made significant contributions to this history), Robert M. Reese, William A. Owens (whose adventures are told in his *Eye-deep in Hell*), George Charon and many others too numerous to name.

In that cold January 1942 class, as we practiced hound-and-hare exercises on the streets, we had to duck into a store or bar every half block to warm frozen hands and face. My favorite was Demet's near Marshall Field, where a cousin of mine worked and where I found refuge in warming up my freezing body with hot beverages.

We survived the training, which included excellent instruction from experts in the FBI, police forces, secret service, and other investigative services, in preserving the chain-of-evidence in a case, how to dust for fingerprints, the use of moulage to preserve evidence, the art of report writing, interrogation tricks, the use of cameras, sabotage investigations, plus what they could of espionage tricks of the trade, such as letter drops, and on and on.

The following was written by a special agent who became a professional editor and writer, and who graphically describes, better than

I, an average day at this unusual school during the hot Chicago summer (as opposed to the winter):

* * *

The Gabardine War[4]

"In Chicago, in June of 1942, six months after Pearl Harbor, I was one of a detachment of some 30-odd agents from the Army Counter Intelligence Corps assigned to take an FBI course that, like so much of my subsequent military training, taught me very little that I would ever again put to use, in or out of the service. In Chicago we learned, among other things, how to pick locks, practice judo, lift fingerprints, make plaster molds of tire tracks, forge documents, and tail suspects. The last of these activities, dubbed surveillance, was the centerpiece of our final exam and remains my most enduring memory of that wartime summer.

"Although we were all sergeants, our uniforms in Chicago were army-issue civilian clothes, purchased by voucher at government-approved outlets. We were therefore identically attired in tan gabardine suits, button-down white shirts, plain-toed brown shoes, and inconspicuous ties. Hot as it was, we had to wear jackets outdoors to conceal our mandatory shoulder holsters containing unloaded .38-caliber police-positive revolvers.

"Our Chicago bivouac was a former YWCA building near the Water Tower on North Michigan Avenue. There were classrooms, a cafeteria, a gym, and double-decker bunks in the single rooms. Also, this being a U.S. Army installation, a formation was held early every morning on the sidewalk. Passers-by were naturally puzzled to see a platoon of apparently able-bodied young civilians in gabardine suits being put through close-order drill by a uniformed lieutenant.

"'Recruits' was his evasive reply to questioners, an explanation that grew less plausible as we were marched around, week after week, in our civilian disguise. But, at the time, the very existence of the CIC was classified information.

"As graduation day approached, we were told that the main event of our final exam would be a 'field exercise' in surveillance, which is the art of tracking someone's movements and activities while remaining unobserved. For this purpose our class was divided into equal groups of hares and hounds, with each hare provided with a mimeographed sheet of instructions designed to give his assigned hound a hard time and perhaps shake him altogether.

"The hares were told when to take buses and taxis, where to get off, which shops to enter and what to buy, how far and in what direction to walk, what movie theaters and restaurants to enter (and how to

---

[4]   *By agent William Attwood, reprinted from June 1988 Chicago Magazine*

depart by rear exits), and finally how to complete the exercise by registering at a designated hotel under an assumed German-sounding name. Our stalking activity was timed to last about two hours and was to take place entirely within the Loop.

"The weather on exam day was hot and muggy, and the older and more sophisticated hounds of our detachment—those over 25—arranged to meet discreetly with their hares in some cool tavern and there concoct plausible reports that would give them both passing grades, reports in which the hare would briefly elude his shadow and the hound would miss a few details (such as what brand of cigarettes did the suspect buy at the cafeteria). But both would get to the lobby of the hotel in time to check in and be observed doing so.

"Most of us, however, being fresh out of college, undertook our assignments the hard and conscientious way. As a result we brought the war closer to home for a good many Chicago cabbies as well as cops to whom we had to show identification to explain our headlong pursuit by taxi and on foot through tangled city traffic.

"'God*damn!*' cried one excited cab driver as I flashed my shiny military intelligence badge and told him to trail my hare's vehicle. 'The Nazi spies are sure out in force today. You're the fourth Secret Service agent I've picked up this afternoon. Lucky for us you boys are on the ball!'

"And off we went, through a red light on State Street where a traffic cop waved us through at the sight of my badge.

"On foot, we hounds stayed about 50 feet behind our subjects, on the opposite sidewalk, crossing at corners if they turned in one direction and pausing if they turned in the other, toward us. As instructed, both of us kept changing our appearance by putting on and removing glasses, jackets, and hats. This is SOP in the spy business but not very effective in our case since by now we knew our classmates' faces as well as we knew our own. At any soda fountain where our hare might pause for refreshment, we lingered at the far end of the counter until he paid before confronting the cashier with questions about what he had ordered and if he paid with coins or bills.

"Curiously, no one seemed surprised or upset by our nosiness. One look at our credentials made everyone instantly eager to cooperate. In 1942, I guess it gave them a sense of participating in the war, if only vicariously.

"Two hours is a long time on a hot July afternoon in Chicago, and the hares gradually slowed down and spent more time sitting in taxis and taking refreshment. But every step of the assignment had to be completed before we could head for the hotel where pseudo spies and saboteurs were scheduled to register as guests.

"Arrangements had been made by the army so that various hotels would have a number of rooms available for this exercise, but there had been a slip-up on our examination day. All the hares had mistakenly received instructions to register at a single hotel—the Blackstone. Consequently, all of us, hares and hounds together, converged almost simultaneously on the lobby, then filled with the traditional potted palms. Ten or so hounds crouched behind the plants while their assigned quarries besieged the reception desk, demanding registration forms that they were to fill out with German names and addresses.

"The paperwork completed, we hounds sprang out from behind the foliage, badges and credentials in hand, and ordered the clerks to show us the forms and room assignments for all the Himmlers, Hindenburgs, Bismarcks, and Goerings who had just checked in. The other occupants of the lobby only looked on with what seemed to be wide-eyed pride at seeing their boys in action against the enemies in our midst.

"The course completed, we all dispersed—none of us, so far as I know, ever to wear our gabardines again. Within a month or so I was bound for Egypt, where Rommel had not yet been stopped by the British, and during the next three years was taught various other skills that I never again put to use—such as bracketing a target with howitzer bursts, beaching a rubber boat in heavy surf, and making a soft landing in a parachute. War's end found me on Okinawa, where our Chicago summer seemed very long ago and far away. By then I'd even forgotten how to pick a lock. But it wasn't all a waste of time. Ask me even today to follow a suspicious stranger through city streets and I'll bet I can stay on his tail all the way home, provided he doesn't walk too fast.

* * *

"So we were now trained, qualified special agents—probably only by virtue of the fact that most of us had been exposed to some form of investigating before we entered the service. There was one former FBI agent with us, many former investigative reporters, lawyers galore, credit investigators, newspaper hounds, police detectives—ad infinitum. The instructions were not necessarily wasted, but served as a refresher for many. *William Attwood"*

* * *

When my group graduated and returned to our Atlanta headquarters in February 1942, Asa Candler immediately dispersed us in different directions to the hot spots in the Service command.

My destination was Alexandria, known as the Heart of Louisiana, now surrounded by four army training camps: Beauregard, five miles to the north; Livingston, adjacent to Beauregard; Claiborne, fifteen miles south; and Polk, forty-five miles west. In addition, the Air Corps had a nearby air field. On weekends, this deep-south city of some 25,000 normal population was swamped by soldiers and an accompanying flood of civilian workers—all looking for relaxation. Included in this horde of fun-seekers was a number of black units from Northern states "unversed in the proclivities and implications of Deep South Jim Crow."[5]

The situation was ripe for what had happened while I was a student in the Chicago training school. It started when a white MP arrested a black soldier for creating a disturbance on Lee Street about 8 p.m., Saturday, 10 January 1942. When the black soldier began resisting arrest, onlookers became angry and physical—resulting in what became known as the Lee Street Riot. Nearby black soldiers joined in, as did other white as well as black Military Police. Additional military police were quickly called in from Camp Livingston, along with city and state police. At the height of the action some 60 MPs, 30 city police and state troopers, and an undetermined number of white civilians engaged an estimated "several thousand black troops along a four- or five-block corridor of Lee Street, also called Little Harlem." Many black civilians were trapped in the two-hour turmoil before authorities brought order out of chaos.

Guns were fired, tear gas bombs were thrown, with the blacks hurling bricks, rocks, and sticks. In the melee some 28 black soldiers were injured, at least three of them seriously. One or more policemen were injured; one black civilian was shot in the hip.[6]

Rumors went wild about the two-hour race riot; exaggerated reports stated that 18 had been killed and as many as 26 wounded. One of the main concerns of Army Military Intelligence was whether the incident was the work of subversive elements or enemy provocateurs. A black CIC special agent was immediately dispatched to Alexandria to check on this possibility.

Knowing I was from that area, in dispatching me to this spot undoubtedly Candler expected me to establish an excellent rapport with loyal citizens, and to build and maintain an effective informant network that would alert us to any further troubles, as well as close out any lingering loose ends.

Early in February, I reported to agent Charles Bruder in the basement of the post office in Alexandria, or Alec as people thereabouts

---

5   From Prof. Wm M Simpson, Louisiana College, Pineville
6   Contributed by Tommy Kohara from files of Daily Town Talk

dubbed it. Also present was Thornton R.Greene, one of the few black agents in CIC at that time—the special agent Service Command CIC had dispatched to investigate the Lee Street Riot.

Bruder was on his way out of CIC into the CID (Criminal Investigation Division, formerly known as the OPMG) of the Provost Marshal. I never knew the reason for his transfer, though it may have been that he had no foreign language ability, definitely a requirement when I entered CIC. So I relieved him as SAC (Special Agent In Charge) and very quickly learned to work with and respect agent Greene, a highly intelligent college-educated Negro born and reared in Alabama, a dyed-in-the-wool Southerner—my kind.

The investigation into the race riot on Lee Street (more or less the border between black and white) was for all intents and purposes practically over when I got there. Greene had been sent to cover the black part of town and the black troops in the nearby four army camps and one air corps field; I followed up on leads among the white troops that Bruder had not yet completed. Greene's findings cleared early fears that the riot was enemy inspired; his report stated "the underlying cause of the disturbances and controversy in Alexandria is not due to any subversive element, but ... to jealousy, hate, roughness, and over-indulgence in intoxicants."

As some white civilians on Lee Street were also involved, it was a case of joint jurisdiction with the FBI. Bruder introduced me to the sole FBI agent in the city before leaving town, as well as to the network of informants Bruder had established. I added to the network with reliable contacts from my previous life in the area, including black Jake Barrett, a loyal worker for my father many years at our abattoir on the outskirts of Pineville on the east side of Red River opposite Alexandria, and my favorite high school teacher, Miss Mary Thornton, who knew more about everybody than anyone else.

In addition to the usual police and detective-type informants, another source believed to be important was the red-light district bordering upper Third Street, north of Bayou Rapides, along the banks of Red River. Bruder introduced me to his contacts there, and I left my address but only heard one peep thereafter from this network.

* * *

One of my first calls on old friends from my high school days was the Kohara family which operated a photography shop in Alec. I had gone to high school with Tommy and Sammy, his older brother. For the first time I learned that Mr. Kohara had died about three months before Pearl Harbor, so Ms. Kohara was the surviving Issei parent who after Pearl Harbor endured a complete inspection of everything in their house and business, conducted by friendly local police acting on behalf of the FBI which was checking on all enemy aliens. Intelligent Mrs. Kohara took advantage of the muscles of the police to conduct a house cleaning! As a policeman finished inspecting each item, she would have him put many into a trash pile, placing her prized possessions and household items in a separate location. She thus managed a thorough, early, spring house-cleaning!

When I arrived, my friend Tommy was away in the Army, probably at Camp Shelby, Mississippi, at that time. But after I was there a few months, his sister Kay came home one weekend from medical school at LSU. She was no longer the little sister of my friend but an attractive young lady; as soon as weather warmed up enough for swimming, I had my first date with her, little realizing that some four years later we would be married.

Most of the pending cases awaiting my attention in the office were routine loyalty and discretion checks. But one of my first new investigations will illustrate problems FBI and CIC were confronted with in the first months following Pearl Harbor. I received a tip from a "red-light" informant that there was someone with a radio sending out signals only at night, from a rooming house next door.

As taught and stressed at the CIC school, "Don't ignore ANY report—check them all out." I made time to case the house that same night, first to determine if the suspect was a civilian employee of one of the nearby bases and thus in my jurisdiction, or belonged solely to the FBI. With the help of the mystified landlady to whom I swore secrecy, I discovered the roomer was not working for the Army and so was not properly in my jurisdiction. But as I stood simply contemplating the surroundings in order to make a clear, preliminary report to the FBI, if necessary, I did indeed hear the dit-dot-dit-dot that sounded like Morse code similar to what I had learned in basic training. Tracing the sound as well as I could by ear, I solved the case quickly. A neon light on the side of the adjacent building was flickering because of a tiny puncture in the tube. The flickering caused an audible sound that aped that of a slow Morse code signal.

I passed the word on to the FBI agent, who was busy enough as it was, so he could avoid devoting any time to other reports of the same incident. At least I saved him footsteps he would have taken had he gotten the tip before me from his network of informants.

* * *

Most of my cases consisted of routine investigations to determine the loyalty and discretion of candidates for highly secret positions, including candidates for the then-secret radar teams, and for those employed on the atom bomb project—not known even to us at that time for what it was. I ranged as far north as the historic city of Natchitoches, and as far south as Lake Charles, Lafayette, and even Baton Rouge, the state capital, on the east side of the Mississippi.

In addition, I maintained contact with the Post Intelligence Officers at all four of the nearby army camps plus the one air corps field. It was through these sources and their in-house counter-subversive networks (CS system) that tips and leads on possible cases of subversion in my jurisdiction would usually come. From CIC Headquarters in Atlanta other cases were referred to me, plus following up on leads to complete investigations initiated by other offices like mine. On a large investigation, one office usually handled only one part; thus we rarely knew the conclusion or success of our efforts—very frustrating to investigators.

* * *

As I wore only civilian clothes, my old friends in the community whom I had to interview on occasion had trouble trying to figure out my status. On official business I was permitted to identify myself as a Military Intelligence Special Agent, but I was prohibited from revealing this even to my own family! I also began to hear the expected not-so-friendly taunts from men in uniform, questioning why a man my age was still in civvies.

When not on the road on a case, I met Greene in our office in the post office basement. It pleased me greatly to cross the street to a restaurant for sandwiches for our lunches; he would have had to go much farther away, or endure probable indignities, had I not been present and gone for our carryouts. In fact, I felt honored at doing this for someone I respected so highly.

I'll never forget the Monday morning when Greene entered the office and gave me a stern lecture; he had observed me walking alone on the previous Saturday night, strolling on Lee Street where the earlier riot had occurred. He confided that he trailed me until I was safely out of the danger zone, but he suggested strongly this was not the smartest thing for me to do alone at night, especially on a Saturday when streets were full of soldiers.

* * *

I finally had a sabotage case within my territory when the PIO at the air corps base called me about a suspected attempt to cause a crash to a plane ferried in from Alabama. The pilot luckily flew the plane in the daytime, and discovered early that something was wrong with his compass; he knew the flight path and completed the trip by visual observations, reporting the difficulty on landing in Louisiana. Inspecting the plane, we found a small magnet that appeared to have caused the compass to deviate. It was not visible, and not quickly discernible, to the pilot. While I initiated the case, I had to refer it for completion back to the field where the plane had been last serviced and taken off. I never heard further about the incident, and can only conclude it was simply negligence, not enemy-inspired sabotage. Nevertheless, following this type of incident, security was always tightened thereafter, especially at the point of origin. This service, though not our primary mission, was rendered by CIC throughout the war, in every theater.

In June, the Eighth Service Command took the State of Louisiana into its territory away from the Fourth Service Command in Atlanta. For a while I thought I would be transferred from the Fourth along with my office, but Asa Candler pulled me out after I surrendered my office and informant network data to Melvin Diggs, the lone agent who transferred in from Texas to take over my territory. For a brief moment in time, I was working in the Eighth Service Command territory. Thornton R. Greene followed me shortly thereafter, and I never saw him until many years later. But he was in great demand, not only in our Service Command but also by others, such as the FBI, which had no black agents at that time.

Before leaving, I received orders dated 2 June 1942, promoting me to the great grade of Staff Sergeant! I did not celebrate.

* * *

Candler next stationed me in a one-man office in Huntsville, northeast Alabama, on the banks of the beautiful Tennessee River. There were two ammunition manufacturing plants located in this area, Redstone Arsenal and Huntsville Arsenal; my job was to protect them from sabotage, etc. Army officers were located at each, and I maintained contact with the PIOs stationed there, to investigate any suspicious incident that might possibly fall within CIC jurisdiction. This of course included all civilians working for the plants.

This assignment was virgin territory for CIC. And it didn't last more than a few weeks. I established an informant network around the two plants, checked out another flickering light case (caused by strong winds moving tree branches between a distant light and the observer), checked out a few incidents of unknown persons seen on the plant properties, and continued handling the loose ends of investigations initiated elsewhere.

We maintained a daily log of every hour of the day, the time we spent on each case, whom we interviewed for any reason, where, and so on, plus our caseload. We had to include even our personal time at the barbers, and were required to report on the four hours weekly of our exercise to keep in physical shape. We mailed these daily to our Atlanta HQ via the "confidential" envelope system.

To my surprise, I had barely arrived and established living quarters and the usual office in the post office, when I received word that I was now a Technical Sergeant as of July 1! I did not celebrate.

* * *

Down the beautiful Tennessee River near Florence, in northwest Alabama, was the Muscle Shoals dam, where in peacetime fertilizer in the form of phosphate and nitrate was fabricated by means of the hydroelectric power there from the Tennessee River. In wartime, this source supplied an important ingredient used in the manufacture of ammunition for our armed services. Thus, plants involved in the process, and all civilian employees, came within our jurisdiction. Atlanta had received a report from overseas of defective, unsafe ammunition emanating from a plant that used the Muscle Shoal product; little pieces of iron filings were found inside the ammo.

I was ordered to investigate, and afterwards relocate my one-man office to nearby Florence to cover northwest Alabama. The investigation was practically completed by a concerned, responsible management by the time of my arrival. But I had to make an official report, so they led me step by step through the entire facility to follow the process. One of the final steps was sifting of the nitrate through a metal screen to keep out foreign objects and large clumps. Any chemistry student knows that this product isn't particularly friendly to metal, and gradually eats it away; thus the screen generally deteriorated in time, and became less effective, allowing bits and pieces of its metal to break off and fall into the finished product.

It was not so much a problem in the manufacture of fertilizer, but could have been, and obviously was, in making powder for our shells. Management was already aware of the cause and had already replaced the old screens. I could discern nothing that indicated anything more than negligence, and so reported to Atlanta. In a case like this, all employees who had anything to do in any of the steps were checked out by CIC for anything in their background that would indicate disloyalty, or even disaffection. I heard nothing further on the case, and assume nothing instigated by enemy agents was uncovered.

* * *

This case apparently brought my name back to the attention of the Atlanta office, for after a stay of only a few days, I was transferred to Anniston, Alabama, to what had been a one-man office with Henry Ingargiola of Baton Rouge, Louisiana, in charge. After I replaced him, he was on his way with his Italian language ability to the first combat

CIC teams in our North Africa landings, and later to Italy.

Now it was no longer a one-man office. Nearby Fort McClellan, a munitions storage facility, and a number of Air Corps installations in eastern Alabama caused it to be increased to three of us within months. In addition, we continued the protection of the arsenals at Huntsville. The Florence and Muscle Shoals area was handled by agents out of Birmingham, under the direction of Major Fuller who after WW2 ended was temporarily head of the Air Corps CIC, later to become the Air Force's OSI (Office of Special Investigations).

In most cities we managed to find free space in a post office. Here in Anniston, however, we occupied a room in a regular office building, with lettering on the door to proclaim we were an insurance agency. No one ever opened the door to inquire about insurance. With help now, I assigned routine cases to the new agents, while I maintained contact with the PIO at McClellan, and a nearby munitions storage facility (its PIO George Hamner later came into and served in CIC many years).

While stationed in Anniston, we received belated confidential news that on the eastern coast on 12 June two German submarines landed eight trained saboteurs with missions to destroy plants in New York, Philadelphia, Illinois and Tennessee. We were ordered to insure that networks were in place around all army facilities that would report anything and anybody suspicious immediately. Outside of some purely innocuous reports, we heard nothing, though we made certain we had covered every possibility.

It was not until after the war was over that I learned all the Germans who landed had already been captured by the FBI even before we got our first alert of their presence. The powers that be didn't see the need to advise us of that, as there was always the possibility of other such invasions by enemy agents bent on sabotage. And indeed there was. On 29 November 1944, a U-boat landed two agents at Crabpoint, Maine, with espionage and sabotage orders. Their mission was too little and too late. It was aborted quickly when the one who was an American ex-sailor turned himself in, and helped the authorities capture the other, highly trained, operative.

* * *

But, finally, in Anniston I ran into the real thing in my specialty of spy catching. Two cases came along, the first being a mere warm-up for the second. Just before Christmas, an officer at Fort McClellan reported to the PIO that he had been approached at a hotel in Anniston by a young lady under very mysterious circumstances. He felt that she had mistaken him for someone else she was supposed to meet, so he played along with her as she asked him searching questions about what was going on at the Fort, like troop training, identity of units, troop movements. The PIO and I agreed that the officer should continue the contact and report to us daily on further developments.

As this looked like it might involve an army officer and a civilian contact who was not an army employee, it was obviously a case of joint jurisdiction with the FBI. I notified the local FBI, and on the day after Christmas a team of three FBI agents was camped in our CIC office. By agreement, and as proper, they began an extensive background investigation of the female, while we huddled with our army officer and gave him elaborate instructions on questions he should pursue and actions he should take. At the same time, the PIO tightened up his internal organization for greater alertness to a possible spy on the post. (In a short time, it paid off!)

Thereafter, this became a daily ritual: we met with the FBI, who used our office to report by telephone every morning directly to J. Edgar Hoover, while we prepared our normal daily reports to our Atlanta HQ and Birmingham offices, listing our activities. We conferred with the FBI daily on plans for that day and night, and relayed the information our officer was providing us. And of course we were trying through the PIO's own informant network (every army unit had such a counter-subversive system, called CS) to try to determine the identity, if true, of that unknown officer the civilian subject had intended to contact.

* * *

As our army officer continued to have dates with the suspect night after night, we knew in advance where he planned to take her. The FBI agent in charge then asked if one of us could get into our army uniforms in order to get closer to the subject and officer. They wanted an independent witness other than the officer, if possible, to every word that was spoken by the suspect. It was a logical enough request as almost everybody in the night spots was in uniform and, unhappily for them, FBI agents looked like FBI agents. I dusted off my uniform, borrowed a second lieutenant's bars from the PIO, and made a date that enabled me to sit unobtrusively not too far from the suspect at the bar or diner, where she was taken on the date.

While all of this was interesting, especially as it lasted through New Year's Eve, the FBI agents and Hoover were becoming more and more perturbed with the lack of any solid information on such an ideal setup for an espionage ring, even though they had thoroughly checked the hotel staff and found nothing to substantiate any sign of a ring. And our continued efforts to confirm the identity of a subversive army officer turned up nothing.

I was not surprised therefore when the FBI voiced their desire to check the living quarters of the subject. As she lived alone in a house with no landlord, to gain entry meant forcing an illegal entrance, which of course the FBI would never do, at least on the information so far obtained. But the mission of the CIC was to prevent harm to our armed forces, so after listening to the complaints of the FBI another day, one of my agents was able to gain entry and invited the FBI to join him. After this inspection, FBI picked up the female for questioning. The final report absolved the subject of being anything but an intense reader of detective and spy stories, with nothing to indicate any connection with anything like an espionage ring; she had been having fun and dates at the expense of the Army!

I cannot recall which one of my agents did FBI's work for them, but that ended this case which proved to be a training refresher for the next, more serious, one.

* * *

In the meantime, on one of the visits to Fort McClellan, my PIO introduced his new assistant, a major who had just come into the Army from his civilian job of mayor of one of the Alabama cities. As usual, the PIO introduced me as Mr. Edwards, never revealing my rank, then of a tech sergeant. The following week I made a routine call on the PIO and found he was out, leaving his new assistant in charge.

The major asked me in to the office, put his fingers to his lips and spoke softly so the soldier clerk in the outside office couldn't hear, "Can I ask you a very confidential question?"

I closed the office door and nodded assent.

"Please tell me, Edwards, what does G-2 mean?"

So this tech sergeant told the G-2's new assistant, a major, exactly what G-2, G-1, G-3 and G-4 meant, all the time struggling to maintain my composure as I, an enlisted man, had to educate a man who had somehow managed to gain entry "the easy way" into the army as a major. All the while, the thought popped into my mind, "Whatever happened to that proposal in Congress to grant CIC agents officer or warrant officer status?" (I eventually heard it was voted down to keep the "army from rewarding unqualified civilians with easy commissions!" Ha!)

The last orders I received in 1942 were dated 28 December, relieving me of duty temporarily in order to attend a 15-day infantry refresher course at Camp Wheeler, Georgia. Our Service Command G-2 was dedicated to keeping his CIC agents fully cognizant of the infantry. I was granted a few days delay until the closing of the ongoing investigation of joint jurisdiction with the FBI.

* * *

Picture of How It Was in the Industrial Northeast[7]

In 1942 our continental United States, called the Zone of the Interior, was broken up into nine Service Commands, each headed by an older General. The First Service Command, for instance, with headquarters in Boston, covered all of New England and part of northern New York State. The Commanding General had wide-ranging responsibilities which military commanders of later years have seldom even discussed. For instance, General Sherman Miles, CG in Boston, was responsible for the orderly continuation of the civilian war effort.

The range of responsibilities handed CIC regarding the civilian infrastructure is difficult to communicate in today's terms. We have not had a *declared* war in our country since 1945. There have been many instances of hostilities: the Korean conflict, Viet-Nam, Grenada, and many others. However, none of these involved a *declaration* of war. And this made a difference. After all, a declaration of war has more to do with one's own population than it does with the enemy. While the declaration does bring into play certain of the Geneva conventions which have to do with the conduct of hostile armies facing each other, the Articles of War take on a different tone. Offenses which under peace time called for imprisonment, in war become punishable by death. Treason, the most despicable crime in our national vocabulary, does not even exist in peace time.

* * *

In the 1990s it is hard to visualize how all-pervasive the war effort had become. Every little machine shop had a government contract to manufacture something for the war effort. One plant which had made tea bags converted to the manufacture of parts for hand grenades. Empty buildings which were of no use earlier were bought up by entrepreneurs and used in the manufacture of any one of the millions of items required to support the war effort. All of these entities involved a security factor. On one hand they could be sabotaged; on the other, merely shut down by strikes. Either way, the General was interested—and responsible.

* * *

Who were the General's eyes and ears in these matters? CIC, of course. The Posse Comitatus Act, generated following the Civil War to combat abuses of the Army's interfering with civil matters, forbade the Army to be used as a law enforcement agency, to monitor polling booths or to investigate civilian crimes. But during a *declared* war this was all swept under the rug and forgotten. The Delimitation Agree-

---

[7]   *From here through next two pages are by Arthur Hurlburt*

ment between the Army, the Navy and the FBI, mentioned earlier, really didn't address the limitations of the Posse Comitatus Act; each went about carrying out their responsibilities as they saw them, at the same trying to keep out of each other's hair, e.g., doing the other's job.

* * *

In addition to war plants, the General had in his bag of responsibilities the continuation of communications, ports, transportation systems, the security of army installations and efforts, wherever they might be. He also had an interest in people coming into the area in out-of-the-ordinary situations. This could mean contractors' employees coming back from such esoteric places as Greenland.

CIC actually had agents in place, working with contractors under cover in Greenland. When a ship bearing returning employees set out from Greenland, our agents there alerted our agents here and the ship was met when it arrived at Boston. A system called "ship paneling" provided for CIC to interview all those coming back into the U.S. to see if they had anything they should report. Further, CIC in Boston was armed with advice from Greenland about what to look for.

Schools and colleges had government contracts for teaching and research. Even Harvard Divinity School was not beyond the pale. CIC had its fingers in a myriad of places in the civilian world where it would be unthinkable in peace time. Or even in time of conflict short of a declared war. What made all the difference was that Declaration of War, making it an all-out effort.

One instance involved the port of New Bedford, Massachusetts. CIC heard there was a possibility of labor leaders shutting the port down, although there were others with interests far divergent from labor's who wanted it shut down. As far as General Miles was concerned this could not be allowed to happen. Aside from the value of the port itself, its shutting down would set a precedent which would be unthinkable.

Two dozen CIC Agents, equipped with credentials from the Gallup Poll, descended on the port city one afternoon with a whole set of questions in their pockets. All they had to do was find the right people to ask.

Their first step was to go through city directories and other sources, pick out civic leaders of all types and make up a list of interviewees. Starting with that list, their next task was to find out what made that city tick. Within two or three days they finished and reported back to General Miles. He then had a good handle on the various possibilities, in their order of probability. Along with that, he had targets for troops to seize and hold to insure control of the port, should that be needed.

As it turned out, that never became necessary. Word got out to those involved in the movement to shut the port down; they decided their interests would be better served by not going ahead. In regular military terms you might say the CIC effort was a "show of force" sufficient "to carry the day."

Every Friday morning throughout the war, the General's Subversive Squad laid on his desk a report on the situation status throughout the First Service Command. This report covered any items thought to be of interest in carrying out the Army's responsibilities. This function was considered important enough that a core of about a dozen agents were held back from any other assignment. The role was played out until VE day when most of the WW2 agents had enough points for discharge.

* * *

The *Only* CIC Officers Candidate School

(What was the turning point in the rising star of CIC, that eventually lead to its abolition as a separate entity? We can conjecture and argue the point, but if the OCS undertaken by MI in the spring of 1942 for its CIC agents had not been abolished after its single session commissioning 30 of its most promising agents, would it have endured until today and beyond?)

Thirty of the most promising, senior special agents of the CIP-CIC were admitted to a new, intensive, officers' training school in the spring of 1942. Apparently the school was improperly established; that is, it failed to secure the prior approval of higher key authorities in the army and thus adhere to the strict rules of the day (or the past; one example of archaic rules, candidates for OCS had to possess a minimum number of teeth!). Those who attended and passed the course were permitted to retain the second lieutenant bars they had earned, but they made history as the *only* graduates of a CIC officer candidate school, ever!

Thanks to Marvin Goff and to Dudley Skinker, we here list for the first time our honor role of those in the only CIC OCS Graduating Class, June 1942. The names of many of these graduates appear in various books and articles about CIC, and many of them, despite the very low TO&E (Table of Organization and Equipment) the CIC was initially stuck with, attained a respectable rank by the end of the war.

Had CIC been provided a more equitable TO&E, such as the *Kempei Tai* had (one officer out of every three), it is believed many more would have made a career in the service, providing it with a large core/corps of experts in the business when badly needed in the Cold War era.

Or so the argument goes.

CIC's New Lieutenants, Station and Home

AULT, Donovan J., MIS WDC Presidio of San Francisco CA; San Diego CA

BARRY, Edward Philip, MIS HQ 6th C.A., Chicago IL; Evanston IL

BOOTH, John Welles, MIS HQ 1st C.A., Boston MA; Newton Center MA

BRITT, Amos Edward, MIS HQ 7th C.A., Omaha NE; Indianola, MI

BROWN, David Rodman, MIS WN DC, Bardstown KY

BUCKLEY, Harry William, MIS HQ 5th C.A., Ft. Hayes; Columbus OH

CAMERON, Jack Bruce, MIS HQ 1st C.A., Boston MA; Boston MA

CASE, John Persinger, MIS HQ 4th C.A., Atlanta GA; Washington Court House OH

CORNELL, Jr., William Burgess, MIS HQ 3rd C.A., Baltimore MD; Albany NY

DICKEY, David Bonnell, MIS HQ 8th C.A., Ft. Sam Houston, San Antonio TX; San Antonio TX

DOYLE, Robert Henry , MIS HQ 2nd C.A., Governor's Island NY; Glen Ridge, NJ

GOFF, Jr, Marvin C., MIS HQ 8th C.A. Ft. Sam Houston, San Antionio TX; Memphis, TN

GRAY III, Arthur Powell, MIS HQ 3rd C.A., Baltimore MD; West Point VA

GRIEVE, William Gray, MIS HQ 2nd C.A., Governor's Island NY; NYC

HOWELL, Joseph Franklin, MIS HQ 3rd C.A., Baltimore MD; Baltimore MD

HUYLER, Coulter Dunham, MIS HQ 2nd C.A., Governor's Island NY; Greenwich CT

JOHNS, William Edward, MIS WDC Presidio of San Francisco CA; San Francisco CA

JONES, Thomas Orton, MIS HQ 6th C.A. Chicago IL; Highland Park IL

KEENAN, Jr., Albert Joseph, MIS HQ 2nd C.A. Governor's Island NY; Brooklyn, NY

KOLB, Lewis Jackson, MIS HQ 4th C.A. Atlanta GA; Columbus GA

MATTHEWS, Dudley McCutcheon, MIS HQ 2nd C.A. Governor's Island NY; NYC

NEUMANN, Albert Francis, MIS WN DC, Washington DC

PICARD, Lucien Leopold, MIS WN DC, Washington DC

RUGE, Neil Marshall, MIS WDC Presidio of San Francisco CA; San Francisco CA

SKINKER, Dudley Graham, MIS WN DC, Washington, D. C.

SMITH, Francis Joseph, MIS HQ 2nd C.A. Governor's Island NY; Brooklyn NY

STANLEY, Charles Haydon, MIS WN DC, Frankfort KY

VANKIRK, Arthur Harris, MIS HQ 6th C.A. Chicago IL; Janesville WI

VINEY, William Elliott, MIS WDC Presidio of San Francisco CA; Covina CA

WALLACE, Jr., William Harry MIS HQ 8th C.A. Ft. Sam Houston, San Antonio TX; Corpus Christi TX

(This was the end, but should it have been?)

1943

General MacArthur had expected to find at least the skeleton of an American Army in Australia when he obeyed orders from the Pentagon to hasten there and organize the effort to defeat the enemy in the Pacific. He was disappointed; there were no *combat* troops awaiting him in 1942 other than the badly outnumbered, hard-pressed but brave Australian troops. By the end of 1942, the first American divisions (32nd and 41st) had arrived and begun to train, but with agonizing slowness. They needed instructions from the Aussies in jungle survival to fight the Japanese then approaching Port Moresby on the southern side of New Guinea.

MacArthur asked for and finally got an experienced field general in Walter Krueger who began the nucleus of his U.S. Sixth Army in Australia in April 1943. The already existing I Corps under Eichelberger with the 32nd and 41st Divisions thus came under his command. These divisions were participating alongside the Aussies by the end of 1942 and early 1943 over the Stanley Mountains in bitter fighting to capture Buna and Gona, two enemy strongholds on the north coast of New Guinea.

MacArthur was gradually becoming cognizant that the Pentagon was bent on defeating the Nazis first, sending the bulk of troops and matériel in that direction. It was a "win" against the Nazis, and a holding action against the Japanese, so the Pentagon spared him a little only when he clamored a lot. After loud clamoring the dribble became a small stream in 1943.

CIC's situation was no different. Only a mere handful of men in that theater even pretended to know much about CIC, though the request repeatedly went to Washington for agents. This response was also as weak as the other requests from MacArthur.

In desperation Thorpe and staff turned to the troops arriving and already in Australia for personnel qualified to meet the high standards for CIC agents. Out of hundreds of applicants, the final screening left only a handful of candidates, who were then trained intensively with the help of Australian experts, especially their Field Security troops now returning from North Africa to fight the enemy approaching its northern territories.

But even a handful was better than none at all.

Essentially the "Eureka" conference 4 December 1943 in Teheran, Iran, with the U.S., British and the Russians, dealt with Germany, but Japan was on President Roosevelt's agenda, and he pursued it. Russian intelligence reported rumors of an attempt to assassinate Roosevelt; elaborate plans were made to thwart any such try. These plans included selecting agent Robert Ebaugh from the small CIC detachment on duty in Iran to pose as Roosevelt, cigarette holder and all, on auto trips to and from the conference. If there were assassination plans, they were indeed thwarted, thanks in part to this enlisted CIC agent and others from the detachment who took part in safeguarding Roosevelt around the clock.

* * *

The Secret Service of course took the credit, with never a hint of army CIC agents being a part. As Roosevelt on departing shook the hands of the agents and thanked them, he most likely had no idea that each of them was an enlisted soldier.

CHAPTER XIII

Luzon—Sakakida Survives

In February 1943, Sakakida was removed from Bilibid prison to the office of Colonel Nishiharu, Chief Judge Advocate (legal staff) of the Japanese Fourteenth Army Headquarters, who evidently had reviewed the story which Sakakida had stuck by without a single variation. The colonel said he was to work in the office, run a mimeograph machine, make tea, help out generally where needed, and during his off-duty time serve as houseboy at the colonel's living quarters.

Although the Japanese seemed to have accepted his story, they continued in devious ways to trap him into an admission that he was in the U.S. Army. One day some one threw him a .45 pistol and curtly ordered him to clean it. Realizing that if he properly disassembled the weapon, it would be an admission of military service, Sakakida merely wiped the .45 with an oily rag and explained that if someone would take it apart he would be glad to clean the rest of it.

Once the officer in charge of counter espionage of the Fourteenth Army abruptly accused him of being a sergeant in the United States Army. Alarmed, Sakakida recovered quickly and denied the accusation convincingly enough that the officer turned to other matters. This kind of threat was ever hanging overhead, so Sakakida continued to exercise utmost caution.

Another officer, a Harvard graduate, seemingly in a sympathetic mood one day asked how much the U.S. Army paid him for his work as an interpreter. Recognizing this as another ruse to learn the rank of prisoners, Sakakida replied he received no money while working under coercion, though he was fed and housed.

The dual job of office work and houseboy continued until the colonel found out Sakakida was dipping (on purpose, just for the result) into his stock of American cigarettes. The colonel banished him from the houseboy job. (During his postwar interview in the 1950s at Fort Holabird, world headquarters of CIC, Sakakida spoke naturally in a soft voice and in an earnest manner, but smiled as he mentioned the colonel's anger at this incident and then added it was a most fortunate change for him.)

He was sent to a civilian barracks, the former English Club in Manila city, under the strict discipline of a warrant officer who took

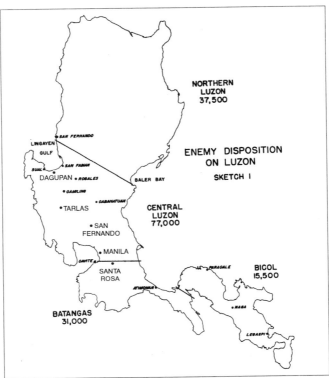

NORTHERN
LUZON
37,500

ENEMY DISPOSITION
ON LUZON

SKETCH I

SAN FERNANDO

LINGAYEN
GULF

SAN FABIAN

SUAL

DAGUPAN • ROSALES

BALER BAY

• CABLING

• CABANATUAN

• TARLAS

CENTRAL
LUZON
77,000

• SAN
FERNANDO

• MANILA

CAVITE •

SANTA
ROSA

PARACALE

BICOL
15,500

• NAGA

BATANGAS
31,000

LEGASPI

Luzon, showing number of enemy on D-Day. Courtesy Marvin D Goff, Jr

roll call at 6 a.m. and 11:30 p.m. and bed check at midnight. The time between midnight and morning roll call gave Sakakida about five hours in which to contact people to whom he could give information gained at headquarters during the day.

After searching, he contacted Filipino guerrillas known as the "ROTC Group" led by a Major Tupas. He then began in earnest to gather shipping information in headquarters, concentrating on ship schedules, and slipping it out to the guerrillas for transmitting to Australia. These messages were forwarded to Pearl Harbor and then on to prowling U.S. submarines. At no time did his captors suspect Sakakida was the source of so much damage to their resupply efforts.

While Allied radio eavesdropping teams in Australia and Hawaii may have learned in late February 1943 of a major Japanese movement of troops from Rabaul to New Guinea, confirming information from Sakakida was welcomed. He had spotted a copy of Japanese plans for such a major movement, so he smuggled it out to his guerrilla contacts. MacArthur's people had definite advance warning of 8 transports and 8 destroyers on the way from Rabaul to New Guinea.

* * *

A combination of American and Australian air might, aided by American PT-boats on the surface and by a new technique of skip bombing by planes, sank all the transports and half the destroyers in the Battle of Bismarck Sea early in March 1943. More than 3000 Japanese troops perished. Found in an abandoned lifeboat on Goodenough Island, northeast of New Guinea, was the complete roster of 40,000 Japanese army officers from Hideki Tojo down to the lowest company commander; we now knew each officer's rank, his unit and job classification. This was the enemy's *order of battle,* a most valuable prize for our intelligence. There was nothing heroic about what he had done, Sakakida explained—he was glad he could do it. He felt fortunate in having made the one contact that made it possible to communicate with the guerrillas as soon as he found himself free for that five hours after midnight.

Once in 1943 Sakakida's hopes were raised when a total stranger approached him to inquire if he would like to escape to Australia. Afraid this might be another trap set by Japanese Intelligence, Sakakida said he would have to talk to the original inquirer. He heard nothing of it again until after the war, when he learned the Anderson Guerrillas had been trying to get him out at the direction of General MacArthur's headquarters. But the message had been garbled and the word reaching MacArthur was he preferred to remain where he was.

Anderson, the leader of the guerrilla force that bore his name, was only one of several bands started by American soldiers who slipped away into the mountains and forests throughout the islands, rather than surrender. A weak radio signal from one of them had been picked up in the States, and the message was relayed to Australia that resistance to the invaders was being organized but supplies of all kinds, including better radio equipment, were badly needed. American subs then began to slip through the net of Japanese warships and delivered vital supplies not only to guerrillas on Luzon, but also to Leyte and Mindanao.

The exploits of these guerrilla bands could fill many books, but we must confine this to the CIC. The only known member of the Manila CIC Detachment to participate in this guerrilla warfare was Drisko, who survived until near the last days before liberation with a price on his head. To have earned that distinction, this CIC agent must have performed deeds that would have earned many Bronze Stars and other awards, if the deeds were but known. But the record is completely blank about him, thus far.

But, in this turnaround year, Kangleon's guerrillas on Leyte, and Fertig's on Mindanao, were—like Anderson's and others on Luzon—learning to survive, and to annoy the enemy more and more, as the stream of aid and matériel from MacArthur continued to increase. Add to that list of valid, loyal, guerrilla units, that of Tomas Confessor on the islands of Panay and Romblon.

* * *

The leaders of the puppet government under the Japanese were Jorge B. Vargas, who had been prewar President Quezon's secretary, and Jose P. Laurel, Quezon's adviser. The latter tried to wrest the power from Vargas so he could became a "benevolent" dictator and bring an end to the growing resistance of the guerrilla bands operating throughout the Philippines. In October 1943, Laurel was inaugurated as the puppet president and remained the nominal head of the Philippines. Both he and Vargas made every effort to convince the guerrillas to cease resistance, but their pleas were answered only by increased resistance.

The puppet leaders' solution was to outlaw the previous Sakdal and Ganap parties and replace them with the government-approved Kalibapi (neighborhood) association. At a special convention, the Kalibapi "representing the people" ratified a new constitution and met September 25 as the newly "elected" National Assembly and named Laurel President of the Philippine Republic.

Laurel then used the remnants of the Sakdalistas to form the republic-blessed Makapili, under Pio Duran. Makapili members fought alongside the Japanese against the guerrilla bands, and as many as 5,000 were reported to be firing at American soldiers when we landed on Philippine shores to liberate the Filipinos. They were guilty of atrocities on their own people in Polo and Obando, Bulacan.

* * *

DANAS was another group of neighborhood associations which Laurel tried to use against the resistance groups. He is recorded as addressing their meeting on 6 January 1943. Another minor group were the Kaigens, associated with marines.

CHAPTER XIV

South Pacific Welcomes CIC

During the latter part of 1943, field duties were added to CIC's mission in the South Pacific Theater, a Navy Theater commanded by Admiral Bull Halsey. Additional training was deemed necessary. As it was never possible to get enough agents to serve with all combat units, there was always a great deal of transferring them back and forth between the detachments as the need arose.

Field duties included the delivery of security talks, publicizing regulations concerning souvenirs, collecting and studying material of intelligence value before its release to the troops, searching enemy command posts and bivouac areas immediately after their capture, assisting in the interrogation of prisoners of war, and assisting technical officers in discovering, protecting, tagging and shipping material to be sent to the rear for further study and analysis.

Although hampered by shortages of personnel and equipment, disease, and the lack of cooperation of some commanding officers, CIC was able to organize an efficient security program in the South Pacific—not a single case of Axis-inspired sabotage ever developed in the area, a really amazing record when the vast expanses of command are considered. On occasions, investigation was necessary to rule out sabotage, which CIC performed with efficiency and professionalism.

As in all theaters and zones in which CIC operated, it first had to "educate" many G-2s and many commanders about the capabilities and limitations of CIC, a new agency to most, its missions still undefined in many military channels. While the strength of CIC detachments fluctuated a great deal in the South Pacific, yet it at no time had more than 65 agents, making it necessary to shift them around to crisis points.

In April 1943, help arrived at Noumea, New Caledonia, on the liner Holland-American *SS Veendam*. Robert M Reese and other CIC agents were the only passengers aboard her, after 18 days at sea with no escort. Noumea was Fleet HQ for Admiral Halsey; but the Army also had a small headquarters at Camp Barnes on the beach outside Noumea, where Art Turner, then a major, had other CIC people with him. Among them were Marvin C. Goff, Paul Hurst, Lowell "Lokey or Loky" Bradford, Don Ryan, John C. Marley, Herman R. Butts, George

Smith, George Crow, and (FNU) Velie.

Turner became Chief, CIC, SOPACBACOM, with Goff his Executive Officer; they worked untiringly the next few months forming CIC Detachments for the various Island Commands. George Crow, then a 1st Lt. had arrived at the same time as Turner, bringing in 20 additional agents, and was later assigned to Efate in the New Hebrides Islands, which included Espiritu Santos.

Robert Reese later became CO of First Island CIC Command, in Noumea (when we prepared to invade Japan, he was CO of the 441st 3rd Region on Mindanao, Philippines). Agents were also assigned to the 25th Infantry Division, and at one time or another also to the 37th, 40th, 43rd, 93rd (black division, with some white, some black, agents) and Americal (which relieved the Marines on Guadalcanal) divisions, the XIVth Corps and 13th Air Force. Some agents were attached to units in action against the enemy on Bougainville, Munda, New Georgia, and Guadalcanal in the Solomon Islands.

* * *

One Island Command was located in New Caledonia, a French possession—an important link in U.S. bases, since thousands of troops passed through on their way to the fighting in the north each month. One of the richest mineral islands in the Pacific, with nickel, cobalt and chrome for exporting, it was of vital importance from a strategic viewpoint as well.

The natives were mixed Melanesians, with a substantial white population. Before the war Japanese indentured labor had been imported, and many chose to remain when their contracts ended, some 1,200 of them. They became influential throughout New Caledonia, gaining ownership of some mines and much of the lumber business. Most but not all were deported to Australia early in the war.

CIC searched former Japanese residences, gathering letters, maps, dictionaries, military books, passports, and magazines. Though impossible to prove they were operating an espionage net, from the amount of information compiled it was evident Japan knew much about New Caledonia and the surrounding islands.

Considering the number of military personnel stationed there, suspected cases of sabotage were relatively few. The most serious: 1 November 1943, an explosion on the Nickel Company docks at Noumea killed 52 and hospitalized 115, while destroying tons of munitions, military equipment and other critical supplies. Marvin Goff was on the scene while debris, including shell fragments, was still flying through the air. He led his CIC team in an investigation into the cause of the explosion, which ruled out deliberate enemy sabotage, exposing yet another case of employee negligence that bedeviled our war efforts around the globe. CIC determined that inexperienced, unsupervised personnel had been handling high explosives stored improperly on the docks.

In April 1943, agents James Franklin and Edgar Lucas went on a 10-day patrol with a native guide, throughout the islands, on a 50-foot vessel borrowed from the Navy, manned by two seamen and one Navy warrant officer. Tahiti-born agent Lucas for some time before the war was a Navy labor recruiter in the islands; he acquired knowledge of the language and the people—excellent credentials for the mission.

They stocked the hold of the ship with provisions to use as gifts for the natives, and also to provide for missionaries in the Islands whose trips for supplies were now irregular on account of the war. The agents checked with native chieftains, missionaries, coast watchers, and plantation managers to learn as much as possible about Japanese who might be watching Allied shipping lanes, while also checking on numerous rumors and reports previously received.

* * *

Archdeacon E. G. Teall at the Melanesian Mission on Aoba reported witnessing a pilot dropping messages in the bush farther inland, but this turned out to be in the interest of romance only: a New Zealand pilot was dropping notes to a teacher friend at one of the mission schools! CIC investigated other suspicious incidents but none had as definite or as pleasant an explanation.

Somewhat later, agents Wallace and Paul Poulin set out to check a report that Japanese had been put ashore from a submarine. Accompanied by a half-caste guide and interpreter, they spent three days in the interior of Malekula with a fierce, cannibal-practicing tribe called the Nambas. The Nambas had been shooting ancient French rifles at low-flying Allied aircraft. The agents put a stop to this bad habit by establishing a better rapport with the Nambas, even though the hunt for the alleged Japanese infiltrators was negative.

CIC operations did not get well underway in Guadalcanal for nearly a year after the battle there began, as it was primarily a Marine-Navy operation. In the entire occupation of that island, CIC received not a single report of espionage and only a few scattered incidents of suspected sabotage, mainly minor, such as cutting communication lines and damage by fire or explosion.

As the war moved northward and Guadalcanal stopped functioning as a tactical command, some soldiers inevitably became restless, increasing cases of disaffection and subversive activity. In the absence of a Criminal Investigation Detachment (CID, agents for Provost Marshals) CIC investigated several soldiers for stealing post exchange supplies from barges anchored along Lunga Beach. Court-martial trials sentenced them to long prison terms.

The Provost Marshal on Guadalcanal began requiring military police who worked on the vessels, piers, and beaches to submit daily reports of all pilferage, a policy soon adopted by Allied security officers in other commands, resulting in a great drop in such losses, and in the threat of sabotage at these critical port areas.

A CIC Detachment worked closely with New Zealand's security intelligence bureau, even sharing the same office for a time. Activities there included port security, routine investigative duties, and some criminal cases due to the absence of CID units in the area. CIC also did a limited amount of work for the American Consulate.

Port security was a vital CIC duty in all island commands as well as in New Zealand ports which were the scene of intense activity from 1942 until cessation of hostilities.

CIC was alert to attempts to leave or enter an area illegally. They apprehended one Australian merchant seaman who impersonated an officer and visited a nearby bar to relate several "hair raising" war tales. The result of his escapade was being escorted onto a transport aircraft bound for Australia where he was wanted on a felony charge.

In another case, a male Red Cross worker had cards bearing the title "CIC Society" printed to pass among his friends for a "laugh," he claimed, with no intent of ridiculing the army or committing a subversive act. CIC stood by while the printer destroyed the plate with a promise not to accept similar orders in the future.

By spring of 1945, most U.S. troops had been sent to bolster General MacArthur's forces on their island-skipping way to Japan. CIC HQ in the South Pacific moved to the Philippine Islands in June. The remaining CIC detachments were deactivated, most agents having been transferred months before into the Southwest Pacific Theater. Finally, all agents came under 441st CIC, SWPA Theater Headquarters Detachment, and many later moved on into Japan for the occupation.

* * *

Thus ends the saga of CIC in the South Pacific.

CHAPTER XV

SWPA Comes Alive

Late in February 1943, USAFFE Headquarters at Brisbane assumed counter-intelligence functions and took steps to build up the numbers in lower echelons. Seven enlisted men, carefully selected and trained, were assigned to the A-2 Section (Air Corps equivalent of G-2) of the Fifth Air Force. In March, Lt. Colonel James N. Jones left his temporary assignment at G-2 USAFFE and took over the CI subsection of A-2.

By February 1943 only 23 CIC officers had reached the theater. Even counting supervisory personnel in the G-2 office, and base intelligence officers, total CIC strength was barely 50, including those procured locally. But the year 1943 saw the Counter Intelligence Corps finally begin to come into its own as an integral part of Southwest Pacific operations. Following numerous ignored requests to the War Department by Thorpe, finally a contingent got to Australia: Major Albert L. Vreeland with James A. Bledsoe and 20 special agents reported for duty 30 March 1943. This shipment was followed in April-May by a group on the *Klip Fontaine*, listing Thomas Ackerman, William McCauley, Joseph A. Whitlow, Bob Frederichs, Ed Thrift, Pete Moloney, Earl Held, Arsenio Trinidad, Tom Costello with Lt. Lou Kohn among them.

This "second CIC detachment" to reach Australia was first quartered in tents in the Ascot Racetrack, Brisbane, for several weeks before quarters were found in houses and hotels.

These reinforcements made possible the physical separation, for more efficiency, of the G-2 and CIC offices—with Vreeland (a NJ Police chief and mayor) as Theater CIC Chief, and Blair P Labatt (who came in the original detachment) as his Executive Officer. From this new CIC HQ emerged the theater-wide 5227th CIC Detachment (provisional) and its successor the 441st CIC. The physical separation in no way diminished the always close cooperation between G-2 and its CI sections. Some of the agents were then assigned to the 32nd and 41st Divisions busy over the Owen Stanley mountains of New Guinea; several were sent to language school to learn Malay, the language universally understood in NEI. This course caused the agents to think that MacArthur was planning to take the route via NEI back to the Philippines.

While in Brisbane, Whitlow recalls working one spy case the subject of which was a German national minister of a church attended by German settlers in the area. This was an ongoing investigation that covered a long period of time. CIC found the minister was heavily involved with "Gertie" who made her living going door-to-door in Brisbane as a photographer, offering to copy photos of husbands, relatives, loved ones, etc., in the Aussie service and prisoners of the Japanese. What better way for a spy to learn unit names and locations throughout the theater? Whitlow was reassigned before the case was resolved, frustrated at not knowing the outcome of a case he worked on, as happened so many times to other agents.

* * *

After completing the Malay course, Whitlow was sent to Milne Bay on the eastern tip of New Guinea, first to Gili-Gili, then to Ahioma down the Bay, for port security work. The importance of checking all allied ships coming into port was well recognized early on. As with other agents *not* assigned to combat troops, he wore a shoulder patch and civilian employee identification, U.S. Army.

Captain Lew Shull requisitioned a 26' harbor tug that speeded up the work of the small detachment, which was to board all incoming vessels and check crew papers. Many were Dutch small steamers under charter, but a lot were Liberty ships, and some British. Joe Weyn, Whitlow's partner, spoke some Dutch. One case of attempted sabotage was discovered: a metal pellet found in one of two oil lines going to each engine shaft bearing, possibly put there by some one at the Iron Fireman factory, Portland. Oregon. It was obviously intentional as it was machined to pivot in the line and cut off the oil. It was reported through channels, but again the final disposition back in the States was not known to the Milne Bay detachment.

One day in October, Whitlow was summoned for an emergency situation on board a ship, to what at first seemed like a rebellion. A clique of young seamen had become very independent and were telling the chief mate how much work they would do, how they would do it, and were writing letters and riding around in a launch when they were supposed to be at work. Their 28-year old leader thought he knew all the regulations and the answers; he had been at sea for six years, and was advising the younger men. The Captain asked this CIC "army civilian" for help with this "mutiny."

Whitlow had a couple of MPs stand by with hands on guns while he questioned each of the clique in turn, and then he read him a list of his "sins" from the log. Each admitted the truth, whereupon Whitlow read him federal statutes on the subject, which showed the seaman liable to a $5000 fine plus a year in the clink, *inasmuch as working for the Army, though a civilian, he was subject to military law like any soldier.* Three of them almost fainted with fright; they didn't know if they were on trial or not, but they got the idea. The ringleader took a martyred attitude and tried to quote the union rules. The others began to turn on him for getting them into trouble.

They spent the night in the stockade and were told they were being held for Army court-martial. The "judge-advocate" finally relented and instead lectured them on the fact of their subservience to military jurisdiction. Apparently none of them, including the ringleader, had ever realized it before. As they sheepishly returned to their ship, they vowed they would spread the word among the rest of the crew. All in a day's work.

Returning to Brisbane, Whitlow joined agents under John Irwin writing and presenting a "Security Show." Vicious rumors and destructive talks about MacArthur and other high officers were spreading. Whether instigated by the enemy or by disaffected soldiers, morale can be adversely affected by this seemingly unharmful activity. MacArthur was worried enough to order something done. Irwin's effort brought into existence six teams of three men each who lectured groups of 20 to 3000 soldiers, showing cartoons on loose talk and rumors and captured Japanese documents.

When lecturing, the agents wore their U.S. jackets but fobbed off the inevitable questions about rank by answering, "We work directly for the War Department." For this reason, they were often mistaken for USO units! After testing the effectiveness of this approach in mitigating the problem of morale around Brisbane, some teams repeated the lectures in New Guinea, and later in the Philippines.[8]

* * *

Galloway was promoted to Major in June 1943 and moved from New Guinea back to CIC HQ which now was in Brisbane. He had run into the almost universal brick wall facing CIC practically everywhere in the Army, at least in the beginning: field commanders resisting CIC because detachments were authorized to communicate directly with their HQ without going through the normal army chain of command (this annoyed most COs). During 1943-44 Galloway made a number of trips to field units trying to smooth the way for CIC units. Once most field commanders recognized the high caliber and skills of CIC, there was a complete turnaround, and CIC became more completely integrated into operational plans.

On 16 August, as G-2 of the Advance Section HQ, Galloway issued the following for the Intelligence Officer, Advance Section

---

8   *Foregoing stories came from Joseph A Whitlow*

USASOS, clarifying CIC duties in New Guinea, to:
a.   Supervise and maintain an integrated counter-intelligence net throughout the New Guinea area.
b.   Maintain contact with Allied intelligence agencies operating in the area.
c.   Interpret policies established by higher headquarters.
d.   Keep informed on all developments in the area pertaining to intelligence and see that base Sections receive required information.
e.   Allocate and shift CIC personnel as needed.
f.   Make recommendations as to checks and investigations to be carried out in the various Base Sections.
g.   Pass on all requisitions requesting equipment, etc. from the mainland. [9]

Theater CIC had been bolstered further by the arrival of the CIC unit attached to General Walter Krueger's Sixth Army, with the second echelon of this new combat command. This unit consisted of 39 special agents, headed by five CIC officers: CO Richard G. Earle, Louis Kohn, Thomas H. Major, Thomas W. Applegate, and Daniel F. McGillicuddy, Jr.

This was the first of a genuine infusion of combat-trained CIC agents into SWPA. To an I Corps CIC detachment at Rockhampton, Australia, came William J. Koenigsdorf with an officer assistant and 11 special agents. To HQ Fifth Air Force were assigned two officers and 11 agents headed by Charles H. "Chuck" Albertson; five agents led by Harold F. Frederick reported for duty with the 1st Cavalry Division; five agents under Phillip O. Roach were assigned to the 32nd Division at Camp Columbia, Australia; and five agents under Victor Cook were sent to Oro Bay, New Guinea, to the 41st Division.

Meanwhile, the influx of American combat troops and units into the Southwest Pacific area increased considerably throughout 1943 and 1944. But, unfortunately, shipments of CIC agents did not parallel the movement of these other troops, and the shortage threatened to hamper plans to send CIC agents into combat zones. And some of those shipments of CIC were adventures to the agents just to get to Australia. The story of the "lost" 201st detachment illustrates the problem, as related by agent Arthur J. Zinsmaster:

"Thirteen of us traveled cross country from Holabird to Camp Stoneman, California. We convinced the PIO that part of our assignment was to monitor bars for loose talk and suspicious characters. As a result, we had 24 hour passes during our stay; the PIO, convinced we were special, classified our orders 'Top Secret' and flew them to alert Australia we were coming.

---

[9]   *This & other data from J Roy Galloway*

"When we boarded our troop ship, therefore, we were not expected, so there was no space reserved for us. We were split up: one to sleep in the ship's clinic, another in the newspaper room, etc. I was put in charge of handing out work details to 48 privates. Within a half-day of Brisbane, Australia, our ship was diverted to Milne Bay, New Guinea.

"As we watched the troops disembark, an officer came up to me and asked, 'Have you seen anything of 13 sergeants around here?' So—off to the jungle we marched! After a day of getting acquainted, agent Alex Duncan went to the camp HQ to find out where we were headed. At that time Finschhaven was ridden with malaria and heavy casualties; hence he was told we were being assigned to the infantry!"

"Even a condemned man gets one phone call, so demanding this right we were allowed to radio Brisbane HQ, which politely responded, 'Where in hell have you been? We've searched the whole South Pacific looking for you!' Thank goodness, we were rescued from an infantry assignment in New Guinea and routed on to Brisbane to do our CIC job."

* * *

Meanwhile, CIC was seeing a bit of stateside type action in some of the larger cities in Australia, as the undermanned Field Security could not cope with all cases reported to it, and cooperated willingly with the Americans. An espionage ring was known to exist in the "Little Italy" section of Melbourne, and one link in it was the Italian proprietor of a tavern there.

CIC loaned agent Frank Collucci (often misspelled Colucci) to penetrate the ring to identify all its members. In civilian life back in Massachusetts, Collucci had been a Ph.D. and could easily handle the Italian language. He determined to get himself accepted by Melbourne's Italian community, and became a habitué of the tavern.

Hearing nothing from him for a week, a CIC officer visited the neighborhood and ran into his undercover agent who had on a dirty uniform, was unshaven and stank of stale wine, outside the pub. The officer put on an act so as not to betray Collucci's cover, and demanded loudly, "Are you a soldier or a drunken bum?"

Lurching back into the tavern, Collucci retorted, "Who the hell wants to know?"

"I'll be back with the MPs to get you, you damn deserter," the officer roared through the door.

Military Police showed up, but on orders didn't search too thoroughly. That night the officer's phone rang and he heard a low voice say, "Thanks! They were a little suspicious, but that brawl with you

fixed me up." Collucci was soon accepted in the Italian ring, and before long all the spies were gathered in.

* * *

An influx of new agents caused new emphasis on local recruiting
and training; a permanent CIC training school was set up at Brisbane
on 28 June 1943, and known to CIC agents as "Palma Rosa Castle."
Under Major Vreeland its curriculum was geared to combat conditions, with field problems simulating jungle battle conditions. Its students also studied Japanese methods of administering conquered territory, learning that firm, intelligent approaches would win the
allegiance of the natives who detested the cruel ways of their Japanese
overlords.

Before MacArthur had solidified a decision to take the shortest
way back to the Philippines, CIC was training personnel for a planned
route through the Dutch East Indies, believed at that time to be lightly
held—amounting more or less to a combat training operation for
freshly arriving troops. The overall strategic plan at this point was that
once winning the war in Europe was at least assured, MacArthur
would have ample troops to liberate the Philippines.

The Dutch placed at the disposal of CIC a unit of some 30 Indonesian and Dutch soldiers who had been trained in civil administration. They were schooled at Palma Rosa, and whether official or not
became known to CIC agents also training there, some later serving
with them, as the "Dutch CIC." They would also be valuable as guides
and interpreters of Dutch and Malay languages. CIC was also compiling, with the help of the Dutch, a black list of collaborators to be taken
into custody. At the top of this list was Soekarno (Sukarno), who later
became president of Indonesia!

Any thought of an NEI operation was scrubbed when word
came out of our guerrilla forces in the Philippines that a large Japanese
resupply convoy had been totally demolished by American submarines. The Philippines now appeared to be ripe for the taking. So the
emphasis at the Palma Rosa CIC school switched to organizing and
training detachments of CIC agents for combat units, and supporting
area teams preparing for the Philippines. A handful of "Dutch CIC"
nevertheless accompanied CIC units, with troops later penetrating
Dutch New Guinea in 1944 through the Hollandia and Biak operations
and other NEI areas.

* * *

CIC began to prepare seriously for its part in the long march to
Tokyo via the Philippines, in close step with, sometimes alongside,
sometimes accidentally in advance of, our front-line troops.

CHAPTER XVI

CBI Theater Warms Up

By early summer 1943 Burma had assumed a strategic importance probably unsurpassed by any other area in the war with Japan. It offered the only life-line to China, whose champion Chiang Kai-shek could not continue to tie down massive numbers of Japanese soldiers, nor hold out much longer, unless the U.S. could get him trucks, artillery, tanks and other heavy equipment.

Major General Chennault's Flying Tigers were desperately trying to ferry 10,000 tons of supplies a month over the Himalayan mountains (the Hump) from Assam, India, to the Yunnan plateau in China. But they could not fly the badly needed *heavy* equipment. If China fell, Japan could exploit tremendous resources without harassment, and when the United States finally applied pressure to the home islands, the Japanese government and warlords could even flee to the Chinese mainland and continue the war perhaps for years longer.

At Casablanca in January 1943, and at the Trident and Quadrant Conferences later in the year, plans were made to build a road through North Burma, paralleled by an oil pipeline to connect with a similar one from Calcutta to Ledo. This would supply Chiang's forces and our B-29 bases to be built in China; the devastating air assaults pulverizing Germany could then be brought to wreak havoc on the Japanese islands. The road and pipeline would make it possible to dramatically increase general supplies to 85,000 tons, and petroleum products to 54,000 per month!

Recognizing the security problems in such a plan, in May 1943 the CBI Theater requested the War Department to provide it with a field grade counter-intelligence officer and a CIC detachment of one officer and five special agents! This was to be on an "experimental basis," a definite indication of the army's general lack of knowledge of, and hesitancy in using, this little-known service. This was 17 months after we had been at war with Japan—and some 25 years after the CIC (CIP) had been created to serve our Army, which should have been long enough for the Army to know about it.

Colonel H. R. Kibler, Chief of worldwide CIC, in Baltimore did not hesitate. He sent Major D. E. MacKenzie early in September, followed on 11 November by agents George L. Wilson, William Comisky,

Carl J. McArdle, Charles F. Gentile, John Nowlan, and Edmond Fong.

* * *

Anticipating the resourcefulness of the men he sent would soon end the "experimental basis," Colonel Kibler immediately ordered a search for agents with special qualifications for this far-off Theater of Operations. On the CIC roster were several with years of valuable experience in the Orient: Ali Mohammed, former resident of Lahore, India, in civilian life a professor at the University of Southern California; LeRoy T. Newland,[10] who spent his first 18 years in Korea, the son of a Presbyterian missionary; Edwin W. Simpson, also a missionary's son who lived in Kolhapur, Bombay, for 17 years and spoke most of the dialects fluently; Thomas H. Kendall, longtime resident of China, whose mother was then a prisoner of the Japanese; and George C. Mah, whose uncle was mayor of Nanking.

In September 1943, CIC agents began slowly filtering into the theater; Japan had conquered all of Burma except for the fringes of mountain, jungle and swamp on the north and west, and were threatening the British base at Imphal and the Bengal-Assam railroad below the base. On these important points the Hump air transport and the projected railroad depended. General Stilwell's famous "walk-out" was now past history and the Allies were preparing for major offensives from both India and China, which had to await the end of the November monsoons.

Before the war the "Burma Road" was the only road connecting Burma with China; it extended 1,445 miles from Rangoon to Chungking. Actually it consisted of a railroad from Rangoon to Lashio, a new motor road from Lashio to Kunming built by the Chinese 1937-1939, and the old highway on to Chungking. Engineers were to build a road from Ledo in Assam, to the Irrawaddy River near Myitkyina, down the river valley around the southern end of the impassable Kumon Mountain Range, to cross the Shweli River and intersect the old Burma road at Mongyu near the Yunnan border.

Early in December 1943, Wilson and his five agents arrived and at once began making security surveys as the danger from enemy agents was immediately perceived as very great. In the meantime Colonel Kibler had received the anticipated requisition and recognized the need for additional agents as also very great. The group he assembled were receiving special training for CBI, as training for combat troops in ETO's "front line activities" did not fit CBI needs for protecting transportation and supply installations.

In November 1943, agent Paul J. McArdle arrived and was assigned to Calcutta, where he found every incident between U.S. sol-

---

[10] *Newland has contributed much information*

diers and natives was being played up out of proportion. When agents Harry Smith (SAC), Richard Klise, Lawrence Hughes and Young Chinn reached the city in June, deliberate sabotage—cutting telephone lines between Calcutta and Kharagpur—was occurring. Klise traveled the 100-mile line, visiting police chiefs and other village elders along the way. While developing their friendship, he also reminded them each village was subject to a fine whenever an accident "happened" to the line in their territory.

A vital gasoline pipeline had just opened between Calcutta and the Ledo Road. This could be a major target for saboteurs, so agents traveled its length, using similar instructions for establishing the responsibility of each village. This security program proved to be worthwhile: for the rest of the war there were only a few minor interruptions in the pipeline's operations.

A short time later Klise met with Commander Benkart, the U.S. Naval Liaison Officer, as Klise had become disturbed over the potential disaster lurking in the very lax security concerning future ship arrivals. Benkart agreed that Naval Intelligence and CIC should make a joint survey with the British, to strengthen security. Klise was then a sergeant!

* * *

Other than in MacArthur's Southwest Pacific, and South Pacific Theater, the army rank of CIC agents was for the most part successfully concealed. In CBI, as in all theaters, enlisted agents had to deal with-high ranking officers, both British and American and other allies, on a basis of equality; for example, the report of one important meeting in CBI contains a roster of the names of high-ranking British officers and railway officials, but only one American, shown as: "Harry G. Smith, Esq., CIC, U.S. Army Base Section." Smith was then a master sergeant!

CHAPTER XVII

Hawaii and Central Pacific

Since espionage always remained a potential threat, CIC in Hawaii organized a system of travel control. By summer of 1943 everyone leaving Hawaii first had to be cleared by the Trans-Pacific Travel Control Bureau. After 25 October 1944 with the abolishing of martial law, this Bureau continued under the Office of Internal Security. This office in Honolulu was staffed by the Navy, but recommendations concerning travel were made jointly by CIC, FBI and ONI. To better control the problem, the Bureau opened branch offices in San Francisco and Seattle, staffed by eight CIC agents from the Honolulu unit.

* * *

Meanwhile, an amazing report from a marine aboard a transport on the way to Kwajalein Atoll in the Marianas: a carrier pigeon alighted on the ship, was captured and found to be carrying a message in Japanese. This vestige of WW1 espionage doesn't seem to have made the history books, and the message has not been made public, but undoubtedly the ONI did something with the information. Now birds had entered the espionage equation for CIC to beware of.

This same informant reported that on Pago Pago in American Samoa a Japanese grocer on the Island of Tuituilla was apprehended for espionage when caught signaling to enemy subs off the north shore of the island.[11]

---

[11] *Last two paragraphs from U.S. Marine Sam Stinson, author and newspaperman*

CHAPTER XVIII

Stateside CIC Banished

After the fifteen day refresher course at Camp Wheeler, I returned to my Anniston, Alabama, office to be greeted with a promotion to master sergeant as of 18 January 1943! I did not celebrate.

The war shifted into higher gear; CIC's workload increased proportionately. Like investigative work in general, most of it was routine: background checking of character, loyalty and discretion of candidates for key positions, including the highly secret, very important Manhattan Project—and especially new applicants for CIC. (One FBI agent stated he had never seen a more complete investigation than CIC made on its own applicants.) We also had an increase in the number of our agents, my eastern Alabama office now being blessed with three agents, with me in charge.

Following the farcical case of the "Lady in the Hotel" which had so perturbed the FBI, our biggest case of suspected espionage up to then came along—entirely within CIC's jurisdiction. Through the PIO's network at Fort McClellan came a tip on a civilian employee of the motor pool. This information may well have come as a result of the PIO's tightening his CS system following the hotel-lady case.

There was no evidence of foul play, only suspicions caused by the fact that the employee always immersed his fingers in weak acids long enough to continually obscure his fingerprints; coupled with the fact he was a loner with a German name. Not enough to get alarmed at, but as taught in our training schools, pass up no reports. After all, the FBI had broken the submarine saboteur ringers the year before within a couple of weeks by paying heed to a single, innocuous phone call.

Hence, we opened a file on our suspicious acting army civilian employee; the further we went into his background, the more interesting and suspicious it looked. As leads we sent out to other sub-offices, especially in Florida, brought data back, we discovered that our subject—now upgraded to suspect—before the war had been convicted in Federal court of smuggling between Cuba and the mainland. He was now on parole, so why should he worry about obscuring his fingerprints? Possibly doing so, of course, had allowed him to being hired as a mechanic at one of our busy camps, where thousands of troops

113

were being trained and then shipped to overseas destinations. A perfect spot for a lower-grade German spy.

What did we have on him that warranted an investigation? The fingerprint concealment was enough for us to continue prying, to see what he was doing in his spare time, who he kept company with, who he was writing to, and why he continued to obscure his fingerprints.

Under these circumstances, we instituted a mail-cover procedure on him through the post office to discover the names and addresses of those with whom he was corresponding, but of course we had no legal right to read the contents of the letters. For the moment, we made no effort to interview his co-workers, as a careless slip could alert him to our investigation. So after the routine of checking records of all kinds at the county courthouse, police department, credit bureau, as well as similar checks back in Florida, our next step was to shadow him as he left work, see where he goes and who his contacts were.

* * *

Using the handy walky-talkies the PIO procured for us, with an agent in each of two cars we tailed him for three nights in succession, while one of us sat in our downtown office as a control center. On none of these nights did he return to his rented room. The first two nights he stayed at one address, the third night at an entirely different one. Our neighborhood checks indicated our suspect was quite a lover—either had two girl friends, at least, or was a bigamist. The morals of the man did not concern us at this point; we were intent on whether he maintained any kind of contact with any person to whom he might conceivably be passing troop information.

A survey of his living quarters was now definitely in order. Swearing his landlady to absolute secrecy, we borrowed a key to his apartment while he was on the job at the camp. We went through every scrap of paper there, leaving everything as we found it so as not to alert him. What we found though aroused our further suspicions: newspaper items had been clipped out and filed in a folder of other mementos. Most of the items concerned the exploits of a German general on the Eastern front fighting the Russians—and the last name of that general was identical with our suspect's! This coincidence definitely intrigued us. In passing, we also noted four new tires still in their wrappers, for which special permits had to be used under the wartime rationing then in existence for such products in short supply. We found no authorization for their purchase, nor record of same at OPA (Office of Price Administration) in charge of issuing them.

We redoubled our watch over the man's activities, though we didn't have the manpower to do so 24 hours a day, seven days a week.

Here we solicited the aid of his co-workers, certified loyal by the PIO. We interviewed and instructed them a safe distance from subject. It was now a game of watch and wait.

Days passed, weeks passed. Nothing through the mail cover; the man simply didn't write, nor receive, intriguing mail, nor did he ever leave town on trips. A mail cover on the ladies with whom he kept company had produced no further leads either. No change in his routine at night, where he favored one address a few nights, then another, then back to his apartment a night or two to rest.

The war went on. We had other cases, nothing as serious as this number one threat of espionage. Troops completed training at Fort McClellan and were moved out, and still no movement by the suspect. After conferring with my supervisors at Atlanta HQ and Birmingham, we finally had to face the fact that our primary mission included the protection of our army from *potential* threats. We didn't have to catch them in the act or with evidence to present to a jury as the FBI did. Nor did we have sufficient numbers of trained agents to maintain surveillance forever. Therefore, we did the next best thing under the circumstances, which was to neutralize him until the war was over. With what we had on him, this was easy enough to do.

* * *

One afternoon as he was exiting the gates of Fort. McClellan, with one of my agents in the background, an MP made the subject get out of the car while a search was made. As we suspected, from the glove compartment the MP brought out a pistol, the possession of which alone was sufficient to cancel his parole. In addition, however, we were able to present evidence of the illegal possession of the tires which were secured without the required permit, which enhanced his prospects for a longer prison life.

While not entirely satisfied, we were content in that we had utilized all of our CIC training in neutralizing for the duration a potential threat to our armed forces. There was no doubt in our minds that if and when the suspect had the chance, or was contacted by a professional enemy agent, he was certain to betray our country. The subject's parole was revoked by a Federal judge and he was put behind bars to serve at least for the duration of the war.

After this case was over, in April I was sent to the seventh Counter Intelligence class at Camp Ritchie in western Maryland where Military Intelligence was training personnel who might be ordered to overseas duty—with instruction directed only toward ETO, at that time. CIC in North Africa, both with combat units and area teams, in the Army and those attached to Air Corps units, had been doing an outstanding job. Some one saw there would be a growing need for more CIC agents trained in the military, and in the military of other governments, both friendly and otherwise.

The emphasis was on the German Army, so those of us in this class could only guess that someday we'd be headed for duty in Europe against the Nazis. That's the logic of the Army—I wound up, as did some others in that class, going the other way, for which Ritchie had not trained us in anything Japanese!

* * *

Following Ritchie, I was assigned to the Columbus, Georgia, office, located in the post office. Fort Benning, the huge infantry installation for training new officers, as well as regular troops, was nearby. I was now in charge of a four-man office including myself. The others were Carter O Lowance, a newspaper reporter (after the war, secretary to the governor of Virginia), Carl F. Savino from New York, and Robert C. Josey III from Scotland Neck, North Carolina.

Outside of normal routine investigations, nothing unduly exciting occurred most of the time, other than encountering on the streets of Columbus a lot of brand new second lieutenants celebrating their graduation. Even though we were in civilian clothes, we got a kick out of walking down the street, and as new "seconds" came abreast of us, suddenly putting our right hands up to brush our forehead. This act invariably caused a new officer to salute us smartly before noticing we were only civilians. (Civilians! Little did they know.)

When French General Giraud visited the States in July 1943, he made an official visit to Fort Benning. Our office had the job of ensuring his security during the visit. This began with the PIO insisting on lending me a first lieutenant's bars, while I got into my soldier's uniform. He had offered captain's bars, as I was to be in command not only of my agents in uniform but also of MPs and other soldiers in providing the security detail. I declined, as I suspected no one would believe my baby face could warrant captain's bars.

We cleared of anti-French bias those working in the areas the General would be quartered and come into normal contact elsewhere. On his arrival we preceded his official motor entourage around the camp with two agents in one jeep, followed by two in a second jeep; we repeated this the following day as he visited a demonstration site and made a few comments in French, complimenting the demonstrators. At each location we visited, troops were drawn up in formation, saluting Giraud as he passed; we could not help but enjoy returning salutes as a share of honor bestowed on this general.

The only sabotage case of any size that I handled personally out of this office was the one in which the paratroopers' jump-tower train-ing cable broke, killing the trooper making the jump. After question-ing all involved in the exercise, we ruled out subversion, and pointed the finger at lack of proper maintenance of the equipment. Bending metal back and forth endless times causes it to weaken at the bend, and if not timely replaced can result in injury or fatality, as it did in this case. Cables were replaced frequently thereafter.

* * *

Some time in 1943, some agent or agents in the D.C. area got us all into hot water, causing the temporary dissolution of the CIC state-side. Communists were high on our suspect lists from the very begin-ning of the war. Many may have forgotten that Stalin and Hitler had entered into a territorial agreement before hostilities abrogated the treaty, but our military intelligence didn't; our suspicions of Russia continued so we kept tabs on communists in the army.

A suspected communist by the name of Lash seemed to be quite cozy with a special lady named Eleanor Roosevelt. CIC was keeping tabs on army officer Lash so that he was closely followed and ob-served. As it turned out, it appeared to be Eleanor's secretary that Lash spent the night with, but CIC didn't know that at the time.

When the tape was played to our President, the roof fell in. Lash was immediately ordered to somewhere in the Pacific; of course, there was no positive proof Eleanor was personally involved, but the mat-ter so irritated Roosevelt that he listened to the Provost Marshal and allowed CIC to be taken away from G-2, with all agents remaining in the States being brought under the Provost Marshal General, joining his CID agents in a new organization known as the Security Intelli-gence Corps, SIC for short. Many in CIC believe this fulfilled an am-bition the Provost Marshal had held for a long time.

Luckily, General Eisenhower had just requested several hundred additional agents for his theater for use in the coming liberation of France and Europe, hence CIC was saved as a separate organization outside the continental U.S.

Before the actual breakup of CIC as such in the States, in October 1943, I was transferred from my Special Agent in Charge office in Co-lumbus into the Atlanta HQ, where I conducted mostly routine inves-tigations for a couple of weeks until my request for foreign duty was processed. I then bid farewell to my CIC officers, agents and other friends, especially Colonel Willis Everett, the assistant to the G-2, who invited me to come back after the war and join his law firm in Atlanta. I left for Camp Holabird on the outskirts of Baltimore, then the stag-ing area for CIC agents headed overseas.

While awaiting overseas assignments, we were exposed to training at Aberdeen and Havre de Grace in such exciting fields as driving tanks and motorcycles, and how to sabotage them, hence how to determine if sabotaged in the event such cases fell to our lot. One of our oldest agents in years was William A. Owens, a professor from Texas A & M University, who had never ridden a bicycle, and so was unable to balance and drive a motorcycle. The instructors put him on a bicycle, which he tried valiantly and unsuccessfully to master. But his pluck in never giving up won our admiration.

After other necessary items, next came vaccinations for smallpox, typhoid-paratyphoid, tetanus, cholera, and typhus. I was assigned to a group under Captain Ermal Geiss headed on a long train ride to Angel Island in San Francisco Bay to await a troop ship to Australia. Another 13 under Jack Y. Canon and Earl Klein also traveled with us.

In my group was attorney Milton "Mike" G. Horwitz, ten years older than I. Shortly after Pearl Harbor, Mike tried to enlist in the Army. The recruiter examined his application and said, "You're one year too old to enlist. Sorry." Mike walked slowly out, around the block, then back and picked up a new form, which he completed showing his birth date one year later. The same recruiter took it, looked at the date, then said to Mike, "Welcome to the U.S. Army!"

Instead of going bananas on Angel Island waiting weeks for a ship, Mike cooked up the idea of getting us into San Francisco during daytime. We were now in enlisted uniforms, with our civilian clothes hidden in our barracks bags. A few minutes after showing badge and credentials to the PIO, Mike had permission for us to hit San Francisco in the mornings and spend time with the city police refreshing and sharpening our skills in finger-printing, interrogations, moulage, and other tricks of the trade.

Thus we escaped the boredom of the army's inevitable waiting, and the turns we would have to take at KP. We learned to shorten the hours at police headquarters and spend more time seeing the sights of the city, enjoying its food and drink. This took us safely through Christmas and New Year's 1943.

1944

This was the year in which the small stream of men and matériel going to General MacArthur began to turn into a creek and even a small river, though nothing like the mighty river that flowed toward Eisenhower to combat the Germans. Japanese still held strongholds in most of New Britain and along the north shore of New Guinea. To hurl troops directly at them would cause us catastrophic losses, as happened when forces under our naval leaders attacked well-fortified islands held by the enemy.

A senseless waste of life—Mac had a better way. For helping in his lifesaving alternative, credit is due the outstanding code-breaking work of our Signal Corps, coupled with fantastic work by our loyal Japanese-Americans in ATIS, translating and interpreting enemy radio messages, captured documents, and interrogating POWs, and to Australian coastwatchers installed long before WW2. And certainly a small nod to CIC for locating and delivering Japanese codes and other written material, i.e., order-of-battle, defense plans, etc., into the hands of ATIS.

MacArthur's staff knew the location of the enemy's strength, the training and quality of the leaders and troops there. Instead of confronting them directly, go around, cut off their supplies and reinforcements, take care of the rest later. Exactly what Mac did! This is not to belittle our men who made lightly opposed landings, such as Hollandia. One bullet from one enemy can be as fatal as ten bullets from ten. But it illustrates Mac's ability to husband limited resources. Whatever else can be said (as much has been) Mac was no sacrificer of his men: the fact that he lost fewer men in his whole march from Port Moresby through the Philippines than was lost in just one head-on battle at Iwo Jima shows his solicitude—and brilliance.

He was convincingly on his way in 1944 to keep his pledge to the Filipinos that he "would return." Before year's end, he would step ashore on their island of Leyte.

Records[12] of the 441st CIC Detachment dated 15 December 1944 demonstrate the continuing investigative activities of special agents of the Corps:

"During October 1944 a total of 1,927 cases (pending and closed) was handled by 24 operating CIC Detachments in SWPA. This figure represents a drop of 584 cases below September, caused primarily by

---

[12] *Located for us by Dr Bruce Saunders,*   119
Fort Huachuca historian

the reduction of agents in Melbourne, Sydney, Brisbane, Townsville, Darwin, Port Moresby and Milne Bay."

The 441st records also show that 3 base detachments and 9 area teams accounted for 1,606 of the cases, 12 combat teams the balance of 321 (considering the role of combat teams, the relatively small number is understandable). Base 3 handled 461, with the 448th and 449th almost tied at 327 and 325 respectively. Among the combat teams, the 6th CIC division team handled 39, and the 214th CIC corps team 205.

CHAPTER XIX

Jungle Tales from SWPA

In late January 1944, 26 experienced agents arrived in Brisbane on the unescorted *SS Matsonia* from the Angel Island jumping off spot in San Francisco Bay. Three officer agents were with them: Ermal P. Geiss, Jack Y. Canon and Earl Klein. Geiss was CO of my group. He was openly proud of his 13 sergeants, stating more than once he was honored to command a group with a total of 18 college degrees among them. However he lost us the moment we checked into CIC HQ.

Palma Rosa Castle housed the new arrivals for several days while HQ was deciding assignments. Some were put to work on Port security teams, a few of the older agents such as Mike Horwitz, and William A. Owens, almost as old as Mike, were assigned to CIC HQ, others to sub-offices operating near army installations and bases. Some of us were thus enabled to open our duffel bags and bring out the civilian clothes we had carried all the way from Fort Holabird, Baltimore, Maryland, and wear them for a few weeks.

Those older agents at HQ were assigned special tasks, such as researching the area of future combat operations, and preparing background information of all kinds for the benefit of combat troops. One important task was compiling black and white lists for CIC agents' future use. Reports from guerrillas and other sources provided names of people known to be working with the enemy, and thus went on the black list; known loyal people, especially those in positions of authority, made up the white list.

The oldest agent specializing in this was Mike Horwitz, the Baltimore attorney who lied about his age in order to be "young" enough to enlist. It didn't take long for Headquarters to appreciate his talents in this new batch of agents. Before he left Brisbane many months later to join the Sixth Army 306th CIC Detachment, Special Agent Horwitz, then a master sergeant, was supervising the work of *four* army captains!

* * *

The month after this group of 26 arrived, 130 agents under the guidance of officer-agent Dudley Skinker[13] pulled into Brisbane's harbor and literally swarmed over Palma Rosa and a nearby race track until assignments could be found for them. With this huge flood of

---

[13] *He has supplied valuable information.*   121

agents, HQ began to fill the slots in the growing number of combat units also appearing. But the vital necessity to protect the inflow of war matériel caused a number of these additional agents to be assigned to port security. The duties, problems and rewards of ship paneling is fully described by Arthur Hurlburt:

* * *

Port Security and Ship Paneling

Why is CIC, strictly an Amy unit, doing Port Security? Doesn't the Navy take care of that? Or the Coast Guard—or somebody else?

Even before the move northwest commenced along the coast of New Guinea, CIC in Brisbane recognized there would be a need for some sort of presence in that area. We are used to thinking that in most parts of the world there are the rudiments, at least, of civilization. That is, most places have local authorities in the form of Customs, Immigration, port authorities, local police etc. But not in New Guinea. Here we had the "mosquito coast," where in peacetime the mail ship stopped every other month to leave off letters and pick up coconuts. If the U.S. Army were to establish facilities in wartime for staging areas, supply depots, port facilities, it would have to establish its own security arrangements.

In April of 1944, agents Arthur Hurlburt, George Ulrich and Joe Rosa landed from a C-47 at the airstrip at the southern edge of Base F, Finschhaven, New Guinea. They had flown that day from Brisbane, starting in the small hours of the morning, stopping at Townsville, Cairns and Nadzab for refueling. Daylight was waning, taking about ten minutes after sundown to convert into complete and utter darkness. A call on the field phone at the air strip raised the local CIC detachment. A jeep was dispatched and the trio picked up and brought to Detachment HQ. One of the remarkable things noticed by these three was the size of the base at first glance. The main thoroughfare was a double barreled highway, with telephone poles installed in the median strip. The poles had over twenty yard arms, with literally hundreds of wires on each pole. The road was surfaced with coral, dug from who knows where. It was constantly wet and slippery. Three hundred inches of rain a year was the norm. The ride seemed endless; it turned out to be about 15 miles.

The next morning they were interviewed en masse by the new CO, Lt. John Emmet. One of his first questions was, "Does anyone know anything about boats?" Hurlburt held up his hand, in spite of advice to every single soldier from the days of Alexander the Great: Never volunteer for ANYTHING. "OK, you are on the boat." What that meant he had to wait to find out.

Next morning he was introduced to a brand-new, spanking, 24-ft boat, built in Australia. It was equipped with a Gray 4 cylinder marine engine and could run around 10 miles per hour, about 8 or 9 knots. He checked over the tool box and gear that came with the boat and was a little surprised to find a kit of wooden plugs, about the size of a bullet, along with a mallet. Apparently, they were for plugging up holes from enemy fire, should they encounter same.

Among the equipment was a number of canvas bags with lead weights sewed in one end. The other end contained a series of copper-bound holes, with wires and lead seals for sealing the bags. Also, there was a pliers-shaped device, along with spare lead seals for sealing the bags. Apparently, the lead weights were to carry the bags to the bottom should there be enemy interference.

* * *

The team had been given instructions about a new activity called "ship paneling," which was simply the furnishing of a presence of local authority on board every ship entering and re-entering every port in the Southwest Pacific Area. It consisted of CIC agents boarding each ship before or as it entered every port. They would approach the ship's Captain, ask if this was his first visit to the theater. If it was, he would be asked to line the crew up for an examination of their papers. This served several purposes. It let merchant seamen know there was a presence (CIC) interested in their being there and warning them not to go about on shore. It identified who was entering the theater who might be on the Coast Guard black list sent from San Francisco. Third, it gave them all a chance to talk and report to a shore-based authority concerning any questionable events that had occurred on board the ship.

Was all this worthwhile? It is hard to prove a negative. Yet, in areas where this effort did not go on, merchant seamen went ashore, hitched rides, sometimes on planes, saw things that were none of their business, and got into and caused all kinds of trouble. This kind of activity was minimized by their just knowing someone was aware of them and watching.

If this was the first visit of the ship in the area, CIC would issue a new Security Log, an ordinary lined school notebook which fitted precisely into the canvas bag. In it they would write a report of the results of the paneling, seal it up and hand it to the Captain and see him store it in his safe. If it was a second or later visit to the theater, CIC would get the previously issued log from the Captain and review what the previous agent had written before commencing work. Each day they would write up a summary of the ships paneled, what was put in the logs, and send it back to Theater HQ at Brisbane.

Usually two agents handled this duty, although from time to time those working in the office loved to get out on the water to escape boredom. One ran the boat; the other climbed the rope ladders and did the work. It could be dangerous: there was no weather service to warn of impending storms. So they went out in bad weather. After one typhoon that lasted six days, the ocean was filled with bobbing 55-gallon drums of gasoline. Gasoline had been stored on level plots of land inland along a river. The intense storm flooded the plain and washed the drums out to sea. That week the Base newspaper came out with a headline, "Lies being spread. It has been rumored that we lost over 100,000 drums of gas in last week's storm. The truth is that we only lost 80,000." In addition to the rough weather the bobbing drums, hard to spot, were dangerous if hit by a small boat.

Another boat like the detachment's, in pulling alongside a ship, had its engine drowned by someone aboard the ship flushing a toilet just at the moment the boat passed under the escape pipe. Fortunately the boat operator jumped clear and swam quickly away, but the boat followed along the contour of the ship and was gobbled up into splinters by its propeller. CIC built a canopy to insure against this.

To give an idea of the magnitude of the job, in this sleepy port prior to the war army engineers had built thirteen piers in three harbors, strung along the coast for about fifteen miles. Each of these piers usually contained two ships, tied up side by side, plus many more at anchor, waiting their turn to dock, or for convoys. Finschhaven turned out to be the third largest port in a combat area in the world, exceeded in size only by Naples and Liverpool. In the month of July 1944 there was in excess of half a million tons of shipping that was completely off-loaded and reloaded, plus several times that much merely waiting for convoys.

To properly handle this huge task, after a time CIC made a deal with some Australian civil marine mechanics for an overhaul of the team's boat, to include a brand new Chrysler 8 cylinder marine engine. This new engine stood the boat up on her tail and pushed along at about 30 mph. The panelers never got through work earlier in the day, but it enabled them to go aboard that many more ships.

Was all this worth it? Agent Arthur Hurlburt elaborates more on this subject:

"Every so often there was an incident that required investigating. And there was no one else present on the scene with the training or the assignment. Or, native inquisitiveness. Most CIC agents were inquisitive by nature. They loved looking into things. They hated a vacuum.

They considered they were along with the Army to help protect them from risks they either did not see or did not have the training or talent to challenge.

"One such incident occurred on a small ship entering Finsch harbor. The Captain was asleep when I boarded and the First Mate was adamant about the subject of the Captain's age and lack of capability. They had left Sydney harbor with orders to go a certain course when leaving. They noticed that other ships, leaving at the same time, going to what they thought would be the same destination, were traveling on a course divergent from theirs. It turned out that their gyro-compass on the bridge was 18 degrees off. Compensating for this they carried on for the rest of the voyage and arrived safely. The Mate was firmly convinced sabotage had occurred.

* * *

"My training as a CIC agent had covered many areas, but not such maritime subjects as gyro compasses. I had to get myself educated in a hurry. All I could think of was to visit a couple of other ships and talk with their Captains and see what could be learned. Very simply put, a gyroscope, with the wheel standing vertically, will gravitate towards the lines of longitude. In other words, it will point towards true North, as opposed to magnetic North. On a ship, the gyro compass is located in a secure area, usually in a room behind the bridge. The compasses in the bridge and other parts of the ship are merely repeaters, wired to the main gyro. When in port for more than a day or two, it was customary to shut the system down. A few hours before leaving port, the system would be started up again and would soon point to true North again. However if the repeaters, or one of them, was disconnected during this restarting of the system, it would lay dormant until reconnected. That could easily have accounted for the variance between the main gyro and the repeater on the bridge in this case. After interviewing the Captain, I agreed with the Mate that he was in his dotage. In addition to our own channels, this information was turned over to the one Coast Guard officer on the Base for his action. His jurisdiction included management of merchant marine personnel and their licensing.

"Yes, the war probably would have been won without our work. We could well have stood the loss, even if the ship had eventually run aground. But I went to bed that night feeling that somehow our presence was justified.

* * *

"Another incident involved an explosion, heard coming from the docks just as we were finishing dinner. (We called it supper then.)

Curiosity drew two of us like a magnet in the direction of the noise, which now was turning into a cloud of smoke with further explosions every few seconds. We met the purser of the ship running towards us, arms in the air, shouting, 'Run for your lives; she's going up!'

"It was a Liberty ship at a nearby pier with fire coming out of number 4 and number 5 holds, just aft of the superstructure. Flames were gushing to a height above the mast, probably 50 to 60 feet. On boarding we looked for the Captain but were told he had gone to a nearby ship to see the movies. The ranking officer aboard was the Chief Engineer. Next to him was the Third Mate. A quick tour showed that the steam lines to the fire-fighting pumps had been ruptured in the initial explosion, so there was no water pressure. The ship was carrying 2,000 drums of gasoline, much of it in number 4 hold, and this was what was going off. Every time a new drum would explode it kept the fire feeding. A visit to the engine room showed the after-bulkhead stretching out above our heads like a pregnant belly. Water was coming in around the drive shaft. I asked the Chief what was on the other side of that wall. 'That's the main bunkers, full of oil for the engines.' And on the other side of that? 'That's the fire. Let's get the hell out of here. We won't be able to do any more investigating if that bulkhead cracks.'

"By this time some Army Engineers from a battalion of LSPs (Landing Ship Personnel) nearby had come aboard to share the excitement. They brought with them a number of five gallon cans of foam for fighting gasoline fires. But it was of no use without special nozzles which would mix the foam with water. We didn't have any water either. By midnight the ship had settled in the stern so the fantail was just awash. Since we were of no help in the fire-fighting, we took time off for some sustenance and raided the Officers' Mess for coffee and cheese sandwiches. Looking back from the vantage point of these many years, it seems incongruous to think of the two of us standing there eating cheese sandwiches and drinking coffee on a ship that was sinking by the stern, explosions going off continuously, flames shooting into the sky. The perceived immortality of youth!

"This fire continued for seven days and seven nights. Long before that we had an imperative to find out what happened. Was there sabotage? How did it happen? Sure enough, a message came from our CO to find out what happened and write it up. The Base Commander was very interested.

* * *

"It was easy enough to find the center of the explosion by tracing the rupture lines in the deck. It had centered just at the after-port corner of the number 4 hatch. This was right at the location of a hold vent, one of those pipes, about six feet high with what looks like a horn on the top of it. We opened the escape door in that vent pipe and went in and down. At the bottom we found what was left of a body, a piece of shoulder weighing not more than five or six pounds. We could account for all of the crew, but there was one man missing from the Port Battalion, people who loaded and unloaded ships. It was the habit of these workers to scrounge what they could from cargoes they handled, whenever possible. It looked as though the missing man had gone down into the hold, before it was opened at the top, to see what he could find. Since the hold had not been vented since leaving Sydney, there were gasoline fumes in a concentration strong enough to have ignited from perhaps a nail on his shoe striking the metal rungs of the ladder, perhaps a defective flashlight, or perhaps he lit a match. We'll never know. Our report listed the possibilities in order of their probability, with sabotage being at the bottom.

"Our report was turned over to the one Coast Guard Officer at the Base for his disposition. He had no need for further investigating but did lift the papers of all the officers except the Chief Engineer and the Third Mate. None of them had ever returned to the ship until after the fire was out, seven days later!

"No, contrary to expectations, the Navy is not always present in maritime scenarios. There is not always somebody else to take care of things. Fortunately, CIC was the agency present in the Port Security phase, ready to fill the needs that no one else seemed either prepared or able to do. And these supplies were essential to the successful pursuit of our war effort, hence the Army—via its CIC—took a hand to insure the safe arrival of this war matériel."... *Arthur S. Hurlburt*

* * *

After a required indoctrination into differences between SWPA and the U.S. mainland, CIC units began to form and become attached to various combat outfits. On 13 March, Galloway was ordered to visit the 41st Division G-2 to discuss placing a "Counter Intelligence Corps Task Force Team" with that division, then located at Finschhaven, on the north coast of New Guinea, preparing for its next operation into Dutch New Guinea (the western part of the island).

This was only one of several instances of preparing combat troops to accept CIC units in future operations. Next, agents tapped for each team were recalled from their civilian clothes assignments, put back into uniform, and again coached at Palma Rosa, both mentally and physically, for the coming operation of the combat unit with which they would be on detached service. Those who could add another foreign language to the one required for CIC tried to do so in the short time at Palma Rosa. A few managed a working vocabulary of low Malay, a patois widely used in Southeast Asia and NEI, handy in Dutch territory where some agents soon were.

* * *

While combat and area CIC teams were forming, there was still work to do in Australia for our men in civilian clothes. An enormous fire, similar to the one in the South Pacific, destroyed the Wallace Reed Warehouse in Brisbane. It was a whole block in dimension. Our 5th Air Force in conjunction with the Australian military had taken over a portion of the warehouse and installed machinery to shred aluminum foil which the Air Force used to scramble and disrupt Japanese radar wherever they searched it out. Also, all the Christmas supplies had just been stored.

Agents Francis S. Furey and Duane Williford were assigned to investigate for possible sabotage. They conducted an exhaustive examination of all possibilities, interviewing every one involved in operating the warehouse. They found that on the night the fire was started that Australians on watch were writing letters home while smoking cigarettes. On leaving the facility, they emptied their ash trays into a wastepaper basket partially filled with paper. Unfortunately some of the ashes were still smoldering enough to ignite the paper and do a complete job on the giant building.

Not only was the building torched but water from the firefighters undermined the foundations of sections of this massive building, even destroying a supply of liquor in the basement. "Our investigation ruled out arson and established negligent cigarette smokers as the cause, but to see firemen go under water in the basement and come up with bottles of liquor stuffed in their undershirts was a sight to behold!" Furey recalled years afterwards.

The two agents were called before a special Board of Inquiry for a verbal report and questioning; the Board then accepted their findings. "It was an unusual assignment for us—but wasn't everything we did?" concluded Furey.

* * *

April 1944 was the actual beginning of MacArthur's leapfrogging Japanese strong points, jumping past the Japanese Sixth Army positioned east of Finschhaven to capture its main supply base at Hollandia, Dutch New Guinea. The loss of these supplies resulted in the Japanese dying by the thousands of disease and starvation in the jungles, with the survivors facing the guns of American ambushes.

For three weeks our planes pasted their stronghold of Wewak, 70 miles up the coast from Finschhaven. B-25s bombed it incessantly; PT "mosquito" boats darted in to wreak havoc with shipping. In the minds of Japanese commanders, Wewak was the next target on Mac's list. In anticipation for this, they reinforced Wewak from garrisons farther up the coast, building its strength to some 70,000.

Bypassing Wewak completely surprised the enemy—like a bolt out of the blue. We easily took their important Hollandia base with airdromes intact. A few hundred combat and service soldiers put up slight resistance to the April 22 landing of two regiments of the 41st Division at Humboldt Bay, our first ground troops into Dutch territory. The 32nd Division landed further along the coast and effectively joined up with the 41st at Lake Sentani and the airdromes. Thousands of seasoned Japanese combat troops were thus left at Wewak to rot on the vine, cut off with no supplies of food, medicine or help of any kind, left to try to make their way around Hollandia to reach other strongholds in the eastern part of New Guinea.

A simultaneous landing by a regimental combat team (RCT) at Aitape, east of Hollandia in British New Guinea, erected yet another barrier for the Japanese isolated at Wewak. If the fleeing Wewak soldiers came too close to the sea, they would run into ambushes by Americans awaiting them at each point where we had landed. With very little loss of life to us, thousands of the enemy perished either from jungle terrors or from our prepared ambushes set up on word from informants paid by CIC agents. The RCT that invaded Aitape was shortly relieved by elements under the XIth Corps with its attached 211th CIC team.

* * *

Illustrative of what CIC agents faced is this data extracted from orders awarding the Bronze Star medal to Clement Read Kennon, a former lawyer and claim investigator from San Antonio, Texas:

"At Aitape from 5 July to 9 September 1944, Sergeant Kennon was Special Agent in Charge of detachment administration, a job for which . . . is authorized a 1st lieutenant. Kennon was also charged with training combat troops in outpost positions in the importance of complying with instructions printed on surrender leaflets being dropped to the enemy. He was often under sniper fire.

"At Morotai, NEI, from 15 September to 9 November 1944, Kennon continued as SAC, in addition to being chief investigator of the detachment. He maintained constant liaison with (Dutch) personnel, assisting them in screening undesirable natives evacuating from Halmahera to Morotai, which resulted in the apprehension of two pro-Japanese natives.

"At Luzon, P.I., from 29 January to 17 May 1945, Kennon continued to carry out the duties of a commissioned officer in maintaining
sub-offices of this detachment, which resulted in the apprehension of
at least twelve pro-Japanese civilians, including four enemy agents.

"Kennon worked much of the time subject to attack by dangerous enemy agents, without regard to his personal safety. He consistently performed duties normally assigned to a commissioned officer.
Offered a direct commission, he refused it.

"This officer has direct personal knowledge of the deeds listed.
Kennon's official status was Special Agent in Charge of the 211th CIC
Detachment (comparable to First Sergeant).

(Signed) Ralph Sims, Major, Cavalry, Commanding "

This tribute from a CIC officer, an Oklahoma lawyer in civilian
life, was typical of the sentiments of most other CIC officers towards
their men, though many did not have the time required to put their
comments on paper, and were somewhat bound by the forewarning
given to new agents to expect no medals nor publicity for their deeds.

* * *

CIC agents began lecturing troops while preparing for landing
operations, trying to convey to every soldier the great advantage of
turning in every scrap of paper with Japanese writing on it. Even as
CIC teams became attached to combat units, teams from ATIS, composed mostly of loyal Japanese-Americans, were translating captured
documents and interrogating the few captured soldiers for valuable
tactical and strategic information.

With few cases of espionage and sabotage in the jungles, CIC had
the mission of getting every piece of Japanese writing and documents
into the hands of these important translators. Most agents couldn't
translate Japanese language, but they could and did recover every
scrap of Japanese writing they could lay their hands on. In this
350,000-piece collection, there were invaluable Japanese navy and
army code books, orders of battle, plans, etc. In tons of paper, which
ones were to be read first? Beginning with landings in the Admiralty
Islands to the north of New Guinea, Aitape, Wakde-Sarmi, Noemfoor,
Biak, and especially at Hollandia, Dutch New Guinea, CIC "captured"
literally truck loads—tons—of Japanese documents that were scanned
by ATIS teams on the spot for tactical value, with "hot" ones being
flown daily back to ATIS at SWPA HQ in Brisbane (later, Hollandia, as
the wave went forward).

* * *

Japanese soldiers cut off from their bases were floundering
through the jungles, taking food from the natives when they could.

CIC organized a large gathering of natives at one place where officers from I Corps offered each native who furnished information on enemy troop locations a silver 10 guilder coin. This resulted in information flowing in a steady stream from natives anxious to cash in on this; it was invaluable in helping mop up remaining enemy troops.

* * *

And there *were* enemy agents in Australia. The Field Security (nearest equivalent of CIC in Australia) called for help from CIC on a number of occasions in attempts to catch espionage agents red-handed. One special gimmick was to utilize agents back from New Guinea and other jungle fronts in investigations in the big cities. Atabrine, the anti-malarial drug, turned the user's skin a sickly yellow color; some agents on leave from New Guinea or being transferred to other units were called on for undercover roles because of this coloration, on the theory they would be unsuspected in the role.

The following stories further illustrate what confronted CIC in New Guinea and its offshore islands.

* * *

The Story of Woodrow "Woody" Hunter:[14]

Woody Hunter was a practicing attorney in Cincinnati, Ohio, before he came into the Army, and inevitably the CIC. One of the 26 agents who arrived in Brisbane in January 1944, he was assigned to a team with the 163rd Regiment of the 41st Division. Agents David Krieger and George Charon from that same 26 went with him. As the 41st was taking Hollandia in April, its 163rd Regiment (reinforced with artillery unit) simultaneously attacked Aitape. Under CO Dean Caziarc, this special CIC team (designated the "G" Detachment) stayed with the 163rd for the later Wakde-Sarmi Bay operation which took place May 17-19. It was here that Woody Hunter was killed.

Attached to a spearhead *company*, May 18 Hunter landed on Insoemanai Isle, one of two islands making up "Wakde." Expecting little opposition, the troops stepped into a hornet's nest, with the enemy dug in, amply concealed and buzzing bullets all around. Woody was an outstanding figure, tall and bulky like a football fullback; the enemy could easily target him as an officer—without knowing he was only a CIC sergeant.

As he was proceeding slowly through a grove of coconut palms, a bullet penetrated his helmet over his eyes, killing him instantly. Machine gun fire could have done that, though Charon did not discount it was from a sniper. Charon had the unenviable task of identifying the body on May 20.

Because of the intense resistance, Charon suspected the enemy

---

[14]   *From info supplied by Dave Krieger and George Charon*

was tipped off. How? In his own words: "We had reports that a leak by an officer in the motor pool back at Aitape, presumably with the 32nd Division (they replaced us), let the enemy know we were headed for Wakde-Sarmi. If we hadn't speeded up our convoy by one day, they would have increased in numbers and been even better prepared. We intercepted a landing craft near Arare that carried wire and material for reinforcing the two islands, with information on our plans to land, and the approximate date. Captured enemy documents, including field orders and interrogation of prisoners, disclosed this. We thereafter stepped up security briefings with any troops we accompanied, using this case as an example."

Fort Holabird named a building after Hunter, first CIC agent killed in action in SWPA—Manila CIC's fate being yet unknown.

* * *

I had met Woody at Fort Holabird in November 1943. Twenty-six of us, including Hunter, were destined for Australia. We stayed together until reaching Brisbane January '44. I did not see Woody after that. I was with the 41st in Hollandia when we got word of Woody's death, but no details. His untimely demise saddened us.

I will never forget the day I first met him. It was at Holabird while we were playing a pickup football game on the parade ground. I'll never know why I joined in the fun, for after a few plays in which I was on the opposite side from Woody, I found myself directly in his path. He was carrying the ball and my job was to tackle him with my 135 lbs. I tackled him all right, but he dragged me halfway down the field while I clung helplessly to one of his churning legs.

* * *

Noemfoor Island (75 miles west of Biak Island)
Diary of Stanley E. Rutkowski describes CIC activities in the jungles.

A Week in the Life of a Combat CIC Agent

30 June—1 July 44: On board LCI (Landing Craft, Infantry) from Toem Village, Sarmi-Wakde, to Noemfoor Island, Schouten Islands group. CIC personnel included Barbee, Caziarc, Charon, Deubel, McCarthy, Williford and Rutkowski, accompanied by Roberts and Brown from Navy's Mobile Explosive Investigative Unit (MEIU).

D-day—2 July 44: At 0630, destroyers and cruisers of the Allied Command commenced heavy bombardment along the northeast area of Noemfoor Island at Kamiri Air Drome. This combined operation continued until 0800, H-hour, when the first wave of the 158th Infantry Regiment (the *"Bushmasters"*) hit the beach in Ducks and Alligators.

CIC agents remained on the LCI, which lay at the edge of the coral reef approximately 400 yards from shore, until H plus 75 at which time we disembarked and started wading ashore over the coral in water of waist-to-shoulder depth.

Enemy mortar and artillery fire was falling throughout the area; one of the shells burst within 60 yards of us, causing considerable mental discomfort. A Duck received a direct hit by mortar fire, fatally wounding its driver and seriously injuring his companion. As we neared the beach, enemy sniper fire whistled above our heads, causing us to immediately seek cover along the landing strip. A mortar shell bursting some 75 yards behind us scored a direct hit on one of our ammunition dumps, causing numerous explosions and resulting in its destruction.

CIC personnel made contact with the Regimental Command Post and then moved out on their respective individual assignments. Within an hour after their landing, Caziarc, Charon, Williford and Rutkowski, who were following the advance of the 3rd Battalion, had searched 45 enemy dead, recovering numerous diaries, documents and identification disks.

While searching these dead enemy, found on the south side of the strip, sniper fire from the opposite side caused us again to seek cover. Several infantrymen in the area quickly moved in and disposed of the snipers. At this point, Rutkowski and Williford returned to Regimental HQ with the documents to be turned over to our accompanying Nisei in ATIS for translation. Caziarc and Charon remained behind to search remaining bodies of the enemy dead.

Task Force Artillery came ashore on Ducks and commenced zeroing in on the enemy, especially its artillery. Air Corps A-20s and P-38s throughout the day assisted the infantry by strafing enemy positions. Brown, Williford and Rutkowski climbed the ridge above Kamiri Airdrome late in the afternoon, to search for documents in several huts that had been occupied by the Japanese. In this area we found three 20 mm AA guns in perfect working condition, along with a considerable quantity of 20 mm ammunition. These guns commanded the beach upon which we had landed; had it not been for the terrific pre-invasion bombardment of these positions by our Air and Naval forces, the landing would have been more costly.

D + 1—3 July 44: Williford and Rutkowski attempted to locate the Intelligence Officer (S-2) of the 2nd Battalion, in connection with the Counter-Reconnaissance Screen. Found that he was out on active patrol, so decided to try to find him. We traced him as far as the front lines, but deemed it inadvisable to search farther. On returning to the Central Task Force HQ we ran across two more enemy dead and searched the bodies for more documents.

D + 2—4 July 44: While the 3rd Battalion pushed on through several villages towards Kornasoren Airdrome, following CIC agents continued searching numerous huts, bunkers and dugouts, finding few documents but a great deal of abandoned ammunition and supplies.

The layout of the enemy's fortifications indicated they apparently had expected us to attempt a landing in this area. Once more, landing where we weren't expected resulted in saving many American lives. Numerous land and anti-personnel mines were uncovered here. On returning to our HQ we encountered our infantrymen scurrying about, and heard a number of shots. A check revealed two more enemy had been killed in an area believed to have been cleared. We searched the bodies, then went on to HQ. That evening ... an enemy air raid.

D + 3— 5 July 44: Barbee, Caziarc, Deubel and Rutkowski accompanied the two MEIU men, Brown and Roberts, to the area southwest of Kornasoren Airdrome to complete a search of enemy installations there, and also to contact the S-2 of the 3rd Battalion. Nothing of interest was found and we returned to HQ to make preparations for moving our quarters.

Author's Addendum: On Noemfoor with the team was George Charon (a college Spanish-French professor of part-Indian, part-French descent), renowned for his talent of quickly picking up languages wherever he went. Within three days after landing, he was talking to the natives of the island in their own tongue, one that was unlike any others in New Guinea. When he left the island, its entire population gathered to wish him farewell!

* * *

A Hollandia Story
Hollandia had many stories; I can only relate a few.

Galloway had prepared the way for the 41st Division to receive its first officially numbered CIC detachment. My first inkling that I had been picked to go with this team was early March 1944. I had been working for several weeks in the metropolitan city of Sydney in my civilian clothes, supposedly on a six-month tour of duty, when David Lincoln and I were ordered to return to Palma Rosa for a special assignment. Jack Y. Canon, one of the three officer agents who brought our group from Holabird on the *SS Matsonia*, had asked especially for us to be on this first numbered team—41st CIC.

As we trained several weeks out of Palma Rosa and on marches into the Australian outback, we learned we would join the 41st Division at Finschhaven, New Guinea, then preparing for the liberation of Dutch New Guinea at Hollandia, our first real venture into NEI terri- tory. Also scheduled was a team from ATIS, though they probably were assigned to the 41st earlier: leader John Tanikawa, Frank Ishida, James K. Sasano, Tetsuya Mayeda, John Sakai, John Mitani, Hisao Matsumoto, Shigeru Iba and Everett Sasaki. One other Nisei at Hollandia (who later came into CIC) was Charles "Chuck" Nakata; whether he was with this team at the time, or with the I Corps ATIS team there a short time later, is not now known due to his death.

I was the senior CIC agent, a master sergeant, with the 41st CIC team under Jack Y. Canon; instead of the traditional Army "first ser- geant" we termed this position the SAC, Special Agent in Charge. We joined the 41st Division at Finschhaven around the end of March, and immediately engaged in a series of lectures on the great importance of soldiers not holding on to any enemy document, letter or diary, urging them to turn everything into intelligence channels.

Arriving at one unit one morning to present this lecture, I found myself gazing in wonder at the circle of GI's surrounding me; on ev- ery helmet there was a skull and crossbones. This was one of the little known "Graves Registration" units, charged with examining bodies of our soldiers to retrieve identifying items such as dog tags, letters, and so forth. Realizing that these men could also do the same with the bodies of the enemy, I redoubled the intensity of my talk to reinforce the value of retrieving and turning in everything with Japanese writ- ing. Our ATIS team told me they had seen Japanese documents held as souvenirs by survivors of earlier battles in New Guinea, which con- tained information of tactical value had they been turned in at the time, saving American lives and shortening battles. I used this ex- ample to make the point with this circle of listeners.

Our detachment participated with the division in practice for the Hollandia operation, in an actual landing along the coast of New Guinea. We traveled aboard Australian ships that served tea and mutton meals not popular with Americans. It is the closest I ever came to being seasick. Once on the practice shore, where boxes were piled in simulation of our actual provisions and ammunitions, I overheard a supply captain arguing with his superior officer, a major. The captain apparently had been involved in actual landings before, whereas his CO was a newcomer to combat.

The captain pointed out that food supplies were stacked too close to ammunition boxes; the major reacted furiously, lambasting the captain for questioning a superior's judgment. I recalled that incident vividly a few days later in Hollandia.

* * *

On April 22, 7:00 a.m., our assault troops began landing initially unopposed on the beaches of Humboldt Bay; the 186th Regiment on the left immediately took off up mountainous terrain for Lake Sentani and Japanese air fields. I was ashore the first hour with Captain Caffey, S-2 intelligence officer of the 162nd Regiment, along with one ATIS Nisei. The 162nd swept to the right, west from the landing point toward the town of Hollandia. I was the sole CIC agent with the 162nd, the rest of the team going with the 186th and division HQ.

With little opposition to the actual landing, there was no CIC work for me until late afternoon of this first day. We three remained on the beach until the leading battalion messaged an interpreter was sorely needed at the front, which had progressed as far as the heights overlooking a little valley containing the village of Hollandia and its post office—the latter being my objective. When the request came in, the S-2 called both of us to accompany him too, though there was no reason for him to go. Captain Caffey was an intelligent, well-informed officer, fully aware of CIC's missions, as well as of the danger to our Nisei. I was under orders to prevent our own troops from mistakenly shooting our Nisei, and work was ahead for me soon.

Shortly we three started out in the gathering darkness, with no other troops with us. The path led over a high hill and through dense jungle; it was not the most pleasant walk for me—I have too vivid an imagination. In the darkest part of the trail, we spied a spring in the hillside, stopped to refill our canteens, then spotted a path leading off to the side and up higher on the hill. Caffey said, "Let's take a look!" So along we went until we reached a small clearing with a Japanese style house visible on its fringes.

Our troops had already rifled it completely, probably for souvenirs, but we found a few documents which our Nisei took charge of. The place obviously was living quarters for higher officers. Hurrying back to the main trail, we managed to reach the forward battalion just as dark closed in for good. Afterwards I realized this side trip had been foolish. Learning later of Japanese stragglers, my imagination can still picture the enemy ambushing the three of us.

We were safe however, surrounded by the 162nd troops, I thought. But there were green men among them, who like me were in combat for the first time. We three latecomers had to share a crowded foxhole together. Sometime during the night, one of those green, nervous troops rolled a hand grenade in our direction. Lucky for us he failed to pull the pin all the way; at daybreak I stared over the rim of our shallow hole directly at an unexploded American grenade, six

inches away! My first, but not last, encounter with "friendly fire"—
something few civilians can comprehend.

Later as we were standing around talking and eating our breakfast C-rations, our artillery opened up on an enemy target on the far
side of the valley. Then a short burst (a defective shell from our own
guns) exploded in our midst, taking the leg off of a GI standing just
three feet from me. After this close call (my second exposure to
friendly fire), I followed with alacrity our troops down into Hollandia
village, and headed for the clearly visible post office, a thatched roof
with open sides. I spotted huge piles of mail, which turned out to be
a gold mine of valuable documents, battle plans, codes and letters.
Our Nisei at the moment was busy assisting Captain Caffey, so how
could I get all this wealth to him, or back to ATIS at Division HQ?

I spotted a bicycle with flat tires, with a basket on its front. In the
equatorial heat any shortcut was desirable, so I "captured" the bike,
and began pushing it to transport as much of the mail as possible back
over the dirt pathway to the Nisei. When he was recalled back to the
landing area, I continued my trips over that jungle road, how many
trips I cannot recall, though I can remember the sweat, the heat and
the thirst.

The next evening, as we were preparing to sleep on top of the
ground in the valley, we were treated to a fireworks display back on
the landing beach. A lone Japanese plane, flying very high, dropped
three bombs, one of which hit a captured *Japanese* ammo dump starting explosions that destroyed 60% of our food rations! I recalled the
earlier landing exercise when two supply officers were arguing over
how to stack these supplies; the "superior" had to learn his lesson the
hard way. Unfortunate for us, because we were soon on one-third rations for several weeks; it would take that long to be resupplied. The
medics weighed us before we left Hollandia; I was down to 110
pounds!

When David Lincoln arrived from division CIC to replace me
after three days, I hadn't begun to finish the task and was working
alone as Caffey could not spare any of the troops from their current
mission. I must have lost ten pounds those days from perspiration
alone, from pushing that bike on its flat tires, loaded with documents.
Being short of rations until we left, took another 15 pounds off.

Lincoln said I was badly needed at division CIC, as there were a
number of liberated Indonesians there, and I was known to have a
working vocabulary of their patois. I was one happy but very sore
agent when I turned the bike and the post office over to Lincoln.

There was no land route from the 162nd's landing beach to the

186th's where the ammo dump had exploded. Barges were busy conveying supplies from our beach over the bay to the 186th's landing. A line of enlisted soldiers were waiting for transportation on a barge. As Lincoln had said, I was badly needed at HQ. I went to the head of the line and for the first time used my badge to gain access on the next barge. Rather than show the badge and risk becoming bogged down in an explanation, I simply flipped it enough for the barge crew to glimpse the gold, and I was immediately motioned on board, "Come on, Major, we can find room for you."

On reaching CIC HQ, I resumed my normal duties as SAC of the detachment. One of the most important involved the great work ATIS was doing in screening the growing piles of documents we dumped in their tent. The Nisei would exclaim with satisfaction as they spotted documents of suspected unusual military value. When closer reading verified the importance, they would bring them to the CIC tent, to be placed in a specially prepared envelope for the daily special delivery mail plane back to Theater HQ in Brisbane. ATIS and CIC worked as a team. High officials were elated with captured documents[15] that enabled us to continue bypassing Japanese strong-points, greatly shortening the war and saving American—and Japanese—lives.

The signature of my commanding officer for some reason was required to authorize this special mail airlift. As time went on more often than not he was not around, so I began signing his name because ATIS told me some of these documents contained Japanese codes and information of strategic value. No one ever questioned this practice, and I never tried to conceal what I was doing. The war had to go on.

As our detachment encamped near the beach a few days before embarking for our next operation, several new members joined us. Among them was a strapping imposing agent by the name of Jerry Alajajian. His story really began on Biak Island, and Hurlburt will help in the telling. On 25 May, we loaded onto an LST for the two-day trip to Biak, an island in Geelvink Bay, New Guinea.

Excerpts from an informal battlefield report of our CO Canon shed light on our team's success: "We got the finance office, post office, bank and Japanese HQ. We have sent back approximately 3500 pounds of documents, letters, etc. Most important documents: code books Blair (306th CIC CO Blair Labatt) told us to look for and a list of Japanese and German agents in the States.

"We have processed 300 Papuans, Hindus, Ambonese, etc., and Indonesians. From the Hindus we have a wealth of knowledge of the Singapore area (including) information on an Englishman who has reportedly collaborated with the Japanese.

---

[15]   *Admiral Koga's "Z" Plan; "A-Go" Fleet Battle Plan*

"From the local talent we have information regarding two Japanese Ambonese agents and have collared both. We have also names of 18 suspects and I am going out tomorrow and drag them back. We have technical equipment I cannot list here. We raided Japanese secret police HQ at Joka. Edwards, Moddemeyer and Smith have done outstanding work, Edwards particularly. Everyone happy and the Dutch boys invaluable."

* * *

On 25 May, the 41st Division was relieved from Hollandia and embarked for a landing on the island of Biak, hundreds of miles to the west and off the main coast of New Guinea. On the LST our agents were on, the Captain declared that due to a shortage he would have to severely restrict water. Straddling the equator this was unusually tough on us, even though we had somewhat acclimated ourselves at Hollandia. But in the afternoon of the second day, with every one complaining to me, I hunted the Captain, casually flipped my collar to reveal the badge as I was learning to do, and requested the Captain to loosen up. "Okay, Major, we're close enough now that I can do so," the Captain replied. Never had water tasted so good!

Biak was better defended, but eventually it had to fight to the last man without succeeding in throwing us off the island. Victory opened up more airdromes for our P-38 fighters and long range bombers.

* * *
Biak Island
Since 1943, Japan considered Biak an important link in its perimeter defense. When Hollandia was attacked, they correctly guessed Biak was the next Allied target. We incorrectly estimated there were possibly 2,000 Japanese soldiers holding the island, whereas there actually were nearly 10,000, now under orders to resist to the death. The Japanese made two mistakes: they did not expect our troops as early as 27 May, nor to land so far from the airfields which were better defended. But they made it tough on our two regiments, protecting the airfields for almost a month after the landing.

* * *

Biak was important to its A-Go Plan, so Japan created Operation KON to retake it. This operation was scuttled on 12 June on news the U.S. was invading the Marianas. Attacking Biak when we did apparently created a commotion at the highest military level, causing redeployment of Japan's land air forces at a crucial moment. But stiff resistance on Biak continued. On 3 June 32 Zeke and 19 Judy dive bombers damaged several U.S. LSTs and LCTs. Within the hour 41 more attacked, damaging two destroyers. 41st Division General Fuller and Sixth Army General Krueger asked for help, and MacArthur ordered a carrier fleet in that direction. We heaved a sigh of relief when the word reached us on Biak that the Japanese fleet had turned around to help its defenders at Saipan and the Marianas.

* * *

On 27 May 1944 our detachment landed in the third assault wave at Bosnek after a 45 minute naval bombardment of the beach area, followed by a heavy pounding by 54 of our B-24 bombers. There was no reception committee waiting, thanks to the enemy's wrong guess as to our landing point and date.

What I couldn't comprehend is why my CO had designated only me specifically to carry his carbine and Colt .45. As I scrambled down the rope ladder over the side of the LST into a waiting Higgins landing boat, besides Canon's weapons I was also carrying my own tommy gun, my .38 pistol, my back pack, and the detachment's sole typewriter. Getting into the landing craft without falling was a miracle; nothing could ever again match that tension. I almost kissed the earth on stepping ashore in the "most interesting operation in Dutch New Guinea."[16]

Our first task was to blast open a Japanese safe found near the beach. We used just enough explosive to open the door, but were disappointed with the contents. Early afternoon, the first of a number of plane attacks hit us. In addition to five low flying bombers, all shot down, I had my first close look at Japan's famed Zero fighter. As it flew in quickly at treetop height with guns blazing, I did what I was trained to do in the infantry: jump into the nearest foxhole, turn my submachine gun on the plane then so close I could see the pilot's face. Leading the plane, I got several bursts off before it disappeared and crashed into the sea. I felt I had made a definite hit or hits, and thus was victorious in my first combat encounter. As a few others also shot, I dared not open my mouth about my action.

As the surprised Japanese garrison got its act together and slowed down our advancing troops, we pitched camp at division headquarters near the landing area. There was little CIC work for us, though agent Recor with the 186th Regiment fighting its way along the coast probably was searching caves and dead bodies. At headquarters, I took advantage of the lull to get better acquainted with the newcomers on the team, especially Jerry Alajajian.

* * *

Biak is 45 miles by 20, covered with low, flat-topped hills supporting thick jungle growth in places, sparse growth over the coral

---

[16] S E Morison's *New Guinea and the Marianas*

areas. The coast is fringed with coral reef, and coral rock extends into the island as we found when we had to dig foxholes. For nine miles along the coast a high coral cliff with many elaborate caves overlooks a narrow strip of land bordering the ocean. For a number of days we were encamped with Division HQ near the beach landing, as the 186th was cut off from us by land by the enemy entrenched in caves overlooking this stretch of coast; contact was maintained with the 186th by landing craft detouring out to sea.

CIC contributed little of value on Biak. We captured relatively few documents compared to Hollandia, arrested no Indonesian collaborators, though the Dutch CIC were with us—it being their territory, but they were not needed either at this time. We simply struggled to survive until some future target where our talents would be in demand. And at night like every individual unit, HQ buttoned up a perimeter around us, and woe to the GI who stumbled around in the dark outside the perimeter. At least one GI was killed by friendly fire.

Nevertheless, our leader Canon began to make trips in his jeep, with a machine gun mounted on the hood; finally he began designating certain agents to accompany him on these "reconnaissance" trips. The result: he received the Silver Star, the first such to be awarded to a CIC agent in SWPA. Excerpts from citation: "Canon with great risk to his life made reconnaissance in a number of caves which had been occupied by Japanese, approaching dangerously close to enemy fire. He recovered more than 11 cases of enemy documents vitally needed for the successful conclusion of the operation. The intrepidity and devotion to duty of Canon reflect great credit on himself and the military service."

Of course, what Canon was doing bordered very closely on I&R platoon work, which I had been taught in basic training was a function of combat troops. And each regiment was supposed to have such a platoon specifically to penetrate enemy lines for combat information. While CIC's mission was in a different direction, we certainly sought documents whenever and wherever our mission took us. But combat I&R platoon duties? Not within the scope of our primary mission.

Some of the agents complained to me, as if I could do something about it. We were not supposed to be an I&R platoon; the Division already had those. But Canon seemed intent on using our agents just for that purpose. We disagreed, but I was not able to reach his mind; nor evidently could he reach mine, even though he had picked me for his SAC and thought he knew me. (I learned later he had made the background investigation on me on my application for CIP.) We began to go in different ways, mainly because I was trained in I&R platoon work, and knew definitely most of our team was not qualified.

Finally, the men started coming to me more often, asking if it was all right to follow Canon's order to patrol with him; on some, I said yes, but on a few that seemed clearly outside our field, I said to forget it, realizing even as I spoke that I could be court-martialed and even shot *if the order were legal.* Hence I considered each one very carefully before deciding.

Another annoying habit of Canon's was to drop an incendiary grenade behind an unsuspecting agent, who would jump almost out of his skin when it exploded with a noise like a giant firecracker. Expensive firecracker! For some reason, he was unable to stop this habit. One morning when I opened the top of the field desk in my charge, in which detachment records were kept, in plain view were three grenades—in a place they didn't belong. And I told him so.

* * *

A few days passed and he called me to his tent to inform me he was sending me up to the 186th Regiment, to replace Loren Recor. At this time fighting was intense trying to break through the defile leading to the nearest airfield; the enemy had blocked the narrow way with heavy gun fire from the many caves bordering the road, cutting off the land route to our forward battalions. Troops and supplies were being carried by landing craft out to sea, thus bypassing the blockade.

Without further comment by either of us, I picked up my equipment and set out. Up the road I was stopped before entering the ambush area and put into a Higgins boat with a squad of soldiers headed the same direction. About half way along the coast to our destination, enemy planes filled the skies, many attacking the scattered boats and ships, with one coming directly at us. Our black boatman yelled for us to lie down; he continued steering while manning a machine gun which accomplished its purpose: the plane veered off and crashed into the sea while our brave boatman gave our vessel the gas and got us safely ashore before other Zeros could spot us. I went up and shook his hand; he shrugged his shoulders as if to say, "It's nothing, just all in a day's work"—as it probably was, for him.

I made it to the S-2 of the 186th and stayed with him for a couple of weeks with only a few dead bodies to search. The enemy was holed up in hundreds of caves, some large enough to hold a 1,000 men. On 22 June, however, while I was in a very shallow foxhole dug with difficulty into the coral, with the rain beating down, the regimental headquarters came under a *banzai* attack. I was about 50 yards away from where our two machine gunners were laying down a field of fire that wiped out all 109 of the attackers. I was busy for a while searching what was left of their remains, but found little of military value, our Nisei said.

* * *

While with the 186th I came under friendly fire on two different occasions. The first came about when one of our battalions got a little turned around in the jungle growth, and instead of aiming at the enemy aimed its rifle fire in our direction. I hit the ground on the first "buzzing of bees" around our heads; luckily no one was hurt by the time communications got the battalion straightened out.

The other friendly fire was from some of our own planes which had extreme difficulty in spotting our positions as opposed to the enemy in the jungle growth, and at times would drop a few bombs around us. They would come in low and fast and disappear almost before we knew they were "friendly." After a couple of exposures to their misguided attacks, our troops automatically began shooting at *every* plane thus approaching, actually downing at least one. The Air Corps was not happy, but neither were we!

The only tank battle in the theater with the enemy occurred on Biak, with our superior tanks victorious. Their fire power helped our troops to neutralize enemy fire from the caves controlling the beach strip back to our division HQ. After the 182nd secured the first air landing strip, Division HQ moved up, putting me closer to the team.

This permitted me to witness a historic first: the use of television in combat. A spotter plane flew over suspected enemy positions, sending back to a set in the HQ staff tent. It was made with crude, experimental equipment, and was a poor spot for a test anyway, as it was impossible to detect any distinctive features flying over the jungle. It failed of course, but as an old science fiction fan from the 1920s, I felt I was witnessing the future.

Finally, Canon called me to division headquarters to advise I was being transferred out of his detachment back to Brisbane for reassignment. (All agents had their work performance evaluated periodically. I learned later, from the high marks Canon had first rated me, his final evaluation was a zero in every area.) Our men did not have happy faces as I bade them farewell. Jerry Alajajian's seemed especially grim. Here is his story, with some information from me, not fully known until recently.

* * *

Jerry Alajajian [17]

"Born in Armenia in 1914, Jerry was a small child when the Turks eradicated their Armenian problem through the simple means of genocide. The Alajajians escaped with their lives and their two small

---

[17]   *Written by Arthur Hurlburt*

boys and found their way to America in 1919.

"As will happen in so many cases, our two lives touched each other again and again during the years of WW2 and after. We first met at "808" the name given the old Cadillac dealership building beside Cottage Farm Bridge on the line between Brookline and Boston. During the war it was headquarters for the Commanding General, First Service Command, and the New England area CIC. Jerry was processed into CIC at Fort Devens, while I came from the Coast Artillery at Harbor Defenses of Narraganset Bay. He was selected mainly because of his language ability.

"There were about 350 of us at "808." Jerry and I met usually at Physical Training sessions on Wednesdays. He was voluble in his hatred of Turks, there being no good Turk except a dead one, he opined. He claimed to have a long, curved knife at home, which was not to be unsheathed without drawing blood. If we wanted to see it, fine, but he would have to prick our finger to keep the tradition.

"After the summer of 1942 we each went our own way and never did our paths cross again until early 1944 on the way overseas. As army logic would have it, Jerry was not to be sent to the Near East, where he was familiar with the languages. Instead, he went to the Southwest Pacific.

"We met at Fort Meade, staged for overseas, rode the train to San Francisco, boarded the *Sea Cat* and set sail for Brisbane, two of a shipment of 130 CIC agents lead by officer-agent Dudley Skinker. That particular group came to be known as "Skinker's Stinkers."

"Unloading from the *Sea Cat* in Brisbane, we marched to the city's outskirts to a tent city set up in the middle of Ascot race track. The next morning we fell out for reveille, with the roll being called by a tarheel sergeant who had no experience with non-Georgia names. He called out, "Brown, Smith, Jones" to a chorus of `Here's,' but stumbled on Jerry's name. First he said, `Allah— Allah—' then gave up, spelling the name out, slowly, letter by letter. A deep voice from the rear rank piped up, `What initial, please?'

"(Two and a half years later, at the first get-together of CIC veterans at the Elk's Home in Brookline Village, Massachusetts, I spotted Jerry across the crowded room. Loudly I shouted, `What initial, please?' Jerry knew who was being called and he knew who was doing the calling. Instantly.)

* * *

"Our paths separated again at Brisbane. I went north to New Guinea first, to a port called Finschhaven, while Jerry was assigned to a CIC detachment with the 41st infantry division. The next time I saw him he was passing through Finschhaven on his way back to Australia for court martial—charged with failing to obey an order in the face of the enemy. He actually was in irons, handcuffs with a chain around his waist, living in mud at a replacement depot. For a CIC agent this was utter degradation. And for another CIC agent to see one of his own in these circumstances was sickening. I knew something was terribly wrong.

"Jerry related that the charge was refusal to obey an order in the face of the enemy. While he had actually told his CO to go to hell, there was good reason for it in his mind. He had been ordered out on patrol for seven days straight, while others in the detachment only went once. In addition he had just received news his brother had been slain back in Boston; there was frustration in not being able to comfort his parents at such a time. Also, CIC agents were not supposed to be sent on infantry patrol at all, per regulations. I was greatly concerned for Jerry. His commanding officer and the man who had brought the charges was an officer named Jack Y. Canon, also known as Cactus Jack.

"Jerry went on to Australia and his trial. Brisbane HQ knew all about Jerry's CO and believed what Jerry told them. The colonel told Jerry not to worry but because of the serious charges they would have to hold the court martial. As the colonel predicted, the Court cleared Jerry of charges and returned him to CIC duty first in Australia, then to the 43rd CIC, with the 43rd Division. The members of the Court went up and shook Jerry's hand, ignoring Canon completely. Via the grapevine, we heard he had beaten the rap but the details had to wait until after the war.

"In early December 1944, I moved on from Finschhaven, 600 miles up the coast of New Guinea, into the Dutch part of the island, Hollandia. New Guinea was about 2,000 miles long, shaped like a giant lizard, or perhaps more like a triceratops dinosaur. The equator cuts right across its neck and all of it is TROPICAL. I mean HOT. Strangely, some of the mountains in central New Guinea are over 17,000 feet high, and even though on the equator, are snow covered.

* * *

"Hollandia became the stopover between Brisbane and Manila for Theater HQ, for both CIC and General MacArthur. It was the staging port for the Philippine invasion of Leyte. While at Hollandia, apart from the initial landings and securing of the place, CIC was in the staging process, forming up new detachments, drawing equipment, selecting Filipino-Americans from the Second Filipino Battalion of the U.S. Army as guides and interpreters for the future landings in the

Philippines.

"Among these CIC preparations and activities, Cactus Jack Canon, commanding a new detachment, thought it would be wise to indoctrinate his men *his way,* by surprising them with quarter-pound blocks of explosives. These would be set off near their tents in the dead of night, just *to keep them on their toes.* And it went on, night after night. These men, though new to Cactus Jack, had been in the theater for a year or more and were already experienced and trained. They hardly needed that kind of manipulation. Cactus Jack seemed to revel in the notoriety, but it didn't do one thing for him in the judgment of CIC agents.

"At any rate, I was glad not to be associated with him as I began to get some understanding of what Jerry had gone through. End of contact with Cactus Jack. For the moment.

"Next we fast forward to 1946, when Jerry and I met again, as mentioned above, at the Elk's Hall in Brookline Village in the spring of that year. We enjoyed a pleasant relationship as members of the Military Intelligence Association of New England, which is what we called our veterans' organization.

"Next step, I was recalled for the Korean War for a 15-month tour of duty, still in CIC. Toward the end of this tour of duty I became a member of SOB (Special Operations Branch) of Second Army CIC at Fort Meade. At the time SOB had an ongoing investigation titled 'Jack Y. Canon.' No one could have been more pleased than I.

"The investigation led us to Fort Lee, at Petersburg, Virginia, where Cactus Jack was stationed. From there it went to the bowels of the Pentagon in search of files that might shed light on his associates in Manchuria. It took us to the Cuban ferry landing at Miami, and through a high speed chase in five o'clock traffic over the Petersburg-to-Richmond highway. Then, having finished my tour of 15 months, it was time to go home and return to a civilian career. Sadly, in many investigations, one often never knows the final outcome, usually because one moves on for one reason or another. But in this case I determined to keep my ears open and see what finally did happen to old Cactus Jack.

* * *

"Every time I met up with an old CIC friend from Texas I would inquire, `Anybody heard anything about old Cactus Jack?' First I heard he had been brought back from Tokyo and released from the Army in a blaze of nothingness. Even though his release had been held up during the investigation, apparently there had never been enough hard evidence to bring him to trial. Some time later rumor had it that he had been charged, tried for shooting a nearby rancher's cattle from Fort Hood in central Texas, and was doing time in a Texas prison. Sounded believable! Later on I heard he had died, also in Texas.[18] Nobody could say for sure that he had been buried. Perhaps he just went up in a puff of smoke.

"Jerry went on to become President of the National CIC Association and the host of their 1960 convention in Boston, with 600 members attending from all over the country. In civilian life he became one of the top executives of Boston Mutual Life Insurance Co.

"Over the years I thought of how these three lives, Jerry, Cactus Jack and I, had formed a triangle, all three of us never having come together at the same time, the relationship between any two of us being independent of the third. And yet, like ships in the night, we met, parted, went on to meet again, the existence of each of us having an impact on another, even if only for a time. And, since I am the survivor, the story is being told through my eyes. What might it have been like, told by one of the others?

"A couple of years before Jerry's death in 1985 a good mutual friend, Iz Zack, perennial Secretary of the Military Intelligence Association of New England, said to me, `In spite of how close friends you, Jerry and I have been these many years, you never told me Jerry was tried for refusal to obey an order in face of the enemy!' The only response I could honestly think of was, 'Should I have?'"

* * *

Author's Addendum: When I heard the news of Jerry's arrest and pending trial, I felt guilty thinking that perhaps my actions as SAC on Biak may have lead to his disobeying an order; I immediately wrote to Jerry, offering to attend the hearing on his behalf. He did not answer, and obviously did not need me.

Years later I came into information on his CIC career thereafter that will show the treasure Canon lost. The caliber of Alajajian will be covered under 1945: Luzon. After the war when I was claim adjuster in San Antonio, Texas, for the USF&G Insurance Company, I contacted Blair Labatt who had been the CO of the 306th before I was assigned to that unit. Labatt said, "I know you and Canon did not get along, Duval, but he is presently in the stockade at Fort Sam Houston, and I think he would appreciate your visit."

I knew Canon and Labatt were acquainted, and I saw no reason not to comply with this suggestion from Blair whom I liked and admired. I called at the stockade. I was refused permission to visit until I stated, "I was his first sergeant overseas in New Guinea, and haven't seen him since." Canon was brought to the visiting area, looking be-

---

[18] *Believed died 1981, an apparent suicide*

draggled with his handle-bar mustache drooping. He was obviously surprised to see me, but thanked me as I handed him a carton of what I recalled were his favorite cigarettes. We exchanged only a few words, and I left.

I was transferred to West Texas shortly thereafter, but received a news clipping from a friend, wherein it was reported Canon produced copies of orders at his trial to show he was not guilty because he was many miles away from the scene at the time. He was freed. At least he had experienced a little of what Jerry Alajajian had gone through!

* * *

I flew from Biak back to Brisbane to report for reassignment, or for ejection from the CIC—I was uncertain which, until I talked with my friends, Bill Owens, Mike Horwitz, and officer-agent Ed McLaughlin. They assured me not to worry, got me on a week's furlough to Sydney where the G-2 to whom I reported, on spotting my yellow skin, induced me to spend a few nights tailing a suspected espionage agent. I did so, but the suspect was suspicious of everyone in uniform; only result, just some meals at CIC expense.

Back in Brisbane, Marvin C. Goff, who had transferred in from the South Pacific, interviewed me about my experiences, particularly with Canon. I held back nothing; at the end he stated, "So far as I'm concerned, a zero evaluation from Canon means nothing to me. I knew him back in the Eighth Service Command. I want you to join my 214th detachment, now on Bougainville in the Solomon Islands." And I did, and never regretted it.

* * *

Galloway became a Lieutenant Colonel 12 August 1944, and was still assigned to the 447th CIC Det but on temporary duty with the 441st as executive officer for Albert Vreeland, CIC Chief in SWPA. As soon as Hollandia was safe, MacArthur moved his headquarters to Lake Sentani near Hollandia, as did the 441st CIC, now officially the CIC HQ detachment under MacArthur— remaining such to the end of the war, and many years thereafter in the occupation of Japan.

By April 1944, the curriculum at Palma Rosa school was directed towards operations in the Philippines. A battalion of Filipinos mostly from the west coast of the U.S. was placed at the disposal of CIC; a number of them were selected for schooling as agents at the CIC school. In September, the school followed headquarters to Hollandia, graduating its first class from that location in October. Among those in this class was John "Jack" Norton, a West Pointer, who was subsequently killed in a plane crash on Okinawa along with the team he was leading into the occupation of Japan.

CHAPTER XX

MacArthur at Leyte:
"I Have Returned!"

When jungle fighting in New Guinea and offshore islands ended, all islands of any consequence between Australia and the Philippines were under control of the Allies. CIC along with its SWPA combat and area units now turned their sights toward the Philippines. Regional and area CIC teams moved in to assume CI coverage in liberated areas, while combat teams continued the intensive security training of the troops to which they were attached.

Four agents of the 40th CIC joined a regiment at Talasea, and two a regiment at Arawe. The remainder of Earl Klein's 10-man crew worked out of 40th Division HQ at Gloucester Bay, preparing materials to aid commanders and intelligence officers in the security indoctrination of troops before, during and after combat operations.

The theater's first airborne CIC, under George B. Spencer, arrived with the 11th Airborne Division in March 1944. It was quickly dispatched to "Palma Rosa Castle," the CIC School in Brisbane, for further training, and augmentation by agents who volunteered for work as paratroopers. On returning to New Guinea they all qualified for paratrooper wings before leaving for Leyte, the first target in the Philippines.

The 38th and the 210th (X Corps) CIC teams, new arrivals in the theater in early fall of 1944, plus the 214th (XIV Corps), the 37th, and the Americal CIC units located in the Solomon Islands, and four agents attached to the 93rd, which had been scattered throughout the Solomons, all began training for new combat assignments.

Four CIC agents left New Zealand with the 43rd Division in June 1944 for training at Brisbane. They returned to Aitape to carry out a full staging program. Finally, the 25th CIC team was formed in October 1944, sent to Palma Rosa in Brisbane for training, and then worked at indoctrinating troops of their 25th Division in intelligence and security before sailing for the Philippines.

While combat CIC teams were pushing through New Guinea and from island to island, preparing for the liberation of the Philippines, the increased flow of troops in 1943 and 1944 necessitated revision of the theater's administrative structure. Lt. Colonel Jennis Roy Galloway left the Advance Base Intelligence Office he had directed at Brisbane to become executive officer to Colonel Vreeland, Chief of the Theater CIC. Lt. Colonel John W Schermerhorn was transferred from Brisbane to Oro Base Section, Major Blair Labatt to Port Moresby.

An increase in CIC strength now paralleled the growth of the combat units. New agents recruited locally included William O. Moddemeyer, highly regarded by the regimental S-2 of the 162nd (41st Division) regiment. By the end of September, CIC rosters listed 73 officers and 381 special agents. However, the theater was still under its authorized strength of 122 officers and 420 special agents.

In March 1944, all CIC personnel were relieved from assignment to the War Department and assigned to the theater. This allowed the organization of provisional detachments only, but the way was now open for establishing a SWPA Theater CIC Detachment, the 5227th Provisional. It was created on 20 April 1944 to operate under the AC of S, G-2, USAFFE.

The provisional status of the detachments was short-lived. On 17 August 1944, the 441st CIC was activated as the theater detachment and the 5227th designation was abandoned. The 39 combat, regional and area detachments were given numerical designations, and made subordinate to the 441st. For the rest of the war and the occupation of Japan, the 441st directed CIC operations in the Far East (USAFFE).

USAFFE HQ began its move from Brisbane to Hollandia in piecemeal fashion; by the end of 1944, Brisbane was designated "Rear Echelon Headquarters," and Hollandia, "Headquarters."

CIC discovered serious leaks of information coming out of Australia. On several occasions papers taken from the enemy implied that the Japanese knew the strength of American units and their plans. Security somewhere, Australian or American, had missed its targets; agent George Charon may have been right about "G" team and Tornado Task Force being expected on Insoemoar!

* * *

Beginning in March 1943, Lt. William C. Shelton, mentioned previously as conducting a security campaign, initiated a highly intensified security campaign. He made use of radio, motion pictures, and posters, and developed new measures to dramatize security, and eliminate the boredom which troops associated with such talks. At Rockhampton, Australia, for example, troops mingling in a crowd at a railroad depot were brought to attention when a loudspeaker blared: "Attention! Attention all troops! This is Military Intelligence speaking. Enemy agents are operating in this area. There's only one way to avoid giving aid and information to the enemy and that is Don't Talk! No matter who starts discussing military information, from motherly welfare workers down to cute little country girls. Be smart! Dummy up! Change the subject. Don't be ashamed to say 'Don't know'."

New lecture teams were formed. By the end of 1944 ten teams were operating and more than 100,000 troops had heard the talks by the time Leyte was invaded in October. This campaign also included personnel of the Australian Army and Air Force, the American Red Cross, and the U.S. Navy. At the request of Brigadier General Bonner Fellers, the Theater G-1, the talks and counter-intelligence briefings were even given to members of GHQ, SWPA.

The first CIC clinical laboratory in the theater opened in August 1944, to operate in conjunction with the photographic lab which had been established in 1943. With special agent David W. Walters, a qualified technician in charge, the laboratory assisted the investigative agencies, from ballistic tests to restoring charred documents and deciphering secret writings. In one instance they identified by analysis of the typewriter type the disaffected author of a letter to General MacArthur. In another case, they determined the presence of human blood that helped to solve a murder case.

At the last minute before embarkation for the Philippines, CIC agents directed inspections of our troops, to make certain they were not carrying personal items that would disclose their unit identity in the event of capture. As troops evacuated their quarters, other agents combed them carefully for any classified materials that may have inadvertently been left behind.

* * *

As in the island campaigns to the south, plans called for a combat detachment with each army, corps, division or other tactical unit acting as a separate task force with the normal strength of a division detachment: two officer and ten special agents, supplemented by five qualified Filipino soldiers trained in CI measures.

Area detachments with the same authorized CIC strength were to be established in the liberated territories after U.S. forces had pushed back the enemy. Initially, these area detachments were to operate under the direction of the Task Force CIC Commander, pending the ousting of the enemy.

The Filipinos who had been exposed to CI at the Brisbane school were for the most part Filipino-Americans from our West Coast. Most of them were not well educated; it was hoped that in the event they could not operate as full CIC agents, they could at least be of some assistance as interpreters. This was not entirely successful either, as there were many dialects in addition to the five principal languages in the islands, and it was rare for one of these men to know the local lingo. A few were qualified in both respects, but the majority unfortunately could not come up to the particular talents required for the specialized work of CIC agents; nevertheless, they contributed in many ways to aid the teams to which they were attached, interpreting when they could but also serving as chauffeurs, messengers, cooks and in other tasks that freed agents from such chores to perform the special duties for which CIC was there.

After the combat phase, regional detachments consisting normally of three officers and 12 special agents were to move into liberated territory to coordinate the area teams. And finally the 441st CIC was to coordinate and supervise all CIC activities in the theater after combat troops quelled the enemy opposition, and combat CIC teams moved forward with their troops.

Agents were assigned far-reaching responsibilities in connection with the civilians. Chief among them was the responsibility for the arrest and interrogation of all known enemy agents and collaborators. Punishment of its native collaborators was the responsibility of the Philippine Commonwealth Government. The Army was to assist in determining which citizens had collaborated, in keeping with the announced intention of the United States to grant the Philippines full independence as soon as possible.

* * *

The presence of population centers not before encountered in SWPA resulted in new duty assignments: civil affairs, maintenance of order, civilian movement control, communications and publications. Together with the Provost Marshal, CIC assisted in operating reception and interrogation centers for non-Japanese personnel, in the investigation of atrocities, setting up civilian pass systems, and supervision of newspaper censorship.

The American landing on Leyte on 20 October 1944 produced one of the most sensational tactical surprises of the war—thanks in part to CIC lecturers who had burned into the minds of American troops the need for strict preservation of security. The plan only a month earlier had been for the first strike in the Philippines to be made at Mindanao, but on the recommendation of Admiral William F. Halsey, Jr., it was changed to Leyte.

The choice of Leyte with its potential airstrip sites, extensive harbor facilities, free and undefended coast on the east, sufficient anchorage area, and good access to the other islands, made the choice a fortuitous one.

Eight CIC teams, headed by the 306th, plus the attached Filipino CIC agents, participated in the initial action with the original Sixth Army Task Force which smashed into the Leyte beachhead. Six other combat detachments, plus the 459th area team, also participated.

Under the 210th CIC, Joseph P. Hurley, CO, were the 801st of the 1st Cavalry, and the 24th CIC. Entering the Leyte campaign came aid from the Central Pacific in the form of the 224th CIC with Harold F. Frederick as CO, plus the 7th and 96th CIC teams.

In one of the war's most dramatic episodes, MacArthur waded ashore on 22 October, with President Osmeña beside him, thus fulfilling his promise to the Filipinos that he would return. On the following day CIC agents witnessed a colorful ceremony in the capital when General MacArthur turned over to President Osmeña control of the Philippine Government. In the same ceremony he presented the Distinguished Service Cross to Colonel Ruperto Kangleon, an outstanding guerrilla leader who already had given CIC an extensive suspect black list compiled by his forces. Then Osmeña appointed Kangleon the new governor of Leyte.

* * *

Following the ceremony, Colonel Irwin with Major Labatt conferred with President Osmeña on CIC's role in the liberation of the Philippines. A part of that agreement was that CIC would investigate all appointees to office, including all constabulary and municipal officials, to clear them of any taints of disloyalty.

Two agents from the 259th CIC were detailed as personal bodyguards for Osmeña. One of these was Edmund Cappucilli, who remained with the President as bodyguard and personal secretary for the rest of the war, and even made several trips to the States with him. But General MacArthur refused a similar offer of CIC bodyguards, as he had done for himself before in Australia—though he did allow them for his wife and son.

Shortly after the Leyte landing, agent Charles C. Deubel of the 801st CIC found that an army unit trying to rebuild a damaged airport was seriously hampered by a shortage of native labor. Finding a large number of Chinese in the area, Deubel assigned agent Humphrey W. Leynse the job of recruiting laborers from the local Chinese, to help complete the badly needed airport. Deubel had good reasons for his choice of agents: Leynse was the son of missionaries of Dutch extraction, had spent much of his life in China, and could speak Mandarin fluently—and for good measure he was known to be capable of bargaining with the Chinese.

Leynse found that the Chinese were willing to work, but wages alone were not inducement enough. Their national pride was at stake. They insisted that their work in rebuilding the air strip should be considered a "representation," a contribution of the Chinese government. Leynse agreed to this, promising a colorful ceremony at which the Chinese efforts would be effectively recognized. He then set about to recruit.

Response was tremendous! More than 150 Chinese reported at 8:30 one morning for the recognition ceremonies at an army warehouse. Deubel made them a speech fitting the occasion. (Was this where Deubel, postwar mayor of one of the New Jersey Oranges, got his political start?), followed by Leynse. Then several of the Chinese made impromptu talks and climaxed the display of patriotism with a colorful parade to the labor office, waving American and Chinese flags along with appropriate banners.

The procession was interrupted by a colonel in charge of the construction project whom Deubel and Leynse, in their haste to recruit laborers, had forgotten to advise of their plans. They quickly explained the situation to the colonel. Delighted, he also made a speech of welcome. The parade continued, and the new laborers were soon working away on the airstrip.

* * *

CIC sustained its first casualties in the Philippines on 25 October. During an air raid, a Japanese bomb scored a hit on an LST on which the 306th CIC agents were waiting to disembark. It killed agent Elvin C. Jensen; agent Daniel J. Coakley was seriously wounded.

On 25 October 1944 all but one of the 24th CIC agents were trapped inside their Headquarters at Palo, by 80 fanatical Japanese soldiers. The soldiers had infiltrated American lines, rushed into Palo, and tried to storm the CIC office in a "banzai" suicide attack. Although caught off guard, the trapped agents hastily set up a defense and repulsed the Japanese, inflicting heavy losses.

Enemy infiltration continued to plague the 24th team, as Japanese soldiers often stayed behind in little towns and villages in the guise of natives; others passed through our lines dressed in women's clothing. CIC patrols began operating to guard against such infiltration.

American forces liberated several towns rather quickly but Japanese resistance stiffened as our troops pressed on toward Limon, the northern anchor of the corridor leading to the enemy's stronghold at Ormoc. Before long, a number of CIC units were swarming over Leyte, including the 36th, 801st (1st Cavalry), 224th, 96th and the 7th. They all went about their routine duties of screening civilians and maintaining the security of military movements; however it was necessary to construct temporary compounds to hold more than 2,000 natives who had fled Tacloban and then returned; it was deemed necessary to screen them carefully while interned in these compounds, to make sure that no agents or collaborators were among them.

One of the first arrested by CIC was in the provincial capital: Pastor Salazar, the puppet Governor of Leyte, who admitted he had secretly conferred with Japanese military commanders even after U.S. troops arrived. Another highlight was internment by the 96th CIC of three public officials at Tanauan, as well as the puppet mayor of Dulag and his entire family.

* * *

The 11th CIC came in with the 11th Airborne Division in mid-November, in time to defend themselves against a surprise Japanese airborne attack near the San Pablo airstrip. This attack lasted five days, during which Dean Caziarc, the popular CO of the 11th CIC was wounded and had to be evacuated. Agent David Finn was also wounded, but was able to return to duty.

The 77th CIC with its Division was headed to New Caledonia after Guam was captured in the Central Pacific Theater, but had its orders changed in mid-ocean and landed on Leyte on 23 November 1944 after which, for about two weeks, the Division underwent training on routine patrol. Then on 6 December 1944, the 77th Division made a surprise assault at Ipil; Japanese resistance on Leyte was all but sealed. Ormoc was taken four days later. The following day the 7th CIC moved into Ormoc to relieve the 77th CIC team.

At the end of November, the 38th CIC reached Leyte and began helping the 210th around Jaro; it then opened a sub-office in Alanjalang. And near the end of November, the 492nd regional team, with Hurst in command, reached Tacloban to assume jurisdiction over CI activities on Leyte and Samar, with these five area detachments under its supervision: 459th, 480th, 458th, 482nd, and the 483rd. At the end of December the tactical units on Leyte were relieved of assignment to Sixth Army and were transferred to the Eighth Army. CIC supervision of combat CIC teams was transferred from the 306th to the 308th commanded by Chapman Turner.

Throughout Leyte, CIC faced hosts of problems not previously encountered. Here, CIC was coping with some 1,000,000 civilized inhabitants, influenced by several years of Japanese propaganda and culture. It also determined an urgent need to secure documents of CI interest, particularly those which were potential sources of leads about enemy agents, instead of specializing on tactical and strategic information as it had in the jungles and islands to the south. In other words, this was much closer to the type of work for which most of them were brought into the Corps.

Some problems were with guerrillas. Some bands were bonafide guerrillas; others were only self-styled guerrillas, opportunists and bandits. The reports of the latter were often inspired by personal vendettas and ambitions. There also was the problem of the justice of kangaroo courts, which was to be expected under the circumstances of the long occupation under which those who had fought the Japanese would be bitter about those who had collaborated.

On one occasion several armed guerrillas reported to a CIC office with a letter which began: "You are hereby ordered to liquidate the following traitors." On another occasion the sole CIC agent had to use considerable diplomacy, much arguing, and several bottles of "tuba," the native liquor, before he could persuade a local guerrilla to deliver his captives to the nearest police stockade, instead of whisking them off to the hills for "trial"—and instant execution.

* * *

CIC agents ran into problems on a daily basis. Even finding among the devastated ruins a building which could serve as an office reached serious proportions. A greater problem arose in an attempt to set up operational controls, mainly because of the almost unbelievable mixture of races and nationalities on this island of some 1,000,000+ people. The Chinese colony alone numbered 18,000. Mixed in with them were large numbers of citizens from every country in Asia, as well as Europe. Sorting out those who had been active agents and party members was a real challenge.

CIC interned more than 200 Germans in special compounds, as well as many Japanese agents, and scores of disloyal Filipinos. Among the more interesting cases handled by CIC on Leyte was that of a prominent police officer of prewar days who had continued in office under the Japanese. He explained to loyal factions that he tried to act as a buffer between them and the military administration; throughout the occupation, he claimed he managed to please both sides, gaining the confidence of guerrillas as well as a promotion from the Japanese. After the American landing, he was selected to retain his office, including his Japanese promotion, since his energy and organizing skills marked him an efficient leader and executive.

Agents confirmed his qualities of leadership. But a study of the records disclosed an elaborate organization of "secret agents," each reporting by number on guerrilla and pro-American actions. Of course, he had to pretend to be serving both sides even if he been really loyal to the guerrillas. However, the discovery of further documents enabled CIC to compare reports from enemy agents with those submitted by the officer to the Japanese in which he omitted nothing! Interrogation of his agents themselves added further evidence of his duplicity, including his dismissal of operatives for failing to apprehend a high guerrilla leader. So confident had he been of his position that after he was placed by CIC in his own jail, it was discovered that he had neglected to destroy further incriminating evidence in the form of diaries and personal records!

Before moving on to Luzon, the Americans invaded Mindoro Island, the most thickly populated of the Islands with 8,000,000 inhabitants. Thereafter, area and regional CIC moved in to take over, including cases the combat teams had to leave behind.

* * *

19 December 1944, at the end of the Leyte campaign—in preparation for the coming Luzon campaign—Blair P. Labatt, chief of the 306th CIC Sixth Army detachment, summed up and distributed the lessons learned by CIC operatives. The major points stressed:

"I—Pre-operational
"1. Reports have shown universal weakness in basic principles of good report writing. Agents have grown careless ... and proved incapable of setting forth logically facts necessary to support serious allegations.
"2. Agents should be capable of performing three basic types of interrogation: of guerrillas and civilians for immediate tactical information, of recovered personnel for general tactical and counter-intelligence, and of suspects.
"3. Personnel should be briefed on the target area from the counter-intelligence point of view.
"4. It is suggested that detachments prepare index cards of suspects and potential informants in their zone of operations.
II—Operational
"5. CIC detachments overrun with guerrillas and zealous citizens anxious to denounce spies and collaborators should question the accuser closely and request an affidavit; obtain names of other witnesses. If a basis exists for suspecting accused is a security risk, he should be detained.
"6. In the confused early stages of an operation, expediency may require detention of suspects on scant evidence; clarify the evidence as soon as possible.
"7. Early establishment of an informant system is an invaluable asset.
"8. Most CIC detachments have been concerned with guerrilla activities. It is important that CIC exercise close control over passes and permits to carry weapons. Only guerrillas on specific missions, police and constabulary should be permitted to carry guns.
"9. Desirability of entering populated places early has been clearly demonstrated in Leyte. PCAU representatives necessarily depend upon CIC to

evaluate the loyalty of prospective appointees.

"10. Philippine Constabulary personnel will be cleared by CIC.

"11. Important for early CIC in a town is securing public records.

"12. As operations progress, division CIC displaces forward, turning over responsibility to corps detachments. To facilitate the transfer, records (must) be kept up to date.

"13. Effective utilization of (CIC) personnel will require that emphasis be placed on (working out of) civilian centers. Detachments should therefore be prepared to subsist apart from an established mess: cooking utensils and burners should be provided.

"14. Release of individuals from internment in borderline cases are to be made by the Army detachment.

"15. Impossible for a considerable period to replace or augment equipment taken into combat. Detachments are urged to take with them all vehicles for which shipping space can be obtained.

Blair P. Labatt, Major, Infantry, Commanding"

CHAPTER XXI

Sakakida Rescues 500 Guerrillas!

Things were not entirely quiet on Luzon, the main island to the north of Leyte. Sakakida had a most interesting 1944, as he continued to watch carefully for any traps the enemy might set for him. And then came the real big break that he had been awaiting.

It happened one day when the wife of Ernest Tupas came to the Judge Advocate General's office and asked Sakakida to translate for her a request to visit her husband who had been captured and confined to a 15 year sentence in Muntinglupa Prison. Sakakida knew that Tupas had formerly worked with the Manila CIP Detachment and since Bataan fell had been working with the guerrillas. Sakakida revealed his identity to her and filled out passes for her and many of the other guerrillas' wives with forms he had stolen from the office where he was still permitted, assuring her that she need have no fear in using them at the prison since the Japanese soldiers guarding the Filipino prisoners couldn't read English anyway.

It then followed that Mrs. Tupas, knowing many of the guerrillas with whom her husband had worked, was able to arrange meetings between them and Sakakida during his "free hours." With them he was able to plan to free Tupas and 500 others who were confined in the prison. Certainly not the normal duty of a CIC agent, but there was nothing normal at this time in Sakakida's life.

He told her to advise Tupas to get a job with the prison electrical department so that at a designated time he could short-circuit electrical facilities, and also to get word to the other guerrillas to case the prison to select the best time for a break. The report to Sakakida was that officers from the Japanese garrison made a tour, something of a security check, each night between midnight and 2 a.m. Sakakida next had the free guerrillas obtain Japanese officers' uniforms in order to carry out the devised plan.

On the big night, Sakakida left his barracks as soon as bed check was over, and with four of the local guerrillas, all dressed as Japanese officers, decorated with ribbons and with swords clanking at their sides, approached the prison's main gate. Thinking the "officers" were making the nightly security inspection, in accordance with Japanese custom, the guards bowed low in respect for their superiors, and found .45s stuck in their ribs. A good tap on the head put them out of commission for a while. Out went the prison lights on schedule and approximately 25 guerrilla members overpowered the rest of the guards and released nearly 500 Filipino prisoners!

Sakakida hurried back to his quarters in plenty of time to make the 6:30 a.m. roll call. While he was at work in the colonel's office the next morning, the Superintendent of Muntinglupa Prison came dashing in to report the break, upon which the colonel hit the ceiling and, when the furor died away, dismissed the Superintendent for his unfortunate mistake.

Shortly after the breakout, Sakakida was able to contact Tupas who had fled to the mountains of Rizal with the other guerrillas and had established radio contact with General MacArthur's headquarters. At last Sakakida had a means of relaying to the Americans a vast amount of information picked up around the colonel's office, particularly data on Japanese troop movements and shipping activities. Probably his single most important contribution was a portion of the plans for a Japanese Expeditionary Force to Australia. Some months later he learned what happened to this Task Force from an officer assigned to the JAG office who had been aboard one of the 15 vessels that had left the Philippines with plans to land at Port Darwin; he returned to the Philippines on the only ship that got back. U.S. submarines and air planes had taken care of the rest.

* * *

During the course of the year, the guerrilla forces had picked up steam, thanks to the supplies now getting through from Australia.

* * *

In December 1944, the Japanese Fourteenth Army Headquarters had to move to Northern Luzon because of heavy air attacks on Manila, and in April 1945 moved further inland. Feeling a growing amount of hostility toward him in the headquarters, Sakakida decided in the early part of June 1945 to escape to the hills. About a week later he met and joined a small band of guerrillas in the vicinity of Farmschol. Ten days later they took a severe shelling during which Sakakida was wounded and was left when the guerrillas escaped.

CHAPTER XXII

South Pacific Winds Down

By 1944 coverage of the New Caledonia Command was fairly complete with additional agents from the U.S. swelling the unit to 30 men. Besides Detachment HQ, district offices were maintained at Hienghene, and the Tontouta and Plaines des Gaiacs Airfields, with agents Alfonso Betancourt, Ralph Morin, and Maurice Long in charge of these three posts.

Immediately after setting up shop in the Fiji Islands, more than 1000 miles due east of Northern Australia, CIC became enmeshed in the political scheming of two rival racial groups. The Islands numbered some 250, covered an area of more than 7,000 square miles, and were inhabited by 277,000 people of whom 5,000 were European. The two dominant factions which caused CIC's big headache were the Indian immigrants and Fijian natives. The Indians, brought in years before by European planters to harvest sugarcane crops, had increased in numbers until by 1944 they were outnumbered only slightly by the Fijians.

* * *

As the Indians were unwilling to cooperate with the British rulers, friction was added; the native Fijians were satisfied with being British subjects. But relations became further strained when the Indians began developing lucrative businesses with the Americans. Madame Orcan, an enterprising lady, gradually cornered the laundry market, finally washing an average of 160 bundles a week at $2 each. The only labor dislocation caused by this $16,000 a year job was to Mr. Orcan; he left his job on the sugar plantation!

But the jingle of American silver in the pockets of some gave other Indians ideas. Early in 1943 they had struck for higher wages, gravely upsetting the sugarcane industry and arousing the bitterness of the British and the Fijians who were fully cooperating with the Americans in prosecuting the war.

CIC stepped on stage when reports, trickling into headquarters at Suva that American servicemen were furnishing weapons in return for women and liquor, were confirmed by CIC's investigation.

When a rash of shootings and unaccountable fires broke out in the sugar fields, agents helped by Fiji police moved in and apprehended two American soldiers who confessed to various misdemeanors and felonies paid for and directed by Indians. The confessions included the account of a conspiracy between the Indians and soldiers to assassinate the Governor of Fiji on one of his inspection trips; to burn several hundred more acres of sugarcane; to destroy the civil courthouse; to blow up a strategic combination railway and highway bridge to restrict the sugar industry; to kill the local British District Commissioner in a feigned auto collision; to burn a Fiji police auto; and last but not least, to steal U.S. Army vehicle tires from a QM depot.

The prime Indian figure was sentenced to five years hard labor by the Fiji Supreme Court; the American GIs were tried by Court Martial and given long prison terms and dishonorable discharges. While crime and violence of all degrees diminished in the following months, the Indians continued to be troublesome.

* * *

Beginning in the last part of 1944, and by the spring of 1945, the majority of American troops had been added to General MacArthur's forces on their island-hopping way to Japan. During May 1945 CIC HQ was alerted to move to the Philippine Islands in June; soon the remaining numbered CIC detachments in the South Pacific were deactivated; most of agents having been transferred months before into the Southwest Pacific Theater. Finally, all agents came under the control of the 441st CIC, SWPA Theater Headquarters Detachment; and many later moved on to Japan for the beginning of its occupation.

By summer of 1944, when the Central Pacific campaigns had gained bases on Saipan, Guam and Tinian, and our forces were getting nearer to Japan proper, CIC activity was lessened in the South Pacific along with the curtailment of military activity. The rigid security measures implemented by CIC had helped reduce the espionage-sabotage threat to a minimum; but the British Crown Colony of Fiji still remained an important supply base warranting retention of a skeleton force of CIC agents, especially those with ability in Hindustani dialects.

The New Hebrides Island Group was important not only because the enemy made its deepest penetration into Allied territory there, by occupying the adjacent British Solomon Islands, but also because of its spread over a vast expanse of ocean making it logical that Japanese would make use of their coast watchers and subversive agents to gather information on Allied troop strengths and bases.

The 437th CIC in New Hebrides was formally deactivated during November 1944 since the tempo of fighting had increased in the north; most agents were transferred to these new zones.

CHAPTER XXIII

CBI Buzzes

Slated for Air Force installations were 25 agents attending a six weeks' Field Service School at Hill Field, Ogden, Utah, for training in detecting airplane sabotage. Some of the group attended short courses in specialized subjects at Holabird's Motor School. Upon arrival at the CIC staging area at Camp Ritchie early in January 1944, all were given instructions in special CBI conditions.

Most of this group sailed from Hampton Roads on 2 March 1944; agents Farris Hardin and Donald Berntson remained behind to obtain additional equipment and supplies for the Detachment. The bulk of the group, nine officers and 99 special agents with Harold G. Gelwicks in command, stopped off for two weeks at a staging camp known as "Lion Mountain" in Oran, Algeria. During that stay, a small group under agent William Hoffman worked with CIC agents in Oran in handling port security problems; they prepared a port security plan which they later used in CBI Theater ports.

On 4 April they continued their journey on a Dutch ship, arriving at Bombay on 25 April 1944. A few more agents were sent later, and a few were recruited locally in CBI, but this group was the bulk of CIC agents for the remainder of the war.

The agents attended a two weeks course at Karachi in British Intelligence—and those to be assigned in Assam, India, and with the "X" and "Y" forces in Burma, were sent through the British Jungle Warfare School in Budni.

* * *

The War Department was adamant in its decision that 12 numbered Detachments be organized for the theater, disregarding Major MacKenzie's plan. His plan, simply, was based on the fact that CBI, while considered a Combat Theater, needed CIC's mission to be a logistical and advisory one. Except for a small group, most CIC agents would not be utilized in a tactical situation; and even that group would not operate with divisions, corps, and armies as was true in other Combat Theaters. It simply was a different war in CBI, so CIC had to adapt as usual.

Since no one could anticipate the changing conditions which would dictate the static areas where they would operate, organization into a single Detachment would make possible the rapid shifting of teams as situations demanded. The War Department's inflexible attitude forced certain Detachments to be set up immediately, and earmarked for their shipment to China; they then sat around for months until CBI was "ready" for them.

On 18 August 1944, 12 detachments set up by War Department order were the 405th CIC Detachment, designated as Theater HQ, with the additional duty of covering the New Delhi area; the 406th, assigned to Karachi; the 407th to Bombay; the 408th, Calcutta; the 409th, Chabua; the 410th and 414th, Ledo, Assam; the 411th, 412th, and 415th, to China; the 413th, 10th Air Force; and the 416th to XX Bomber Force, Kharagpur, India.

Some agents earmarked for China and the Air Force were placed on TDY with other detachments after it became evident the wait would be long, but efficiency and morale suffered in the meantime.

The constant shifting of personnel from one detachment to another as well as the liberal use of detached service and temporary duty made administration a highly complicated procedure. At times half the agents working with a detachment would be on TDY orders from another detachment, while several members who actually belonged would be with yet another outfit. Directives sent to these units for filling out the Army's required Morning Report must have seemed as confusing as an explanation of the theory of relativity to the Company Clerk who had to figure them out!

* * *

Agent Grieve sold the services of his detachment temporarily to the Air Transport Command (ATC), and begged from them a flight to the Services of Supply (SOS) HQ in China, in an effort to speed up his detachment's departure for that area. Grieve reported meeting with the S-2, who seemed completely unaware of the meaning of security, and said the few incidents they had were turned over to 14th AF investigators. Grieve added this in his written report of the visit: "The 14th AF has no investigators known to this officer." He related that the S-2 added that later on, "when the supply problem is lessened," he would like to have a CIC detachment, but doubted that he would need six men. Grieve recommended that negotiations for a detachment be taken up with higher authorities.

Although duplicated in many places around the globe, this S-2's attitude seems strange when it is remembered that eight months before, numerous reports stated that the Japanese sent not only espionage agents but also trained saboteurs in large numbers to operate in the vicinity of Kweilin and Kunming; that the Japanese had organized an assassination squad of some 200 men, their targets being British and American officers in CBI with rewards per target of 500,000 to 700,000 Chinese dollars; and that the Japanese were introducing poisoned liquor and cigarettes in the theater for sale to American troops. In addition there had been numerous incidents of sabotage to telephone wires, including occasions when lines in the air warning net were cut just before raids at Hengyang on 10 December 1943 and Yunnanyi on 15 December—a sure sign of espionage nets.

To all these groups the first task was "selling" themselves to the people under whom and with whom they were to work. It was the same old story CIC confronted whenever it first arrived anywhere—few persons had more than a vague idea of CIC's mission and few preparations had been made for their arrival.

(It recalls what happened to the first CIC detachment sent to Brazil, an important link in the early airplane supply line to North Africa. The intelligence officer was so confounded that he ordered this highly confidential team to a hotel, not to move outside of it until further orders. So they lived it up in the hotel until finally the officer was educated to their true function and then put them to proper use.)

* * *

CIC agents soon set up liaison with the British and with other staff sections, plotted their own missions, and soon so demonstrated their value to the military mission of the theater that before long they had warm commendations from practically everyone from the Commanding General on down.

Their pathway was smoothed somewhat by the publication of a directive containing operational prerogatives which had been won by CIC agents in the North African and European Theaters only after long, bitter struggles. On June 1944, over the Command line of Lt. General Stilwell, a directive was published authorizing the wearing of civilian clothes and the necessity for the protection of identities and ranks of CIC agents.

Political unrest, nurtured by hatred of the British by Hindu and Burmese nationalists and played upon by communist agitation, provided fertile ground for Japanese propagandists. This combination of circumstances made sabotage protection CIC's most important mission, a danger particularly hard to control as it could come from so many directions.

Security was an engrossing problem for all CIC agents, but of special importance in the New Delhi area under the command of special agent James Lyle Beauchamp. Working with him throughout most of this period were Bernard Auer, George F. Lynch, Norman Brasseur, and James D. Brooks. This detachment was credited by MacKenzie with making a "vast improvement" in the area's security, working "against the inertia of men who mistakenly felt that Delhi was too far from the combat areas for security to matter."

The men of this detachment not only attacked the problem with vigor in their own area but made their program felt throughout CBI Theater. Auer especially was credited with establishing a field-wide program of security education, and as a result probably became the best known CIC agent in CBI. He designed security posters which were duplicated and sent to all detachments for use in their areas; he wrote slogans and persuaded the Army Radio Service to use them throughout their daily programs; and he obtained British security-trained lecturers to address troops from Karachi to Ledo. The Theater Chief of X-2, OSS, added his words of praise for the program, which he rated "of exceptionally high caliber."

* * *

CIC assigned to 10th Air Force was activated on 9 June 1944, with Farriss Hardin in command. The group left Calcutta early in July in three groups. Hardin, along with Don Berntson, Jack Hockman, Lionel Hall, Francis Krauser and Milton Musick, went to 10th AF HQ at Kanjiloa, Assam, near the India-Burma border. Thomas Kendall and Joseph Fuchs later joined them.

The second group was attached to the 7th Bombardment group at Kurmitola, India, near Calcutta. The SAC was Donald C. Mauro, with agents Harold McGovern, William J. Adams, Walter B. Baker, Jr, Harold Fetters, and Press C. Southworth, Jr.

To the 12th Bombardment Group HQ at Feni, east of Calcutta, went SAC William E. Hoffman, with agents Joseph A. Smith, Norman Albright, John McDonnell, Earl Snyder, and Robert Vautrain.

Shifting of personnel was continuous, based on need and available manpower. But in November 1944, because of progress in the Burma military operations, there was a complete reorganization: CIC HQ moved to Myitkyina in Northeast Burma; Krauser and Musick set up a field office at Dinjan, Assam, 32 miles west of Ledo within driving distance of four airfields; and Berntson and Southworth went to 80th Bomber Group HQ at Tingkawk, Burma, to direct security at four airfields along Stilwell Road.

Because of increased Air Force jurisdiction, CIC was assigned to Theater AF in December, and several new members were added; Hoffman, Mauro and McDonnell were sent to the 412th which was finally going to China; each time an airstrip was taken over from the enemy, an advance CIC team moved in to check physical security of the location, plus communications and native personnel.

In October 1944, another reorganization of CIC units took place. Most Detachment agents were formed into Combat Interrogation Teams (CIT) of two to three men each. Native interpreters from OSS Detachment 101 completed the teams. Each team was equipped with necessary camping equipment and food in order to travel unhampered throughout their assigned territories. Their mission, again, was to apprehend enemy agents and collaborators, obtain names of suspects to add to the black list, secure enemy documents, and, in general, obtain all possible information about the enemy.

* * *

CIT No. 1 began operating out of Mohnyin, south of the Stilwell Road between Myitkyina and Indaw. This team consisted of Carl Manwell, LeRoy Newland, Jean Curran, and Wah Foo Quon. The first of several interesting cases was the capture of the leaders of a Japanese-operated gang that had captured and tortured many allied soldiers. Leader Saung Swe and his second in command were tried and executed. CIT #1 made 26 arrests in this area, resulting in three death sentences, four life imprisonments and two of shorter duration.

In mid-December, Manwell and Curran moved down to Indaw while Newland and Quon formed CIT #4. Old team #1 moved over to Katha near the Chinese border, between Indaw and Bhamo, an area seething with intrigue. In Manlai village there was a gang which had tied an American soldier to a tree and burned out his eyes. CIT #1 arrested ten of this gang, meanwhile making friends with the peaceful ones in the village; this later effort was so successful that the local leaders, as a mark of honor for Manwell and Curran, dubbed them respectively with the names "Bo Gyi" and "Bo Gale."

CIT #2 was organized at Myitkyina on 8 November and moved to Schwegu on the Irrawaddy River, halfway between Bhamo and Katha. On this team were James Carr, Sick Foon Woo, Robert B. Edris, and an interpreter, augmented from time to time by personnel from the 96th Signal Battalion for radio communications, and by Kachin Rangers from OSS Det. 101. The team was given a boat with a motor for use along the river and neighboring streams. Where the boat couldn't go, they used foot power as there were no roads.

They investigated suspected collaborators, searched for radio transmitters reportedly operating in the area, and set up a block in an attempt to head off and capture an enemy radio team rumored to be escaping down the Kaukwee River. They checked out rumors of looting of Burmese villages by Kachin and Chinese guerrillas and various Japanese-inspired societies among the natives. One of the major tasks was uncovering a so-called anti-Fascist League, organized by disgruntled members of the Thakin League.

* * *

CIT #3 on November 19 was composed of agents Fong, Edwin Belknap and W. F. Davis Gebhart, plus two interpreters from OSS #101. On that date it joined the Chinese 48th Division HQ 10 miles north of Bhamo, ready to enter that city as soon as Chinese forces recaptured it. For a time Fong could not get the G-2 of this Chinese division to cooperate with CIC's mission; the G-2 was jailing collaborators, and turning enemy agents over to civilian authorities. He also resisted the team's efforts to form a civilian network; the G-2 ordered all civilians to move outside a five-mile radius of Bhamo! The situation improved, however, when a colonel of the First Chinese Army, acting as liaison officer with high Chinese officials, was able to make the G-2 understand CIC's mission and turn over to trained CIC agents all enemy counter-intelligence targets.

One month later CIC agents entered Bhamo, even though Japanese snipers were still active. The team set up office in Minlha village in coordination with the Chinese, arrested 43 Japanese agents and collaborators, and uncovered many documents of G-2 interest.

Team #5 was activated in mid-December 1944 to meet security needs of the NCAC (Northern Combat Area Command) Forward Command Post at Nansin. Its agents were James Lucas and Seymour Abeles, with two interpreters supplied by OSS #101. They began by screening the population for enemy agents and making plans for protection against mobs of Japanese stragglers working their way south. Since the enemy had not actually occupied this area, there was no prepared black list, nor friendly "white" native list. So the agents began giving all the village head men in the area the responsibility for reporting all information coming to their attention on Japanese and friends.

Late in December the team moved to Si-U to perform security for the 50th Chinese Division, as well as NCAC Forward CP. Acting as liaison with the natives, and as a pro tem Civil Affairs team gave them the opportunity to gain the good will of the natives; this good will was necessary in order to provide an avenue for reporting information to the team.

On 22 December1944, the CIC advance party of agents Harold Gelwicks, Everett White, George Mah and Francis Barnhart reached Chungking. By then, the Japanese had made their deepest penetration westward toward Kweiyang. If they took Kweiyang, they would cut the main overland supply route between Kunming and Chungking.

CIC realized the enormity of its task: danger to security came not only from the Japanese but also from dissidents within the Chinese forces on our side of the front. Certain Chinese dissidents, notably communists, seemed less interested in defeating the ostensible enemy than in promoting their own future. CIC agents knew instinctively that utmost tact and diplomacy was to be called for.

* * *

Diplomacy also was needed in coping with the Chinese Army's complete disregard for security, and in dealing with competing local law enforcement agencies as well as between these agencies and the military authorities.

Into this hotbed of jealousy, bickering, red tape and jockeying for power Major General Albert Wedemeyer, CG of the newly created China Theater, brought the Counter Intelligence Corps. He assigned it the mission of protecting U.S. military installations and U.S. military information, which was to call for all the ingenuity, tact and wisdom the agents possessed, since they, like all U.S. military then in China, could act only through the appropriate Chinese authorities.

On 28 December 1944, the General, via a directive, granted the CIC greater authority and freedom of movement than that enjoyed by CIC at that time in most other theaters during the war. He defined CIC's mission "...to furnish appropriate commanders with carefully selected personnel, especially trained and equipped for investigative Field Security functions incident to the prevention of neutralization of the activities of enemy agents."

The directive put teeth into CIC's status with "CIC personnel are authorized to call on all military and civilian personnel of this command for any assistance they may require in the performance of their duties. Personnel of this command will extend to CIC personnel such administrative assistance and other facilities as may be necessary to protect the identity of CIC personnel and expedite the accomplishment of their assigned missions."

* * *

This was not a "paper" directive, according to Major Farriss Hardin. He reported that everyone, including administrative personnel so often the ones to create problems in regard to CIC identity, went out of their way to provide the means of handling CIC problems without a hitch.

CHAPTER XXIV

Central Pacific Becomes MID-PAC under MacArthur

Early in May 1944 the Hawaii Detachment launched a counter-intelligence seminar for all commanding officers and intelligence officers in the 7th Air Force to acquaint them with counter-intelligence problems and methods of handling them. The Detachment also conducted a large scale security program consisting of security talks at the larger bases and comprehensive surveys of guard facilities on all 7th Air Force installations.

An AF 9-man team participated with other CIC units in the invasions of Saipan, Tinian and Guam where in addition to their regular missions they found a large quantity of enemy documents and materials of considerable value. A number of lessons were learned: more comprehensive advance intelligence on the operation and attack plans; attaching CIC agents to the highest overall intelligence echelon; acquainting all personnel with the CIC mission and obtaining sufficient cooperation of troop commanders to carry out that mission; plus adequate transportation during the initial stages of an operation in progress.

* * *

The 81st Infantry Division boarded ships for Hawaii, remaining there until it began its participation in fighting in the Central Pacific. In charge of the 12-man 81st CIC detachment was William F. Aimone, a graduate of the January 1942 CIC Chicago school. The commanding general of the division called Aimone into his office and said, "I have no idea what CIC is supposed to do in my division!"

Aimone replied honestly, "Neither do I, sir, but let me tell you what we are trained to do." And he did, whereupon the general added he also had a detachment of 12 Nisei enlisted men with no officer in charge; therefore, he was putting Aimone in charge of the language detachment as well! Actually it would have been an excellent working arrangement elsewhere, as CIC in SWPA worked closely with the Nisei there—and one CO probably would have been even better at coordinating the two units.

On the morning of 7 September 1944, two regimental combat

teams of the 81st Infantry Division landed simultaneously on two beaches of Anguar, a small coral island in the Western Carolines, and an important Japanese airbase. At 8:00 a.m. on D-day plus 1, the 81st CIC unit under Aimone landed with the advance party of Division HQ and dug in with the G-2 section on Red Beach. Others with the detachment were agents Sam Helman, George Baker, Harry Kidder, James Davis and Stanley Evans; the enemy front line positions were only 200 yards away!

* * *

By 6:00 a.m. on D-Day plus 2, the G-3 situation map indicated that the troops on Red Beach would likely advance into Saipan town, the only village of any size on the island; whereupon Aimone and his men set out in the direction of the village, following an old single-gauge railroad through dense jungle and swamps. Infantry troops were engaging snipers along the route, and the unit frequently had to take shelter behind advancing tanks.

At 10:30 a.m., the 81st CIC team entered the village, just a few steps behind the first wave of advancing infantry; at the north end of the town, the agents inspected the offices of a large phosphate mining company and warehouse and from there proceeded to the main group of buildings where they discovered a large volume of records, blueprints, books, miscellaneous documents, files, 40 bags of mail, and two large safes, both locked. When the safes were forced open the next day by the Division's ordnance men, a quantity of genuine paper money and coins were found. The most important papers were forwarded to G-2; military police posted to guard the buildings during the night killed one Japanese soldier who was trying to reenter them. With the exception of some 190 natives captured and confined to a civilian stockade, the entire civilian population had been evacuated by the enemy before the Americans invaded. On 18 October, CIC moved with Division HQ to Peleliu, six miles to the north, where the Japanese were holed up in a pocket in the hills, until the action was finally completed and the island secured.

* * *

On 1 August 1944, the Counter Intelligence Division (the old Security, censorship, and Counter-intelligence Section) began substantial participation in the combat phases of the war. Seventeen agents were selected to staff three CIC units attached to the 7th Infantry Division, the 27th Division, and XXIV Corps; prior to this only a handful of CIC agents had been assigned to combat units in this theater. Eleven agents went to the 310th attached to the Tenth Army which later saw action in Okinawa. Four agents went to Iwo Jima, 12 to the 968th, and

12 to the 969th on Oahu.

In mid-September 1944, the 7th CIC detachment sailed with its 7th Division, this time as part of the huge armada preparing to join MacArthur's forces in his "I shall return" operation on Leyte.

By the time agents were assigned to the 27th Division, it was engaged in mopping up operations on Saipan, so the new detachment did not join it until it had been withdrawn to New Hebrides. Agent Ernest Halford of Theater HQ had been transferred to the 27th CIC unit in April 1944 with the mission of conducting counter-intelligence operations during the Saipan campaign, the first instance of the invasion of territory with a substantial Japanese population.

Saipan was pronounced secure on 9 July, but remnants of enemy military still remained at large, accompanied by numerous civilians making necessary some psychological warfare. Halford also was charged with directing the efforts of interpreters inside the civilian compound, with the main objective of uncovering those who were soldiers masquerading as civilians. Halford remained on Saipan long after the fighting was over, carrying on his CI duties with the Army garrison force, later designated as Island Command, and finally as Western Pacific Base Command.

* * *

On 1 August 1944, USAFCPA was superseded by U.S. Army Forces, Pacific Ocean areas (USAFPOA), into which all groups formerly under U.S. Armed Forces in South Pacific (USAFISPA) were incorporated, with the Central Pacific Base Command (CPBC) established as a subordinate administrative command. This change created a certain amount of difficulty for CIC, as it now had no more official jurisdiction over internal security of the Islands, and it also became harder for the Theater G-2 to requisition and provide CIC units for Army ground forces in the western Pacific. In June 1945, action was initiated to raise CIC to theater level with all CIC detachments in the theater being assigned to USAFPOA.

At this same time, all Pacific areas were coordinated under General MacArthur, with the new command designated as U.S. Army Forces in the Pacific AFPAC (so USAFPOA was redesignated U.S. Army Forces, Middle Pacific USAF, MIDPAC), with General Richardson its commander. Orders were then issued assigning all CIC units in the theater to the new command, and a circular was published covering the mission of CIC and responsibilities of the commanding officers of units to which CIC detachments might be assigned. With this command change, the G-2 of MIDPAC had control of all CIC in its territory.

CHAPTER XXV

Stateside: SIC (Security Intelligence Corps)

CIC was put out of business as a separate entity in the States (known as Zone of the Interior, or ZI in military lingo) by the end of 1943. Those agents not guarding the Manhattan Project, or attached to Air Corps or Transportation Command units in the ZI or on the way to overseas destinations, came under the Provost Marshal General who combined them with the agents already working for him as CID (Criminal Investigation Division). The combined unit was given the title of SIC, Security Intelligence Corps, though for the most part the former CIC agents continued to handle matters they were trained for.

Documentation of the specific activities of the SIC in the First Service Command, the New England States, has come to hand, and is believed to have been fairly typical of SIC elsewhere in continental U.S. This area was saturated with industrial plants under contracts to supply our Armed Forces with all types of supplies, and were thus expected to be prime targets for enemy agents. The following report[19] on SIC-CIC illustrates the performance of these agents in protecting this vital area during the two year period (1944-1945) these agents worked together under the SIC banner.

There were 28 CIC special agents on duty 31 July 1942 at First Service Command HQ in Boston, Massachusetts. In the next nine months this small unit was boosted with almost 300 more at 808 Commonwealth Avenue, the HQ. The actual strength reported to Military Intelligence Service, War Department, in Washington on 1 March 1943 listed 328 enlisted agents, with grades ranging from 6 master sergeants down to 195 corporals.

By the end of 1943 all but 30 of these agents had shipped out. The remaining agents joined 30 Provost Marshal (CID) investigators to form the Security and Intelligence detachment for the First Service Command.

During that nine-month growth period when 300 agents worked out of Boston and its field offices, specialty squads were organized. A group of 24 formed the Subversive Squad, under the leadership of Special Agent Zack. It was a lively, dynamic group with outstanding

---

[19] *By Isadore Zack, former newspaper man with Quincy Ledger*

language abilities, newspaper training, foreign travel backgrounds and advanced scholastic training. After the loss of so many agents by the end of 1943, there were only 11 men left in the squad; it became the Counter-intelligence Group (CIG) in SIC for the Service Command.

The major function of this CIG squad was to collect intelligence and write the Weekly Intelligence Summary for the Commanding General (CG). The summary usually ran 2500 to 3000 words and covered Subversive Activities, Racial Disturbances, Labor Relations, Sabotage, Foreign Language Press, Riots and Domestic Disturbances, Foreign Affairs Pressure, and Miscellaneous Incidents. The report was distributed to over 100 military, civilian and government law enforcement organizations in the New England area.

The G-2 assigned the task of preparing the Summary to CIG ex-newsmen Cornelius Dalton (Boston Herald), Joe Indio (United Press), Dillard Stokes (Washington Post), and Zack. Other experienced writers on the CIG squad were Elwood S. McKenney (Harvard), William D. MacGregor and Jack Lawlor. Important material for the Racial Situation section came from black CIC agents Paul Davis and Jim Buck who were undercover during the entire war. Buck worked in the black community, while Elwood McKenney, also a black special agent, used the cover of a theology student to infiltrate various groups suspected of impeding the pursuit of the war. McKenney had been in North Africa with CIC but had returned and was stationed at Service Command HQ. He and Davis were the key writers for the Domestic Intelligence memorandums.

* * *

CIG prepared a total of 50 summaries in 1944-45, drawing the attention of the CG, Army Service Forces, who issued this citation to the unit: "The information contained in your Domestic Intelligence Memo #14, dated 26 August 1945, is timely and valuable to the War Dept. The members of your division should be commended upon their alertness and efficiency in keeping the proper agencies informed regarding new trends in the production of subversive material and propaganda by persons who publish articles not in the best interest and well being of the United States."

A key portion of the Weekly Intelligence Summary was the Subversive section, which covered communist activities, German, Japanese and Italian activities, and Pacifist activities, Socialist, Labor and Trotskyite, Italian Fascism, Jehovah's Witnesses, and Sedition.

The Racial Situation Annex of the report covered Negro activities and incidents of anti-Semitism. The Foreign Affairs Pressure Group Annex covered Polish, Irish and Italian groups with heavy emphasis on Armenian groups covered by agent Sam Toumanyian who was on loan to CIG. The largest Armenian community in the U.S. was situated at Watertown, Massachusetts.

The CIG squad handled Incident Investigations directed to the G-2 from military units in the Service Command area (all of New England and part of northern New York State). These agents also were used exclusively by General Miles on undercover investigations: Zack on a 4-month assignment, MacGregor 3 months in Greenland, McKenny twice on major incidents involving Negro troops, Indio and Lawlor frequently when civilians threatened strikes and slowed down production of badly needed war materials. The Army had the authority to seize these plants and prevent the workers from striking. CIG became the CG's eyes and ears for week-long periods, with special scrutiny of war plants in Fall River, New Bedford, Taunton and Salem MA.

* * *

As if they didn't have enough to do, CIG agents made periodic weekend checks of clubs and bars frequented by military personnel on pass or liberty in Boston, a key Navy base and Embarkation port. It was this close coverage by CIC of the bars that nearly cost several agents their lives on the night of the famous Coconut Grove fire in November 1942. By chance, agents scheduled to go into Coconut Grove to replace a team that had just left were late and were outside when the murderous fire killed nearly 500 patrons.

Over the two years SIC's CIG operated, it investigated 182 incidents reported to the G-2. General Miles, who had been G-2 of the Army on Pearl Harbor day, was cognizant of his CIC men, and made extensive use of their talents. He made his own rules about involving the agents in matters of intelligence and even public relations. For instance, when he wanted to showcase the new Signal Corps film "The Negro Soldier," he had black CIG agents prepare the invitation list. He also paid close attention to mail from civilians complaining about the conduct of the military in communities around Army bases. In many instances he by-passed the MPs and used CIC for follow-up and counteraction.

Examples of the kinds of Incident investigations CIG covered: German and Italian POWs held at various Army installations in New England; atrocity letters from soldiers overseas; homosexuals; draft deferments at Watertown Arsenal; subversive personnel at Camp Niantic CT; dim-out regulations; illegally delivered mail to military personnel; WAC rumors; rumor clinic investigations; distribution of anti-Semitic literature at Fort Devens; false information relating to servicemen; Army impersonators; confidential maps found where they didn't belong.

The following agents made up the initial CIC Subversive Squad in the First Service Command: Fred Agentta, James Cate, Paul Davis, Andrew Donnelly, Edward DuBois, Charles Gubellini, Alfred Havighurst, William P. Holden, Arthur Hurlburt, William B. Leong, Simon Y. Levovsky, William D. MacGregor, Peter Marks, Tony Mastrollilo, Elwood S. McKenney, Phillip F. Poirer, Jr, Robert Rawley, Richard St. Onge, Harry I. Sinnott, Stephen Smyk, Ralph Wilde, and SAC Isadore Zack. Lts. Paul Gaughran and William "Bud" Uanna assisted in training and assigning of missions.

Of that original group only Davis, MacGregor, McKenney and Zack remained after the big shipments to Camp Holabird late in 1943. They were reinforced by Cornelius Dalton, Joe Indio, John Lawlor and Dillard Stokes. Later, Jim Buck, a Mississippi school principal, joined and went undercover in Boston's black community.

* * *

One of the most important investigations involved the mass AWOL of the 483rd Port Battalion from Camp Kilmer, New Jersey. The Secretary of War[20] ordered a SECRET investigation to be conducted by *field grade officers* to determine: Was the AWOL enemy inspired? If so, who was responsible? Thanks to the Service Command G-2 and his CI aide, who advised that CIC was best able to handle it, General Miles authorized the use of CIC. It is unknown whether the Secretary of War ever knew that his order for field grade officers (major and higher) to investigate was disregarded and the incident handled by two CIC special agents, Iz Zack and Elwood McKenney, both tech sergeants at the time. They were commended for their comprehensive, clear report, here set out:

* * *

The Case of Mass AWOL of the 483d Port Battalion[21]

The 483rd Port Battalion was at Camp Kilmer, New Jersey, preparing to embark for the beaches of Normandy June 1944. It never got there!

In a 48-hour period in mid-May, almost 220 Negroes of the 483rd went over the hill in a mass AWOL that shook the Pentagon. In late May most AWOLs surrendered voluntarily to MPs and were shipped to a stockade for "AWOLs from Ports of Embarkation" located at Camp Edwards, Cape Cod, Massachusetts, known as the East Coast Processing Center (ECPC). Army Service Forces General Brehon Somervell ordered a high priority investigation. Colonel William P. Grey, Office of the Director of Intelligence, Washington, D.C., assigned the case to the Security Intelligence Division of the First Service Com-

---

[20]   *Even the Secretary of War and advisors were ignorant of CIC!?*
[21]   *By Isadore Zack*

mand in Boston. Colonel Grey told Captain John Booth of the SID: "We are concerned with the reason *why* those fellows went out and particularly if the AWOL was instituted for subversive reasons."

The case was assigned to CIC Special Agent Isadore Zack, who took with him Elwood S. McKenney, one of his three black agents, who joined in the report, produced after the CIC agents spent 8 hours interviewing prisoners, officials at the stockade, and others.

Boston, Massachusetts, 29 May 1944

* * *

MEMORANDUM FOR OFFICER IN CHARGE

Subject: Mass AWOL—Camp Kilmer, New Jersey

The following report was made after a close study of existing circumstances and investigation at the East Coast Processing Center, Camp Edwards, Massachusetts. At the direction of the Chief, Intelligence Branch, Security and Intelligence Division, First Service Command, Special Agents Isadore Zack and Elwood S McKenney went to the East Coast Processing Center on 27 May 1944 and made a survey of the situation which included interrogation of suspected key figures in the mass AWOL, close inspection of 180 signed sworn statements by the soldiers, and interrogating the officers of the ECPC.

Their mission was to attempt to uncover evidence of collusion or subversion on the part of the soldiers involved. ECPC officers turned over to the agents 180 signed statements taken from 184 members of the 483rd Port Battalion, at that time prisoners in the stockade.

It is the combined opinion of the officers involved in handling the colored personnel in this mass AWOL that the reason for the act was their desire to rid themselves of their commanding officer, Lt. Colonel Peter Miller. Every list of grievances made out by the soldiers contained adverse information in regard to Colonel Miller's practices and attitudes towards the men. All but one man stated the desirability to again serve overseas under any other officer. All the men pointed out that the morale had been very high after Colonel Miller left the outfit in Alaska to go to General Staff school.

It is the opinion of these officers that the AWOL soldiers are excellent men, half had overseas training and their value to the Army Service Forces cannot be overlooked. They have been model soldiers in the stockade and their training has left little to be desired.

Inspection of the sworn statements reveals the soldiers told almost the same story, all being careful to note that they had gone AWOL on their own volition and there had been no meeting or urging by any other party. The agents selected 15 soldiers for questioning on the basis of information noted in their statements. Chief interrogated were the top First Sergeants of the 64 noncommissioned officers already apprehended. First Sergeant Ernest J. Cain of the 656th Port Company was the main witness called here. Interrogated at two separate times during the day by the agents, Cain admitted he preferred any punishment rather than going overseas with Miller, and refused to change his story given to Major Potter of the ECPC, which reads:

* * *

"I was a member of the 656th Port Company, one of four making up the 483rd Port Battalion. The other companies were the 657th, 658th, and 659th. The battalion was activated at Indiantown Gap, Pennsylvania, 30 September 1942. They stayed there two weeks and then went to New Orleans, Louisiana, 13 October 1942. We left for Seattle and then Excursion Inlet, Alaska, 5 May 1943. Lt.Colonel Peter M. Miller arrived on 6 June 1943. The battalion remained in Alaska until January 1944 and later to Camp Kilmer, New Jersey, 4 March 1944, until about 7 May 1944. When they embarked, about 100 men from the 656th Company went AWOL at Camp Kilmer about 3, 4, and 5 May 1944; about 65 were noncommissioned officers. I took off 5 May 1944. About 150 men from the other companies went AWOL about the same time. The reason was nobody would go overseas under Lt. Colonel Miller. I understood that when they sailed Miller had been removed as Commanding Officer." Cain said he went to New York and Philadelphia and returned to Camp Kilmer on 15 May 1944. He understood most of the AWOLs stayed in hotels in New York. Most surrendered about 14 May.

He stated he was one of the last to leave his company, going over the hill the 5th of May after several morning reports showed a steady increase in AWOLs, that he gave the matter considerable thought before he finally left. He stated that on the night of the 4th he was so aggravated by the situation that he lay on his bunk and cried. On the 5th he told his company commander he was going over the hill. He stated he told Lts. Miller, Weiss, and Kurse that he was going. He claims that none sought to discourage him. Cain several times repeated that as far as he knew there had been no meeting and no plan to reveal that the battalion as a whole was upset when Colonel Miller returned to take command. While Cain could not remember the persons concerned, another noncom told him that he had been told by a certain officer that the best way for the outfit to rid themselves of Colonel Miller would be if half of them went over the hill. He could not substantiate nor give any other leads in this matter.

* * *

Sergeant Cain said that the leading complaints voiced by the

AWOLs were as follows: 1) A colored man's wife who was quite light would not be allowed on the post by Colonel Miller. 2) The colonel refused to allow any of the men from the Battalion to attend Officers Training School. 3) Miller refused to sign an order authorizing the Sergeant of the Guard to turn a man over to civilian authorities, but told Sergeant of the Guard to do so. 4) Men marked "quarters" by the medics, were, on the following day, marched to sick call under guard, and when returned marked "quarters" were made to dig holes 6 ft. by 6 ft. 5) Colonel Miller ordered the MPs to arrest all colored soldiers walking with white girls in Seattle. 6) The colonel forced the men to go to church. 7) If the men would not play ball after retreat they were forced to police the area. 8) Men had to walk guard without arms in a Theater of Operations. 9) The recreation room was closed and furniture removed. 10) The colonel stopped the soldiers from playing softball with teams from white units. 11) The colonel told Captain Kramer of the 656th Company that the only way he could get a promotion was to work the "niggers" hard and keep them working. 12) Men on night duty from 7:00 p.m. to 6:00 a.m. had to stand inspection by their beds when the inspection officer came through at 9:30 a.m. The men had to lie on the floor and were not allowed to use the bed until after the inspection. 13) The men were made to buy their own raincoats, at $10 each. 14) The men had to take down their pin-up girls. One colored soldier drew a picture of Lena Horne and the colonel made him take it down and draw one of the colonel and put it up in the mess hall. 15) Two warrant officers (colored) had to eat with the enlisted men. 16) When General Dennison was to visit the unit, the men were told to sing or laugh. 17) The men of the 656th Port Company built their own theater but Colonel Miller ordered that the colored and white be segregated therein.

The above statements were corroborated by Staff Sergeant Bernard T. Wright and Sergeant Alvin Molyneaux. In their signed statements almost all the soldiers repeated the above or named others, such as, "I was one of those to sign a petition asking for an interview with an Inspector General, and as a result I was afraid Lt. Colonel Miller would have it in for me."

In regard to the petition circulated in the battalion during April 1944, the following was learned through interrogation: The men of the battalion can be described as army-regulation-wise and by their admission "knew the score." Almost every soldier interviewed could quote regulations and Articles of War by number and paragraph.

It appears that previous attempts had been made to contact and speak with an Inspector General relative to conditions with the battalion. The soldiers claim that on one occasion an announcement was made that an Inspector General was in the camp, but they were not given an opportunity to see him because they were sent on a road march. At the time when they could have spoken to the Inspector General, the entire battalion was 8 miles from camp. Late in April following a petition, an Inspector General visited and interrogated many at length.

The mass AWOL took place four days after the Inspector General's visit, the feeling being that Colonel Miller would take exacting discriminatory measures to "get even" with those men who had signed the petition. Added impetus to the mass exodus took place when, following the Inspector General's visit, the battalion was alerted for overseas and restricted to camp.

Then there was a rumor that Colonel Miller was to place Military Police about the area of the camp to enforce the No Pass restriction. This, coupled with the feeling of revenge on the part of the colonel, started the mass movement.

T-4 Robert W. Craig, ASN 12090811, Clerk of the 656th Port Company, was twice interviewed under pressure and, after first stating that he knew nothing about the petition, changed his story and stated that he had typed out the petition which he presented to the Company Commander after it had been signed by numerous soldiers. Informed that he was a deserter, Craig remarked that he had no intentions of deserting and considered that he would be punished as an AWOL. The agents reminded Craig that under the 58th Article of War, going AWOL from a Port of Embarkation is desertion and the punishment could be death. Craig informed the agents that he preferred death to serving with Lt. Colonel Miller. He revealed that he was a Northern Negro and not used to the kind of handling practiced by Colonel Miller who was a Southerner.

The second of the two 1st sergeants who were AWOL was interviewed and the result was identical with that of 1st Sgt Cain's. This man is Theodore R. Smith of the 659th Company, a college-educated Negro whose militancy and hatred for Colonel Miller was very obvious to the agents. He said he realized that he would lose all his rank which he had earned through hard work, but he considered it a small sacrifice to make in the face of existing conditions when he went AWOL.

General information considered pertinent to this case was gathered by the agents: 1) The AWOLs' claim that their battalion set records while active in Alaska and under the command of Major Dillon who replaced Colonel Miller during the latter's period of schooling in the states. 2) The soldiers' claim that the two colored warrant officers and the two white officers from the battalion went over the hill for the same reason that the enlisted men did. 3) The leading noncommissioned officers expressed their "surprise" over the number of personnel involved in the AWOL. 4) All realized by direct statements that there is no justification for going AWOL.

Interrogation and investigation lasted for a period of 8 hours and culminated when the agents had exhausted all leads. The agents feel that they were successful in their efforts to erase the feeling of collective security among the men by reminding certain key figures that they can be charged as deserters.

* * *

AGENTS' NOTES AND RECOMMENDATIONS:

In view of the fact that the prisoners are allowed to write letters, it is felt some information regarding the mass AWOL will eventually leak out and should it reach the Negro press, the incident would be distorted into an inflammatory story to reflect against the Army. This was doubly important in view of the fact that the Negro press has carried some hint of the mass AWOL including a statement that a public relations officer at Camp Kilmer stated that the situation was merely gossip and rumor.

Secondly, as these men are considered to be trained and efficient soldiers, and as any element of subversion can be ruled out as affecting this incident, it is recommended that the men involved be maintained as a unit to the greatest extent possible to prevent their story being spread among many units and that they be delivered overseas without further incident.

All the signed sworn statements of the men involved are in possession of the Judge Advocate General at the East Coast Processing Center. The bulk of the men surrendered voluntarily.

Isadore Zack, Special Agent, SIC, 1SC
Elwood S McKenney, Special Agent, SIC, 1SC

(Many cases of suspected subversion continued to be reported to MI and directly to CIC. All had to be fully investigated by our Special Agents, even though time-consuming as in this instance. To find no evidence of enemy involvement was also important—and a relief!)

There was more serious trouble from a few blacks in another service command, the Fourth, headquartered in Atlanta. Many of our army training camps were scattered throughout this command, so when an ambitious young black soldier started his own secret army which he called "The Afro-American Army," our Military Intelligence was rightly concerned. This type of case fell into the category of, at the very least, disaffection, and certainly was subversive activity within the "old" CIC's mission. Real disaffection hurt the Army in a number of ways, and could lead to outright disloyalty, harmful to the training of our soldiers in this service command.

Black agents George Kennedy and Thornton R. Greene were assigned to penetrate this "army" and secure evidence needed to end its existence. They each contacted the "General" and paid the asking fee for officer's rank that certainly far exceeded their enlisted grades.

When they had accumulated enough hard evidence of the extent of the secret army's operation, this was turned over to prosecutors who had the ring leader arrested, put on trial and convicted; he was sentenced to a number of years in prison.

Years later, agent Greene expressed his opinion that the black "general" was in a number of ways sincere in his opinion that the blacks were entitled to a portion of the Deep South states for themselves, and this openness in court was sufficient to ensure his conviction. But of course his activity was an impediment to our war efforts, and had to be stopped—which CIC-SIC agents Greene and Kennedy neatly did.

1945

Our Armed Forces in the war with Japan were now hitting their stride. Despite Germany's last effort in the Battle of the Bulge, the Pentagon could foresee the end coming shortly in Europe and now was in a position to fill any needs that MacArthur requested.

Actually, with the victory on Leyte assured, he was confident he was prepared to push ahead vigorously with the landing at Dagupan on the Lingayen Gulf, Luzon.

Activity began to wane in other theaters where Japan no longer threatened, such as in the South Pacific where CIC agents were finally absorbed into SWPA and the Central Pacific.

But even in the Central Pacific, the fighting was coming to an end, with captured islands now being used as bases for our Air Corps to turn its might on Japan.

* * *

The China-India-Burma situation however grew in intensity along with MacArthur's Theater, and CIC activities kept pace with increased military action and diminished where such action was becoming a minor factor. This huge theater is usually treated as one—CBI, but actually Burma-India was a separate sub-theater integrated with China.

CHAPTER XXVI

Central Pacific

On 19 April 1945, two CIC units were activated, the 968th and 969th, their personnel with a few exceptions being drawn from the old Security, Censorship, and Counter-intelligence Section. Wayne Stanard, executive officer of the 969th kept in touch with the 607th detachment on Oahu attached to Army AF Pacific, and with the 98th CIC; he also communicated frequently with CIC units in the field: the 7th, 27th, 96th, 224th, and 310th.

The 7th, 27th, 77th, 96th, 224th, and 310th CIC detachments were staffed mainly by agents in Hawaii, and left from there for the Okinawa invasion. By the end of May 1945, 70 agents had been sent to combat units from Hawaii, among them four with the Iwo Jima garrison force.

* * *

With the end of the war, most of the remaining agents in Hawaii were sent on to Japan, with the small detachment left on Oahu conducting routine CI duties.

CHAPTER XXVII

CBI Booms

January 1945 saw agents Steptoe and Monro of the 409th CIC headed for Calcutta to coordinate with CIC there plans for a security survey of the Chittakong-Tansukia pipeline. Two days after their return to Chabua, Monro and Voorhees set out to cover the upper end of the line, to meet the Calcutta agents covering the lower end.

Later in 1945 the detachment was called on to question some 2,000 refugees from French Indochina, for strategic and other intelligence information. Luckily, a Myitkyina-Bhamo area CIC team had three agents fluent in French: LeRoy Newland, Julian Nixon and Maurice McMahan. They joined the 409th team to lend assistance in these important interrogations.

There was also William W. Tyng, son of a long line of Chinese missionaries who had spent eight years in China and spoke several dialects fluently and whose sister was in China at the time. The difficulty was that Tyng had been sent to North Africa and thence on the invasion of Italy. It required a lengthy exchange of cables to get him released in time to join the China detachment early in the summer of 1945.

As the famed Ledo-Burma Road (later called Stilwell Road) was pushing into Burma, the strategic significance of this doorway into the Burma combat zone became of vital interest. CIC undertook the planning for security, which meant controlling movement along its 1,120 miles. In February, agent Simpson journeyed the entire length of the newly-completed Stilwell Road, from Doom Dooma, Assam to Kunming, China. He went with the 610th Ordnance Company, the first unit to make the complete trip. His task consisted of security planning and collecting counter-intelligence information from Indian soldiers and civilians, aided by his ability to speak excellent Hindustani.

The most effective control CIC set up was the establishment of a Control Post at Hellgate, Assam; here, it could be readily ascertained if convoys were carrying undesirable cargo or humans in either direction. CIC made periodic inspections at this vital checkpoint, as well as drafted regulations to cover any weaknesses in its operations.

An unusual case was investigated when Quartermaster Corps

reported that four of the seven battalions in the 45th QM were having to replace trucks at a far lower mileage than the others. Were saboteurs at work? CIC reviewed charts and graphs of performance and repair records, and conducted carefully selected interviews with key personnel; to CIC the solution became obvious: willful neglect of first echelon repairs due to a very bad morale situation.

Agents Redman and Nebo had conducted the investigation. They recommended improvements in living conditions and recreational facilities; a thankful Base HQ accepted the recommendations and immediately put them into effect, with a noticeable upturn in morale. In addition, the telltale charts and graphs were publicized, to make those who had been willfully negligent aware of the seriousness of the situation.

A definite CIC gain came out of the survey: it revealed a number of disaffected persons, suspected of deliberately causing the problem. One case was a private with a unit along the Ledo Road, who was getting letters from a woman in New York claiming he had fathered her illegitimate child and urging that he desert the Army. Another was a master sergeant, who had been suspected of disaffection, but who turned out to be mentally ill. Another item from the survey: a need for security education. Nebo then put on a special program along the lines used elsewhere, and set up a program to more closely process civilians working in and around American installations along the road.

* * *

In June 1945, all the units in Assam and Burma were combined operationally under Steptoe, CO of the Chabua unit; but considerable shifting of agents began soon thereafter and continued until the deactivation at the end of October 1945.

A practice man-hunt by J. Lyle Beauchamp's New Delhi detachment during an "Allied Security Week" in February 1945, aroused the interest of the entire area. In advance of this stunt, 1500 posters carrying the picture and description of Norman Brasseur as "wanted" were distributed, five particular areas being designated as ones through which he would pass. He would be wandering about in varying uniforms ranging from private to colonel, with a War Bond prize for the first person in each of the areas to recognize and "capture" him!

In February 1945, agent Auer toured Burma and India, putting on well-planned, week-long security drives wherever there were high concentrations of U.S. and British troops. In his drives, he used every possible type of activity designed to make one security conscious: films, lectures, posters, daily news sheets and menus in hotels and restaurants, banners suspended over streets, slides in movie houses, radio talks by high ranking officers, including the Commanding General, and a security contest to increase the vigilance of installation guards. This last was judged by many to be the most successful, with one security officer reporting that for the first time in months, his guards were closely scrutinizing every person entering the installation.

Several other agents were assigned to New Delhi for various periods: Philip Detweiler, Keith N. Peterson, and Francis S. O'Neill. Also carried as members were James F. Murray, who performed security duty throughout the war along the Calcutta to Ledo railway, with a private car as his residence; Charles Shultz whose duties concentrated on the CBI Postal Office; and Eugene Redden who was assigned for several months to railway security in the Assam area.

The Karachi CIC detachment ran into a little more trouble than did some of the others, because they were in a very remote area where even officials were not receiving orders from higher headquarters. One special problem involved fending off attempts to place them directly under control of the local Provost Marshal. They solved that one, and proceeded to provide badly needed security for all installations in the area, except Air Transport Command, until early in November when the Detachment was reassigned to Myitkyina.

* * *

Meanwhile, in Bombay the 407th ran into probably the greatest of all snafus, which seemed for a time to be incapable of solution. But as with many other detachments in CBI, the agents managed to win over all the other units, both British and American, to the point that they gained absolute authority to do everything they felt necessary to insure greater security for the area.

Typical of many places, Bombay was plagued by a flood of rumors derogatory to the U.S., some of which were printed in pamphlets and newspapers. The Bombay Sentinel and the Free Press Journal, both English language, were particularly scurrilous. Some of these rife rumors were about outbreaks of leprosy, impending air attacks, influx of Japanese espionage and sabotage agents, as well as the unfounded one about peace being made between Germany and Russia. It was routine for CIC to deal with such a flood of rumors, as many were apparently maliciously inspired to lower troop morale and increase civilian unrest. Exposing lies and countering rumors became automatic, while always alert to pinpoint the source if possible.

Although security was now constantly stressed, there were always a number of people unable to keep their mouths shut. One incident of loose talk involved a warrant officer who ran a stencil giving instructions for an impending large-scale operation planned for 11 February 1945, making it known to unauthorized eyes. Fortunately the story was caught before passing to many people, but the unthinking warrant officer was fined $50 a month for 12 months in a general court martial, and those who had repeated the story were given stern warnings.

British Field Security referred a similar case to CIC. An American glider pilot had discussed a planned operation with an Indian woman, who in turn passed it on to a British officer. The guilty pilot had already left the theater, but the case was forwarded to his new unit with a request for disciplinary action.

An interesting document prepared in February 1945 lists briefly the 32 types of activity performed by the 407th in India and Burma, with "close contact" and "liaison" being the key words in nearly every such activity. How much this constant stress on liaison influenced the successful operations of the detachment cannot be estimated, but it is significant that there is no mention of the occasional petty though annoying types of difficulties encountered by other detachments.

Even more significant is the warm commendation by Major General Howard C. Davidson, 10th AF Commander, as the unit prepared to leave for China. He praised the devotion to duty of CIC agents, as exemplified by the high esteem held for them by 10th AF personnel and described them as a major asset in the maintenance of Air Force security. Endorsing this, Major General George Stratemeyer, Commander of Theater Army Air Forces, added: "You have justifiably won the respect and pride of the Services."

* * *

Paul Ward's 410th CIC was sent to the secret base of the XXth Bomber Command at Kharagpur. They found their principal problem there to be lax security. The unit was credited with considerably improving the situation through security surveys and general security education; aiding them in this pursuit, Major General Curtis LeMay backed them "to the limit." They encountered and handled an interesting variety of suspected sabotage, such as loose bolts in the magneto housing of aircraft, "old shot bags" in a parachute, and fires at breaks in an oil pipeline—plus numerous espionage cases.

As mentioned above, the 411th, 412th and 415th units had to wait before going to their assigned areas in China, so in the meantime they found CIC work to do in Calcutta. Grieve and his 412th team succeeded in selling their expertise to ATC, and later to the AF.

After several delays made it clear that even Gelwick's small unit could not get to China for some time, Gelwick went through the British school at Karachi while his 411th was merged operationally with Dailey's 415th. By October most agents in these three groups had been sent to the NCAC, and at last were alerted to get ready for China on 5 January 1945.

* * *

The NCAC at first was doubtful about accepting a CIC unit, but after John H. Thorne, Officer-in-charge, flew to their Shadazup HQ and conferred with the G-2, G-3 and Chief of Staff, NCAC changed its decision, and even requested an additional detachment for General Frank D. Merrill's Marauders. The Marauders' code-named GALAHAD Task Force had cut off the Japanese ahead of General Stilwell's Chinese Division, and laid siege to Myitkyina.

Thorne flew on to Myitkyina port, where officials were preparing to receive his CIC team. Still later, the 405th, 407th and 408th were brought in and though they kept their unit identities, they operated as one unit under Thorne. Also, agents from the group waiting to enter China were brought up to join the NCAC detachment.

The specific mission for NCAC CIC was outlined by the G-2, Colonel Joseph W. Stilwell, Jr.: to install an effective, rapid system for classifying the natives into "black" (watch them!) and "white" (friendly) categories; to apprehend enemy agents, collaborators and saboteurs; to maintain security at the front as well as rear areas; and to effect close liaison with British Civil Affairs.

Thorne, with LeRoy Newland, Carl Manwell, Jean Curran and James Carr of the 414th joined GALAHAD Task Force in time to enter Myitkyina with the first assault troops. They found two-and-a-half tons of documents in enemy headquarters; many more of possible great military value had been destroyed by the Chinese through ignorance. The team started clearing local citizens for army employment, while hunting persons wanted on the black list. They located the first three working for Civil Affairs, who knew they were on the list but insisted that their special qualifications warranted being hired. Following a report to NCAC HQ on this unexpected obstacle, CIC arrested and sent the three back to India for trial.

Other arrests of the black list suspects were not quite as easy. One outstanding case was conducted by agent Edmund Fong. Accompanied by a Burmese sub-inspector, he set out September 21 to pick up one Sinwa Nawng, on the list as head man of Kansi village in North Burma. A notorious collaborator, Nawng was charged with seizing, disarming and handing over to the Japanese, 15 native soldiers, plus American pilot Lt. Stewart Walker.

Though suffering from malaria and jaundice, Fong traveled with his companion for two weeks by plane, jeep, motor boat and on foot. Reaching their destination, their first contact was the local Chinese liaison officer, who on learning their mission protested their doing it. "He had been helpful in obtaining foodstuffs and laborers for them," he claimed. "If he helped the Japanese in any way, he was simply forced into it."

Fong was unable to totally convince the liaison officer that Nawng's good deeds was typical of collaborators. Sensing that most of the local Chinese had been taken in by Nawng and would not permit the arrest, Fong came up with this subterfuge after persuading the liaison officer to go along with it: "We have come," he told them, "to escort Sinwa Nawng to Myitkyina, because the people there have heard that he can relate some experiences during the Japanese occupation that can be extremely valuable to our winning the war!" It worked. He and his Burmese aide left with Nawng in tow, under "escort." And on the return trip they picked up another wanted person on the way, plus two more from other units. At Myitkyina, Fong turned in the four prisoners and went immediately into the hospital for treatment of his malaria and jaundice.

* * *

The next location for CIT #1 was Tigyaing. Thomas P. Wheeley, who had been with the Karachi CIC, joined team #1 here. There was work for all three. They arrested many Japanese collaborators, among whom were five natives who had ferried a party of Wingate's British force to an island in the river, and then betrayed the location to the enemy. Leaders of the local chapter of the Thakin League, composed of women, had collaborated wholeheartedly with the Japanese, among other things acting as procurers for them; CIC arrested 12 of them for giving "aid and comfort" to the enemy.

In February, CIT #1 was ordered to join the 36th Chinese Division then operating midway between Katha and Mandalay. Though the team were told by natives (who considered a trail through rice paddies to be a motor road) that a motor road was in existence for their trip; nevertheless, in several places they had to stop and hire natives to build rafts to get across the Schwei river. CIT #1 accompanied the forward troops of the division in the occupation of captured villages; by the end of March it had made 18 arrests. One of these had been traced from Mohnyin; another was charged with the capture and betrayal of Lt. Joe Wilson of the U.S. Air Corps. Team #1 then set up a listening post in Mogak to cover the area between there and Stilwell Road.

In February the team journeyed to Moda Gyi village and arrested six members of "Wa-Bat," a raiding gang trained by Japanese in jungle warfare; Wa-Bat had sabotaged the railroad line above Mawlu, Burma. In addition, the team developed incriminating evidence against most of the remaining 40 they had arrested as collaborators.

For 12 days agents Edris, Carr and Wood, with their interpreters and radio men, slogged over 120 miles of barely discernible trails through rough mountain terrain. They visited 15 villages, interviewing the head man and elders to find out their attitude toward the Allies, learn of their food problems, check on reports of Chinese guerrilla raids, secure any intelligence about the enemy, and ascertain the extent of collaboration with the enemy. The monthly report containing this information concluded with "the physical condition of CIC personnel continues to be stressed."

* * *

CIC agents moved into Namhkam with the Chinese First Army on the heels of the retreating enemy. Their stay there was for only two short, pleasant weeks. The natives, particularly the Shans, were so happy to be rid of Japanese oppression that they forgot their petty grievances against the British, and dropped their feud with Kachins of the hills in appreciation for their help in driving out the Japanese.

The team reluctantly departed Namhkam, to go to Muse near the border between the northern Shan states and Yunnan, where they found little counterespionage and allied work to do. It did find that two gangs of Chinese bandits were operating across the border into Burma in the guise of intelligence agents, pretending to be hunting Japanese spies, but the only persons they arrested under this pretext were wealthy, and were released after paying a ransom. Leaving 23 collaborationists in jail from Namhkam and Muse, in late February the team moved on to Kutkai to replace team #5 which had set up shop there with the fall of that city.

Early in March team #3 divided: Belknap and an interpreter went to Hsenwi area; Gebhart and Julius Nixon to Lashio. Belknap developed information on a school run by Japanese for administration of the Shan states, and also arrested a Burmese who had betrayed an American pilot shot down near Kulong.

Gebhardt and Nixon found Lashio to be a hotbed of Japanese espionage and political activity. The first two weeks they apprehended 20 suspects, guided by a list compiled by HQ and by leads locally obtained. These were for the most part collaborationists, the Japanese having taken most of their trained agents with them. The team also captured a Burmese, long sought as an officer in the Japanese army, and who had fought actively throughout the Hukawang Valley campaign. Interviewing 20 escaped Indian POWs produced a wealth of valuable military information.

* * *

Meanwhile, Newland and Quon, the new team #4, arrived at Katha three days after the fall of that city. While there, they added two interpreters and a Kachin guide to the team. A brigade of the British 36th Division and a company of Kachin levies were in Katha for two weeks; when they moved on, team #4 was left in control except for a British Civil Affairs team. They had some trouble at first with Civil Affairs as the British insisted on handling Japanese collaborators under peacetime rules, while CIC insisted on holding them in jail until their investigation was completed sufficiently to make a decision. CIC quickly won the respect of the population, as the saying became common: "If one was picked up by the CIC jeep, one did not come back."

Team #4 arrested 21 outstanding suspects but found the Japanese had moved their HQ 30 miles down the Irrawaddy River two months before the Allies moved in. But to collect much sought after enemy documents, the team staged a contest, making awards to the persons turning in the most documents; this paid off with a number of valuable documents and propaganda leaflets!

As the only American unit in the area for a time, team #4 was called upon for a variety of tasks, from acting as an information center for incoming Americans to making a ruling on the disposition of 18 elephants with drivers trying to make contact with their unit, the Kachin levies. An assault boat with an outboard motor was added to their equipment for use on long trips on the Taiping River, but gas was scarce so they traveled mostly on foot.

Early in March they proceeded to Bhamo, and from there Newland and Quon moved south to join Team #5.

* * *

India-Burma Wrap-up

In January one member of CIT #5, accompanied by two interpreters and two Kachins, started on the active hunt for one Ushikawa, a notorious Japanese agent reported to be operating in the general Nansin area. The team failed to capture him, but their pursuit kept him on the run, until finally he left the territory completely.

Then in February team #5 followed the NCAC Command Post to Bhamo where agent Fong from team #3 joined them. In Bhamo they made several arrests, added a number of suspects to the black list, and set up a security network by visiting on foot the head men of all villages within a 15 mile radius.

On 15 February, the team learned that two Americans had been caught in a Japanese trap six miles south of Kutkai. Agents Lucas and Abeles volunteered to rescue them, but the Americans had been killed before their arrival. As the team began digging out the bodies, the enemy fired on them; the team escaped the ambush, but Abeles was wounded by machine gun fire, acquiring the dubious distinction of becoming the first CIC agent in CBI to "win" a Purple Heart.

A few days later, Lucas and Fong flew to the Chinese 50th Division, and marched with it into Panghai while that city was still receiving enemy artillery fire and in which snipers were still active. Agent Joe Breechen who had come from CIC headquarters at Bhamo on business became the second Purple Heart recipient when wounded by a splinter from an enemy shell.

As this area was also the center of Indian Independence League activities, team #5 was extremely busy. It arrested 25 collaborators in the first two weeks, added numerous suspects to the black list, set up an informant network, and "captured" many military documents. Its interrogation of many Indians and Shans filtering in through enemy lines produced much valuable tactical military data. By this time agents Newland and Quon, having seen service with teams #1 and #2, had joined team #5 with Eugene Redden. Shortly afterwards Lucas was hospitalized; Newland took charge of the team.

As in all theaters CIC was often called upon to perform missions far beyond the field of their recognized primary mission, but such special assignments usually paid off by creating goodwill for CIC in many areas. One such assignment by Newland, Carr, Gebhart, and James Lucas consisted of comprehensive surveys of comparative figures for supply and cost of food stuffs during British and Japanese rule, specifically to furnish the Office of War Information (OWI) with good propaganda material.

A further example of this interservice cooperation was an "urgent request" to CBI CIC HQ for a copy of the Koran "to extract some proverbs to be used in pamphlets for the OWI." The request was complied with immediately!

Agent Charles Farris was used to strange calls for assistance. In October 1944, before the CITs had begun their labors in Burma jungles, he had taken care of an overnight request for 12 colored silk "escape" maps of Burma, such as those used by the Air Corps, needed because they would not deteriorate too quickly in the damp jungle climate.

While the interrogation teams were ranging throughout the combat zones on special missions, other agents with NCAC were engaged in a variety of counter-intelligence activities. One included the investigation of a break in the Myitkyina to Bhamo gasoline pipeline; if not deliberate sabotage, an intentional break would still deter the allies' war efforts, and all such cases had to be checked out. Agent William Adams found containers of gasoline in three small villages which natives had appropriated from the pipeline to use in their lamps, and in the fermentation of a rice liquor (Burmese moonshiners at work!).

Through astute questioning Adams identified two people who had made the gasoline available; he then called the three head men of the villages together, and warned them that should such an incident recur, a large fine would be levied upon the villages. The civil police added their warning: there would be a burning of the villages involved if pipelines were again broken into by the natives.

* * *

By July 1945 CIC had completed its tactical mission in India-Burma, and the bulk of China-bound detachments had crossed over the Hump. There still remained the tremendous task of protecting the supply line, the Life-Line, to the forces in China proper. To this task was added reporting on the increasingly serious political situation.

By early August all CIC detachments in Assam and Burma, the 406th, 407th, 409th and 410th, were combined operationally under Steptoe; the 408th returned to Calcutta. Major MacKenzie returned to the States at the end of the war, and Major Wilson became Theater Chief of CIC.

With the cessation of hostilities, CIC became responsible for gathering information for the War Criminals branch of the Judge Advocate General's office. All agents who could possibly be spared from their normal duties at Calcutta, Assam and Burma were put on this task, to process our liberated U.S. prisoners quickly so that they could return home after years of imprisonment in Japanese camps.

* * *

Between 17 August and 31 October 1945, CIC interviewed some 750 former prisoners of war, taking more than 200 statements and depositions for use as evidence of atrocities by Japanese soldiers and Korean guards in Japanese prison camps. A lengthy "rogues list" on wanted Japanese was thus compiled. Most of our Americans held prisoner in this area had been on the USS Houston, which was torpedoed 1 March 1942 in Sunda Straits, or were members of the 2nd Battalion, 131st Field Artillery Regiment which was forced to surrender at Garato, Java, on 9 March 1942.

No sooner had this trek homeward begun than it was realized that the services of CIC, now reorganized into the 405th with headquarters in New Delhi with six sub-offices throughout India, were now needed on a complex mission, even more than before.

Many wartime jobs were now being canceled, and rumors were starting of wages in general being lowered. These factors, plus the natural tensions that had existed throughout India for many years, provided fertile ground for subversive groups such as the Communist Party, to stage riots and demonstrations. It was an ideal situation for communists to use every evidence of dissatisfaction to its own advantage. CIC's powers of observation were called on, "observing" being their only official activity permitted as they had been warned not to be drawn into either camp. On 24 November eight Americans were hospitalized and 20 others treated for injuries in Calcutta, but it appeared that all the violence was actually directed at the British. The Americans suffered only because they happened to be nearby.

CIC had won the respect and trust of high-ranking American officers to the extent that close attention was paid even to these observations by CIC agents, as well as their general observations in the field of diplomacy. An example took place in November 1945: a U.S. Service group had stored a large quantity of ammunition in a water tank where it could easily be identified and seized by local subversive natives. The British objected vigorously to this cache in its vulnerable location, but were met with the response of the S-4 of the U.S. unit that "The matter has been investigated. The condition that exists is normal and shouldn't concern anyone." But CIC agents knew from their careful observations that there was indeed cause to be concerned, and that this kind of attitude might well endanger the careful liaison they had developed with the British.

Richard Klise, SAC of sub-office #3, warned the U.S. government officials that they might some day be charged for damaging the water tanks, which in most instances were the only sources of water for villagers. The decision of the S-4 of the Service unit was reversed.

Klise also recommended to Intelligence Officers at the Calcutta Base Section, at AAF HQ, and at ATC HQ, that adequate steps be taken so that U.S. salvage dumps and other disposal areas NOT make certain types of equipment available to the general public, especially radio sending and receiving sets. His recommendations were seriously considered, with no indication of any rejections. In fact, Bennett, now the Theater G-2 and Chief of the Military Observer Group, described Klise's critical reports as "the best of its type that we have had to date," adding that some of them had been forwarded to Chief of Military Intelligence Service at the War Department. At the time, Klise was a 2nd Lt., having been an enlisted agent until 13 March 1945.

Bennett's comments were typical of those towards CIC agents throughout CBI, by both British and American officers.

* * *

Throughout India unrest was growing, rapidly propelled by the coming All-India elections in December and provincial elections in February. The British were expressing a willingness to give India its freedom from British rule, if a government could be set up that was capable of taking over and running the country in a democratic way. Klise's associate, James M. McTighe, was also the recipient of Colonel Bennett's praise, for a weekly press analysis that Bennett credited with revealing "a rare talent for eliminating the mass of extraneous detail presented by a strongly partisan press" and rated it as being of great value in determining the "local attitude toward the United States military establishment in India."

While agents in the Base Sections in India were observing and reporting on the touchy political situation, agents in North Burma found themselves in a number of roles, one of which was chief native relief dispenser.

Gradually the detachments in Burma and Assam began closing out their activities, and in mid-November were deactivated, with only a few agents left in Chabua to operate a sub office for a short time.

Klise's predictions proved to be correct: the riots began in earnest in the following February, with CIC charged with observing and giving timely warnings if U.S. personnel or installations appeared to be in danger. The rest of the story is well known: several American newspapers crying "Bring the GIs home" reached India-Burma in full force, so CIC agents found themselves with the extra burden of observing and reporting the various aspects of the newspapers' campaign, while investigating in detail the origin of numerous pamphlets and other literature flooding U.S. troops.

In March 1946, lst Lt. Carl Manwell, who had arrived in India with the 108-man detachment in April 1944 as a corporal, became CO of the remaining CIC in India. He was followed shortly in that position on 16 April by lst Lt. Richard Klise, also a member of the original group as a sergeant. And on 30 April 1946 Klise wrote the last summary report for the theater, predicting that the trouble would continue. On that date the last CIC detachment was deactivated and all personnel reassigned home except for the CO who remained for a while as assistant AC of S, G-2.

CIC had closed another chapter of its history, and judging from the letters of commendation in its files, a most successful one. Records indicate that a large number of the Burma-India detachment were commended at one time or another for some specific task performed well, far too many to include in this account. But CIC veterans can be proud of the part played by their fellow-agents in keeping the Life-Line to China open.

* * *

At first, CIC detachments in China were scattered among several headquarters, but it soon became apparent they could not operate effectively with this arrangement. On 28 March 1945, all units were placed under Theater HQ with operational control by Theater G-2. Subordinate commanders were instructed to request CIC personnel on a temporary duty basis, and resident agents were also authorized.

In some places, CIC found security exceedingly low, but met with instant cooperation from installation commanders in accepting and implementing CIC recommendations, a spirit no doubt enhanced by the widespread knowledge of the Theater Commander's broad, and clear, directive.

The request for CIC agents to be assigned was so great that the solution was to establish resident agents at various SOS and Air Force headquarters throughout China. By the middle of April resident agents were in business: James Brook and George Reynolds at Chengtu; Lawrence Ballou and Eugene Tilley at Hsian; William Boggs at Paoshan; Lawrence Hughes at Yunnanyi; William Hoffman at Chanyi; Robert Scott at Kweiyang; and Kong Louie at Peishii.

The responsibilities placed on these agents is reflected in the directives quoted above, and in the command letters sent ahead of each agent telling the commander of his expected arrival and requesting quarters, rations, office supplies and vehicle maintenance.

Typical of this was the letter to the SOS area commander at Chanyi, advising him of the assignment of Hoffman as resident agent: "Mr. Hoffman has received specialized training in security matters and related subjects. His services should be of great value in improving conditions at your headquarters and in your subordinate commands ... His mission is of vital importance, for it is essential that effective measures be taken to prevent the enemy from obtaining information on our projects and installations."

The letter went on to explain that the agent's reports concerning security conditions were to be forwarded with endorsement explaining action taken on the agent's recommendations, but added that wherever security violations had been corrected at once, they need not be included in the agent's report—further evidence of the recognition given by the command to the judgment and ability of CIC agents.

* * *

At many installations, especially air force, CIC agents were credited with establishing cordial relations between American and Chinese; and in some places even bringing about a certain amount of harmony between purely Chinese agencies, an almost unheard of event.

From the beginning, U.S. personnel were keenly conscious of the vulnerability of information given to Chinese unit commanders because of the weakness of Chinese military counter-intelligence. In an effort to devise a plan whereby CIC could be best used to overcome this fault, agents Edward White and George Mah were sent in April 1945 to survey the situation in the Kwangsi command. During their 30-day trip, they visited Poseh headquarters and all the subordinate units except guerrilla battalions, interviewing most of the Chinese generals and ranking members of their staffs, American liaison officers, members of the French military mission in Tingsi, and representatives of OSS.

Throughout the command the agents found a most pleasant relationship between the Chinese and their U.S. Advisory Teams, which the Chinese seemed most anxious to extend to them also. But the agents found an equally serene disregard of an appreciation of the importance of security. They discovered the telephone was the principal means of communications, with its wires running in plain view over mountain trails rarely patrolled by repairmen, and often shared by civilians. Daily intelligence reports from division and regiments to higher echelons, and directives for tactical operations, all went over these lines—not in code, but in the clear. Often directives to troops en route were delivered to the village householder who had a telephone, to be relayed to the unit commander when he arrived.

In all the subordinate command headquarters, the intelligence and situation maps showing Chinese and enemy troop dispositions, routes and direction of movement, hung unprotected and clearly visible on the office or bedroom wall of the CG or chief of his operations staff. Unit moves were usually preceded by drinking parties to which festivities the townspeople were invited to help celebrate!

* * *

One of the tremendous problems recognized by the Chinese, but considered insoluble, was penetration of the area by literally thousands of Japanese troops disguised as Chinese coolies and sometimes as Chinese soldiers. These Japanese performed combat and reconnaissance missions, ambushing Chinese patrols, attacking Chinese units on the flanks, and often seizing villages in advance of Japanese troops. They often infiltrated a village, mingling with valid refugees until at a signal they would turn on the defending troops and "subdue" them.

The thousands of infiltrating "refugees" were natural barriers, defying identification as the enemy since they were so similar in appearance to the local Chinese. As Colonel Harwood Bowman, commander of U.S. forces in Quansi explained, the Japanese "have a genius for infiltration ... God Almighty might have identified them, but no one else could."

Various Chinese agencies working alone with no coordination with other agencies were engaged in half-hearted attempts to combat these sabotage and espionage agents. To CIC agents' surprise, numerous Japanese agents were being captured. But when CIC tried to discuss with Chinese officers the advantage of training a special group in various methods that had been proven most effective, the Chinese only commented that their suggestion had "merit."

About the only thing the agents were able to accomplish was an agreement that CIC teams could be attached to liaison groups. They felt this arrangement would at least enable them to tighten security within U.S. liaison headquarters, in some of which the Chinese philosophy had become a part of life.

* * *

At about the same time, Agent James Hunter, a Chinese linguist with long experience in China, was studying how the Chinese Services of Supply HQ protected highly classified information. They didn't! He ran into one amusing, though dangerous, example of Chinese handling of a TOP SECRET document:

Knowing of the U.S. Army's rigid control system, the Chinese made only one translation of this document, and added to it an appropriate cover sheet listing the names of Americans who should have access to it, but at the same time made an unlimited number of copies in Chinese and distributed them around headquarters with NO RECORD of their distribution.

Hunter laid much of the blame for this lackadaisical atmosphere on many U.S. officers who would not try to get along with the Chinese, consistently showing an air of superiority and a complete disrespect of Chinese rank.

As in the India-Burma Theater in the beginning, almost prohibitive losses of fuel were occurring through numerous taps along the gasoline pipeline. This line was one that began at Calcutta, continued up through Chabua in Assam and following generally the Stilwell Road through the mountains of Burma, entered China at Wanting and terminated in two branches at Luliang and Chanyi. Between 27 June and 13 August 1945, agent William Holland covered every foot of this line, arrested several culprits and gained information for future precautionary measures.

As a result of the survey made by White and Mah in April and early May, a seven-man detachment was assigned in early June 1945 to work with the Chinese Combat Command. This was on an experimental basis, with the threefold mission of a security survey of all American installations, setting up an educational security program for all Chinese units under training in the Command, and gathering counter-intelligence tactical information. SAC of the detachment was William Tyng, newly arrived from the North African Theater, with agents Frank St. Angel and John Bates (also new), James Carr, Edwin Simpson, Robert Edris and William Borga, who had come up from the jungles of North Burma. In addition to this team, agent Bernard Kotulak was assigned to the Command, with the specific duty of adapting American training methods in a program of security education for Chinese troops.

* * *

Agents Bates and Edris entered Kweilin on 29 July on the heels of the first Chinese Combat troops, the first Americans to enter the city. They found a complete traffic jam paralyzing the movement of military vehicles. They not only untangled the mess, but did so with such tact and diplomacy as to win the complete cooperation of the large number of Chinese commanders in the area. This enabled them to set up a refugee control plan quickly accepted by the Chinese; they also gathered a number of valuable enemy documents, and obtained considerable amount of positive and counter-intelligence information, including an impressive amount of order of battle data.

Operation of CIC's Resident Agents was rated as one of the most valuable activities in the China Theater. These residencies, which had been set up in April in seven different locations, handled not only espionage and sabotage cases, but also security clearances for civilian employees, collected counter-intelligence information, and performed many "diplomatic-type" missions. Their results were considered so valuable that by 1 August 1945 CIC agents were assigned to operate in 17 different locations, in addition to Theater AF HQ.

Some of these agents had barely moved in to their new locations when the Japanese surrender caused a complete reshuffle of personnel along with a change in CIC's mission to one of political reporting.

* * *

Communist plans to continue the war until their own objectives were won had long been known to Americans in China. But the flood of Soviet agents directed at learning everything possible about U.S. forces and intentions in China had scarcely been anticipated. Investigating employees infiltrated into U.S. installations ranked in importance with a hunt for war criminals and collaborationists.

In an official comment on the situation prepared in May 1946, Colonel Ivan Yeaton, G-2 for U.S. Army Forces in China, stated "Features of the existing situation during the entire period of CIC operations and activities in China have no real parallel in any theater of operations..."

Well before the end of 1945, CIC in China was daily encountering incidents and reliable information to prove that the Soviets were playing for big stakes in China. Agents were constantly deluged with reports disclosing that the undermining of U.S. interests and prestige was high on the Russian priority list.

In their unremitting efforts to eradicate any traces of American influence in China, the Russians were leaving few stones unturned. The 415th CIC detachment reported that a group of pro-Russian journalists and reporters met at the Soviet club in Shanghai on 8 July 1946 to discuss means by which political news could be obtained or suppressed. A Soviet expert in control of the press and reporters was charged with the mission of setting up a centralized procedure for the control of all news.

News releases under a Soviet-controlled press were to stress the failure of the Americans to take up for the Chinese people in Indo-China; all incidents of friction among the Americans and Chinese were to be exaggerated; and emphasis was to be given to the number of dead and wounded as a result of American aid to the Nationalists.

* * *

On 30 September 1946, the 415th CIC was officially deactivated. The personnel remaining were designated as the Security Control Section of the Army Advisory Group, with Major Fred Eggers in command. HQ for the section remained in Shanghai with three agents, and field offices operated in Nanking with three agents, and in Peking, with four agents.

In a report to the Director of Intelligence, WDGS, on 2 January 1947, Major Eggers explained: "Due to the requirement of General Marshall that no intelligence work be done within the American Forces in China, the identification of the CIC was changed to Security Control Section and no positive intelligence or counter-intelligence work is done where the Chinese Forces are concerned."

Practically the last case reported upon by American Counter-intelligence personnel in China was one that was merely reported as a fact, and not investigated because to do so seemed rather pointless. It concerned a shapely blond, apparently of Russian extraction, whose specialty was boarding U.S. vessels docking at Tsingtao, approaching Navy and Army officers aboard and asking them to visit a jade store where she could get them a discount. She would ask the officer to fill in his name, rank and service number on a card she gave him; jotting down similar data on a card she retained, she would explain that when he visited the shop his card would be checked against her list and she would receive credit for his purchases. A great way to accumulate names and ranks of U.S. services!

* * *

In April 1947, the CIC detachment was slowly closed out, while assisting the orderly evacuation of American civilians from troubled spots as the Communists continued their advance. In January 1949, when it became evident that all of the Chinese mainland would soon fall to the Communists, the last few CIC agents departed along with the remainder of the Army Advisory Group. Thus ended CIC's sojourn in China. Besides their regular missions, they had performed many "diplomatic-type" missions with results considered very valuable.

CHAPTER XXVIII

Lingayen to Manila

The dilemma CIC faced on Leyte and Luzon was the result of MacArthur and most of his staff having spent many years in the Philippines before the war. They had formed strong friendships with various Filipinos, some of whom had definitely collaborated with the Japanese. Were they compelled to do so through threats and blackmail? Or did they do it willingly, "buy-and-sell" opportunists taking advantage of the situation to enrich their own coffers? Those were the questions CIC agents faced when investigating prominent Filipinos. These cases had to be handled very, very carefully — like porcupines making love.

A classic example was the capture or "recovery" of those who served in the puppet government under the Japanese. As they came into the custody of CIC they would be taken to a "guest" house in Manila. Then the newspapers were watched: if a press release said the individual had been "captured" by the CIC, we knew he was one of the bad guys and proceeded openly with full investigation. But if the press reported "recovered," the caution signal was up, so we knew we had to use utmost caution in developing evidence.

For the most part, CIC was not interfered with, though there were some instances when it seemed to walk a tightrope. For instance, the Philippine Legislature tried to resume its sessions but was reported to be short of a quorum because CIC had so many of its members locked up. Temporary releases eased this situation for a while; ongoing investigations were not halted.

* * *

A vexing problem in Manila involved the local Chinese community which was engaged in a fratricidal war, with CIC in the middle (it was sometimes difficult to distinguish between some Chinese, Japanese, and Filipinos). Often vehicles driving by CIC locations hurled badly beaten or dead Chinese into the doorways.

In preparation for the work awaiting CIC on Luzon dealing with collaborators and potential spies, on 29 December 1944 MacArthur issued this:

MacArthur's Proclamation Preparing for Luzon Landing[22]
General Headquarters, Southwest Pacific Area

PROCLAMATION: *Providing for Military Measures to be taken upon the apprehension of citizens of the Philippines who voluntarily have given aid, comfort and sustenance to the enemy:*

WHEREAS, evidence is before me that certain citizens of the Philippines voluntarily have given aid, comfort and sustenance to the enemy in violation of allegiance due the Governments of the United States and the Commonwealth of the Philippines; AND

WHEREAS, military necessity requires that such persons be removed from any opportunity to threaten the security of our military forces or the success of our military operations,

NOW THEREFORE I, Douglas MacArthur, General of the Army, United States Army, as Commander in Chief Southwest Pacific Area, hereby do publish and declare it to be my purpose to remove such persons, when apprehended, from any position of political and economic influence in the Philippines and to hold them in restraint for the duration of the war; whereafter I shall release them to the Philippine Government for its judgment upon their respective cases.

Done at General Headquarters, Southwest Pacific Area, in the field this twenty-ninth day of December, 1944.

Douglas MacArthur
General of the Army
United States Army Commander in Chief[23]

The policy regarding enemy consulates and diplomatic installations was clarified by the following issued 19 January 1945, by

HEADQUARTERS, ADVANCE ECHELON—U.S. ARMY FORCES IN THE FAR EAST, APO 501 (FEGB 091.112):

SUBJECT: Policy with Respect to Consulates and other Diplomatic Installations

TO: Commanding General, Sixth Army, APO 442

Commanding General, Eighth Army, APO 343

1. Enemy consulate or other bona fide diplomatic installation not in the hands of a neutral or protecting power will be sealed and maintained intact. This headquarters will be advised of such cases and will issue instructions for final disposition.

2. Enemy consulates or other bona fide diplomatic installations in the custody of a neutral or protecting power will be left in the hands of the protecting power, and the facts in each case reported to this headquarters.

3. Neutral or allied consulates or diplomatic installations that

---

22 *CIC arrested 5000+ on this authority*
23 *This and following document found in papers of Wm Owens*

have been seized by the enemy will be sealed and reported to this headquarters. Full description of condition in which they are found should accompany reports. Such installations will be given necessary security until they can be returned to proper authority of the interested government. The return of these installations will be made only on direction from this headquarters.

By Command of General MacArthur
(SIGNED) Leonard S. Carroll, Lt Colonel., AGD
Ass't Adjutant General

* * *

On 9 January 1945, elements of the Sixth Army invaded Luzon, the main Philippine Island, going ashore at Lingayen Gulf at the exact spot where the Japanese had landed three years previously. Although the Japanese had greater numbers of troops, they were taken completely off guard. They were expecting our solders to land elsewhere, as nearly every major hostile unit was in motion—and not towards Lingayen when we landed.

Here for the first time in SWPA, CIC discharged its missions on a tremendous scale. It employed 29 CIC detachments, of which 16 were combat teams, in the fighting phase and the days immediately following. Assault troops from the 40th and 37th Divisions under XIVth Corps stormed ashore at 9:30 a.m., D-day, with their attached CIC detachments close on their heels. At the same time, the 6th and 43rd Divisions under I Corps with their CIC landed on the left flank.

As in Leyte, the 441st CIC at Theater HQ in Hollandia exercised administrative control. But again the combat operations were directed by Sixth Army's 306th CIC under officer-agent Blair Labatt. As combat troops passed through villages and cities, a dozen area teams moved in to relieve the combat CIC units and assume CI jurisdiction under supervision by the 493rd Regional Detachment under CO Lowell "Lokey" Bradford.

CIC teams from the 201st (I Corps) under officer-agent Victor Cook, the 6th under officer-agent James R. Webster, and 43rd under officer-agent Ray Hodgson were on Luzon soil within an hour after the first assault troops hit the beaches. Elements of 214th CIC (XIVth Corps) under officer-agent Marvin C. Goff, Jr, including the 37th under officer-agent James E. Stilwell, landed later that day on the south shore. As the 40th Division occupied Bolanio Peninsula, its CIC under officer-agent Earl A. Klein was on its heels. The advance echelon of Sixth Army's 306th CIC landed the following day.

The second day after the landing, the 214th agents opened an office in Tarlac province; agents of the 21st and the 442nd came in a few days later. First Cavalry's 801st CIC, plus the 32nd, 33rd, 901st (attached to 158th Regimental Combat Team), and the 902nd (with the 112th Regimental Team) soon came ashore.

CIC operations began quickly as each unit landed. One of the first prisoners turned out to be a Kempei Tai agent, who led CIC to two others in hiding; they also confessed and gave information which led to the capture of the organization's executive officer. Convinced that Japan was losing the war, this officer then led CIC to a cave occupied by the Kempei Tai.

The 214th's Goff and his corps team were also busy from the very beginning. Among the first to greet them was an American soldier who had been operating as a guerrilla during the war. He rode up to the 214th's tent in an old topless vehicle, shouting words crudely printed on a banner: "Tapos na! Tapos na!"—Tagalog for "It's all over now." We questioned him on potential enemy agents among the civilians—who had collaborated with the Japanese, who were Sakdalistas, and other pro-Japanese organization members. He was then sent on to higher headquarters for a complete debriefing.

Suspected collaborators began to be brought in by loyal Filipinos happy with the arrival of our troops. Agent Roger W. Mullin was the first to use his skill at eliciting information from a suspect. While he was busy, local guerrillas brought in another, whom I undertook to question.

Securing confessions at this stage was comparatively easy. Being brought in by neighbors who knew of their pro-Japanese activities, suspects quickly broke down and usually made full confessions, in effect throwing themselves on the well-known mercy of the Americans, not aware that though CIC arrested them, the Philippine government would prosecute them. The subject I questioned confessed he had led a downed American flyer straight to the headquarters of the Kempei Tai, who executed the flyer. I conducted the questioning in Spanish through a Filipino who understood Spanish and the dialect of suspect. This was the only time I had to use this foreign language which had qualified me for CIC. But, I had studied and practiced Tagalog, the widespread trade language of the Philippines, on ship all the way from Bougainville, with the Filipinos attached to the 214th.

Movement of the leading divisions down the highway toward Manila was so swift, it was at times difficult for the 214th CIC to keep up. At the town of Tarlac there were a few days of rest, and here it was that the weakness of the Filipinos attached to CIC became fully apparent. They for the most part spoke and understood only Tagalog, the principal language of the five main ones. There were literally dozens of different dialects not classified as languages. From the Dagupan landing at Lingayen to Manila there were two or more dialects unlike Tagalog and impossible for our interpreters to translate.

We had been existing on army K-rations. The agents began to hunger for a real meal daily. I spotted a tent on the outskirts of Tarlac that was serving officers. Recalling memories of news from Europe on the "civilian" status of CIC agents there, plus more recent memories of using my badge in the jungles to get things accomplished, I took three of our hungry agents into the tent, cautioning each to be sure his badge was in position under their fatigue lapels as mine was. We four sat down to a sumptuous feast.

Before finishing, I finally took my eyes off the food long enough to look around—and spotted Lt. Colonel John N. "Jack" Irwin II at a nearby table looking in our direction. We continued to eat and had almost finished when Irwin got up, walked over to our table, put a hand on my shoulder and said, "Good to see you boys. Hope you had a good meal—but please don't do this again. If what you did gets out, it can cause CIC HQ a lot of trouble."

Then he left. As requested, we did not repeat the incident—but I have never forgotten his kindness in allowing us to finish our meal; from his demeanor I felt he was on our side. I knew the army policy in SWPA was not what most of our dedicated CIC officers would have wanted it, and we with combat teams had to endure the status quo.

Perhaps Irwin reported this to Goff, though Goff never said a word to me and the others about it. Goff did however find among our Filipino team a couple who said they could cook, and we established our own mess from then on. This served us well, right through the battle of Manila, where our headquarters was only a few blocks from the fighting to cross the Pasig River into Intramuros, the old walled city where the Japanese troops were holed up.

* * *

Agent W. David Krieger was with the 6th CIC team, and his story paints more of the life of a combat agent at the front on Luzon:

"My tour of duty in SWPA began in March 1944 when I joined the 6th CIC in Port Moresby, New Guinea. I stayed with 6th Division's 1st Inf Regiment until time to load up ship for the liberation of Luzon, landing there at Lingayen Gulf on 9 January 1945. After this landing, Leon Mohr, John Nugent, John Walker, a Filipino and a Nisei joined the unit on the drive to Manila. The 1st Cavalry Division had landed and was the spearhead down the main road to Manila, with 6th Division protecting its left flank. My unit followed the 1st and 20th Reg. on

6th Division's left flank.

"As towns would fall to our leading troops, CIC agents worked with PCAU (Philippine Civilian Affairs Unit) to set up local governments; this brought temporary order out of chaos caused by military operations. We uncovered and arrested three collaborators on our march south toward Manila, one quite by accident. While going through the town hall of a middle-sized city, we came across records and speeches that implicated an important local person using an assumed name.

"When we picked him up and interrogated him, he at first denied being involved; after further questioning he finally admitted he was collaborating but only because he was being forced by the Japanese. Our additional investigation revealed he and his family enjoyed a very good life under enemy rule. Interrogation was through our Filipino interpreters. We delivered him to the division MPs for internment.

"In the first contacts with the notorious Hukbalajaps, we thought they would cooperate with us in establishing order. The two other cases we picked up were with the help of local civilians including the Huks. As our troops liberated towns, we were met by various groups of citizens and the Hukbalajaps were among them; all were anxious to gain control of power and leadership and our problem was to determine whom to believe. In both cases, the "small fry" who were loyal to the enemy during the occupation would betray the loyal Filipinos. We were quickly disillusioned by the Huk's machinations in installing picked men in strategic spots while doing away, permanently in most instances, with their perceived Filipino adversaries.[24]

"The fourth collaborator we arrested was Jose Tomas, a waiter at the Army-Navy Club in Manila before the war who claimed he was treated as a slave by its officers. He became sold on the Japanese philosophy: "Asia for Asians"—and abided with that theory. He spoke Japanese and English fluently, and could read and write English.

"Tomas was brought to our office in Marikina, a small town east of Manila on the Pasig River. Our soldiers had caught him crossing rice paddies from our area headed toward enemy positions in the hills. He carried a crude map showing the locations of our units in Manila and surrounding area. He also had Japanese invasion pesos.

"I conducted the interrogation in a room on the second floor of our office, which was a fine concrete block home with a two-car garage, with little war damage. After patient, consistent questioning he finally admitted to spying for his friends the Japanese. Since he could write English I invited him to write his own "statement" (a better

---

[24] *Provost Marshal's CID agents were unhappy with CIC arresting murderers, but CID agents were rarely as close to the front as CIC which had to stabilize towns.*

word than "confession" I thought) of what he had done, and exactly why. I left him alone, thinking this would create a better atmosphere for the truth.

* * *

"While downstairs congratulating myself on the catch, I remembered a fully loaded tommy gun standing against the wall of the room he occupied. I called upstairs and asked his progress, and got a positive answer. So up the stairs I went, with my .38 ready, entered the room—and observed he was still writing—so picking up the tommy gun I left him to finish. When he had, I read the statement aloud and then asked him to cover other items we had discussed, and he obliged. I had him write also "This statement is made without threat of prosecution or promise of immunity"—signed and witnessed by me. Later he was charged with treason.[25]

"After Manila was liberated, my unit was stationed in Marikina. Surviving Japanese troops were in the mountains to the east, and the 1st Infantry Regiment had the mission of driving them out and preventing their retreat to Baguio to join with the troops there. CIC helped establish a temporary but stable government in the area as well as in the portion of Manila under our team's jurisdiction."

* * *

Recall the problems that agent Jerry Alajajian had with Canon in New Guinea? Jerry was now with the 43rd CIC detachment as it landed parallel to Dave Krieger's 6th. Here is his story on Luzon:

From the 9 January landing to 26 February, Jerry was assigned to establish and maintain liaison with a group of guerrilla intelligence agents to obtain tactical and counter-intelligence information. At times he and his detachment worked in an isolated barrio with no combat U.S. troops nearby, with Japanese soldiers infiltrating the barrio, some in civilian clothes mingling with the civilians. Guerrilla Captain Diego Sipin became ill and asked Jerry and another agent to take charge of his battalion. Jerry obliged.

* * *

At times coming under artillery and small arms fire, plus the nightly infiltration, he was able to direct the guerrillas in locating and neutralizing the enemy artillery, plus securing sketch maps of the enemy's troop dispositions. And thanks to his liaison with this guerrilla unit, Alajajian was responsible for apprehending two notorious enemy collaborators.[26]

He also spent time with another guerrilla unit known as Marking's Guerrillas, headed by a Colonel Marcos of the Philippine Army. He was with this band when it received the mission of attack-

---

[25]   *Krieger received Bronze Star for this and other cases*
[26]   *For which he was awarded the Bronze Star*

ing Japanese to prevent them from blowing up an important dam. The guerrillas recruited 75 local natives as supply carriers for the operation. At the last moment, the carriers balked and wouldn't follow the guerrillas. Jerry grabbed a bull-horn and gave the carriers a 20-minute dressing down, using all the native language terms he had picked up, in an effort to shame them. After his impassioned speech all 75 picked up packs and carried the ammo and supplies! No medal for that great speech, but Jerry felt rewarded.

* * *

On 16 May 1945, Alajajian was with an officer and an enlisted man in a jeep, trying to cross the Angot River, Luzon. In mid stream, the wheels of the jeep dropped into a hidden hole overturning the vehicle and throwing all into the water. The officer could not overcome the swift current and was being carried down stream when Jerry spotted his trouble and immediately went to the rescue, pulled the officer to safety after the current had carried them more than a hundred yards. For his thinking and initiative above and beyond the call of duty in a non-combat situation, Alajajian was awarded the Soldier's Medal.

* * *

On 29 January 1945, CIC units landed at Subic Bay, Luzon, with XIth Corps and the 38th Division which moved to cut off the Bataan Peninsula from use by the Japanese. Two days later the 11th CIC made an amphibious landing with its Airborne Division at Nasugbu Bay, south of Manila. The vise was closing in on Manila.

Initially Lt. Colonel John N. Irwin, as field representative of G-2 USAFFE, supervised and coordinated CI work in Luzon, while Major Labatt, Commander of the 306th CIC, was responsible for CIC.

The drive on Manila became a sprint in late January, with the lst Cavalry and the 37th Infantry Divisions racing toward the Philippine capital from the north, and the 11th Airborne advancing from the south. CIC agents followed their host units closely in a rapid push across the Luzon plain toward Manila. At each town on the way, CIC agents placed prominent and reliable citizens into municipal key offices, aided greatly by black lists and white lists prepared in advance of the operation by Theater HQ.

* * *

John Irwin made this special report to General Thorpe on CIC from landings through the drive to Manila:

"On the 13th I set up our office at the food market in Dagupan, i.e., two tables and chairs, and then went to find CIC. The 214th CIC had a 4-man sub-detachment at the Municipal Building. The 37th Division had taken Dagupan and Lt. Duven, second in command of the 37th CIC, took charge of the town and set up the local administration (no PCAU yet). Duven did an excellent job. As the 37th CIC moved forward, the 214th took over. Many collaborators left with the enemy to Baguio, but two were picked up plus one Japanese in civilian clothes (unknown whether a soldier or not, but probably is). The governor will be picked up today or tomorrow. He is still in the area. The people in town speak well of him, but he swore allegiance to the puppet government, and has played the politician, so he comes under MacArthur's proclamation. Some Japanese moved to Tarlac, which appears to be the first position they may defend in strength.

"The 214th CIC, in addition to the office in the Municipal Building, has located one house. I had Kelley locate others, envisioning one for CIC and one for Censorship. Labatt showed up, went over the CIC situation with the Agent in Charge, gave them necessary information, instructions, etc. He had spent the nights of plus 1 and 2 on White Beach, under mortar fire one night and dug a foxhole down to water level with his helmet!

"Labatt and I drove over to Binmaley, and spent a couple of hours with 214th CIC and the Corps G-2. All seems to be going well with the 214th and with the 37th and 40th under it. Labatt went over everything with 214th's Goff and Spencer, who had not received MacArthur's proclamation, USAFFE letter or the Japanese and German civilian one. We also saw Stilwell of the 37th.

"For the first time I met the C-in-C and General Sutherland and was able to show him some enemy codes captured by the 185th Infantry at Sual. The situation is moving very fast. They hope to be in Manila in 30-40 days. Hollings should drop all studies except Manila and get copies to me as soon as possible and I will see Labatt gets them for distribution."

After Tarlac fell, Lt. Colonel Irwin sent Thorpe this follow-up report:

"Yesterday I drove to 201st again with Labatt to discuss with Cook disposition of detachments when GHQ and USAFFE move to Tarlac. Labatt plans to put Geiss' area detachment in Tarlac, leave Swanson in Dagupan under Cook. Cook will then cover all areas north of Tarlac with the 25th, 6th, 43rd, 201st, Swanson's area detachment and Recor's 158th. Labatt's 306th and Geiss' area detachment will cover Tarlac and area behind 214th, 37th and 40th."

"Because of the fast movement, CIC is spread rather thin. By the time we reach Manila, Labatt could use three more area detachments in addition to Goodrick's area team. Does CIC have them available? If you can get them from Hollandia to Leyte, we can get them over here."

"One thing the 37th and 214th failed in Dagupan was seize constabulary, municipal, etc., records. Labatt is putting out instructions: the most positive proof of collaboration is documents. The fine example of this was McColl's case versus Major Reyes, the constabulary head in Tacloban. Papers and records are just now beginning to turn up in Dagupan; one example: the governor's reports to the Japanese Military Police. They are by far the most damning evidence against the governor. That sort of thing CIC must pick up immediately.

"Three things division CIC should do (simultaneously, if possible!): pick up known collaborators, seize all municipal and Japanese records, newspapers, post offices, and establish municipal government and order (this last, if PCAU not yet there). The way 801st CIC took records in Tacloban and McColl's area detachment followed is a good example. Situation here is more difficult; 214th CIC's had combat duties and could only put a few agents in Dagupan. That is the great advantage of having area detachments. In this case Geiss' 442nd area had not yet landed. That was no fault of anyone, just that we advanced faster than people guessed. Labatt is moving an area team into Tarlac as soon as possible, then things should be smooth there."

* * *

As our troops fought on south toward Manila, CIC agents were gathering information on collaborators and enemy agents, while making contact with guerrilla leaders who also were supplying them with vital data. Search and seizure teams located and took charge of documents and counter-intelligence equipment in the public buildings and former Japanese garrisons—especially when they found a former site of the Kempei Tai. Here were often lists of names and evidence of collaboration and disloyalty to the Philippines and U.S.

CHAPTER XXIX

Mindanao and the Floating CIC

In the final months of 1943 MacArthur was blessed with two armies, the Sixth commanded by Krueger and the Eighth which Eichelberger now commanded. While the Sixth was recovering Manila and mopping up elsewhere on Luzon, the Eighth headed south. The next major Allied objective in the Philippines was Mindanao, second largest island of the Archipelago. Although scattered areas of this island, especially in the north, were already in the hands of pro-American guerrillas, the liberation of the entire island proved third only to Leyte and Luzon in magnitude and special difficulties faced. Aside from its vast size and rugged terrain, Mindanao presented one new perplexing puzzle: the large Japanese civilian population.

Agents of the 41st CIC landed on the beach on an April morning immediately after the first assault elements. After setting up an office in Zamboanga, they established liaison with all other allied units and guerrillas, and by D-plus-4 had completed most of the urgent CI targets. Within a month a CIC-approved panel of citizens was governing the city of Zamboanga, and CIC was following the tactical teams into the province to search out enemy command posts, and enforce security regulations.

The second major phase of the Mindanao operation began on 17 April 1945 when, after air and naval bombardment, General Eichelberger sent Xth Corps of his Eighth Army ashore at Malabang. Joining in the landings with 210th CIC were the 24th CIC, beaching on 17 April, and the 31st, which went ashore five days later with their combat troops.

Three days after landing, the 210th CIC team learned the unpredictable Moro tribesmen were gathering at Dalican, posing armed threat to the allies. The Task Force commander dispatched a message to the leader of the more than 100,000 Moros, demanding that he come at once to Task Force HQ. Three days later the Moro chief showed up with eleven of his followers; after a conference, he agreed to surrender the 400 firearms held by his tribesmen "as soon as the area was cleared of the Japanese."

Davao city was known as "Little Tokyo," home of most of the Japanese nationals living in Mindanao. When the 210th CIC entered

Davao, they expected to find an unusually tense atmosphere in the Japanese community. Instead, it was mostly empty, as most of the Japanese citizens had followed the Japanese troops into the hills. CIC interned and interrogated the few who had remained.

Five agents of the 40th CIC team splashed ashore in the initial assault on Panay Island, on 18 March 1945; others went to the other main Panayan island of Negros. Important finds on both islands included numerous collaborators and spies, plus an incriminating file of letters written by Panay's puppet governor.

The last remaining major islands of the Philippine Archipelago, Cebu and Bohol, were recaptured by early April 1945. As in Manila, Cebu City had been burned and sacked by the fleeing Japanese, and a large number of suspected collaborators began turning themselves in for fear of retaliation by local guerrilla elements. A total of 156 were arrested on Cebu. On Bohol, CIC found that the guerrillas had already arrested 250 suspects. CIC released some of both of these groups, following preliminary investigations.

* * *

To the south of Mindanao, in July 1945, the Australian 9th Brigade began dealing with the Japanese troops in Brunei, British North Borneo. The Field Security team attached to this unit had requested and received the loan of two CIC agents. Agents George Charon and Charles D. Baker were the two CIC men assigned to this operation that kept them there until the war was over. The very first day Charon spotted a local Japanese the Aussies were hiring as an interpreter, and recognizing the name immediately as being on the wanted list the 441st had put out, placed him under arrest!

CIC investigations required securing testimony in the form of written statements from witnesses to acts of collaboration, if time permitted, before interning suspects for the Philippine government to put on trial later on. The guerrillas often interned fellow Filipinos on mere suspicion, nothing more than a hunch by our standards. This is why CIC released some suspects which the guerrillas had jailed. Some were picked up again later on, when CIC turned up further satisfactory evidence.

By summer of 1945 combat operations in the Philippines had ended except for skirmishes with isolated pockets of fanatical Japanese soldiers still hiding out in mountain caves. Some combat CIC detachments had already pushed on to Okinawa, while teams that remained in the Philippines were training for Operation OLYMPIC, the planned invasion of Japan.

Regional and area CIC units that were hopping from island to island found transportation to be a tremendous problem. They partially solved this when Thorpe, now a general, obtained for these CIC units a 105 foot air-sea rescue boat, provided by the Transportation Corps. He placed this boat in charge of Region 2 CO Paul A. Hurst, who then organized an 11-man "floating detachment" under Jack Y. Canon (to keep him out of the way, it was rumored).

* * *

CIC's only Floating Detachment[27]

"The Battle of Manila was over, the enemy hiding in mountains and on numerous islands of the Philippines, but CIC's mission was far from over. Another 1,000 or so enemy spies, saboteurs, and collaborators were yet to be caught and added to 4,000-plus already in prisons awaiting trial and judgment. Still few in numbers, CIC agents with combat and area teams were scattered throughout Philippines' major islands. Communication, transportation of prisoners and supplies were ever present problems. That was CIC's dilemma as summer 1945 approached.

"441st HQ was concerned on how to maintain liaison with all the agents; neither manpower nor equipment from Army or Navy existed to serve this vital need. CIC, resourceful as usual, went hunting. It found and captured the unseaworthy but available 105 foot QS-6, built by Ventnor Boat Works, Ventnor, New Jersey, originally for the Air Force for a Rescue Boat; the AF had then rejected it as unseaworthy! CIC was welcome to it. Two Packard engines gave it a 24 knot cruising speed. CIC office and living quarters were in the stern, where agents enjoyed deep bunks with innerspring mattresses, and the luxury of an ample galley and refrigeration system. A far cry from foxholes.

"441st created a special team under the supervision of the 492nd, and set it on the QS-6 to cruise Philippine waters and bring CIC detachments closer together. Jack Y. Canon was CO, with SAC David McCarthy, and agents William H. Sloan, Henry M. Malden and Dixon Palmones completing the CIC roster. The men operating the ship were a U.S. Army engineer unit captained by WO (jg) Harry M. Campbell.

"QS-6 CIC contacted agents in remote cities, towns and barrios, inaccessible by road from area detachment headquarters. It also shifted CIC personnel from one place to another as needed, and carried supplies to isolated teams. It moved through Philippine seas without escort, as the Japanese Navy was believed to be nonexistent.

"Floating CIC's maiden voyage was in May 1945, touching at ports in the Mindoro-Palawan islands. Its second trip included stops at Panay, Mindoro, Romblon, Masbate, Marinduque, Busuanaga, Culion, Simara, Tablas and Luzon. Shortly before VJ day, disaster

---

[27] *Contributed by David McCarthy*

struck between Leyte and Samar, in San Juanaco Straits. McCarthy was not at the helm at the time, though he had been on several occasions. QS-6 went aground when McCarthy and agent Frank Seiter (traveling from Tacloban to Bacolod, on the island of Negros) were in their bunks. Damaged but still above water, QS-6 limped to a repair station on Mactan Island. It was there this CIC unit celebrated VJ day, awaiting repairs to their sub-office, the QS-6.

"Tiny Mactan is notable as the burial place of Ferdinand Magellan. It also was the site of Dad Clelland's Dry Dock & Ship Repairs; it was Dad himself who patched up the PT boats commanded by Lt. Bulkeley in the process of transporting General MacArthur, wife, son and staff from Corregidor to Mindanao.

* * *

"Clelland's boatworks was the premier operation for building, repairing and maintaining water craft, in existence over 30 years when MacArthur's party paused there for repairs on the way to Australia. They invited Dad to join them to avoid capture, but he declined to leave the home and business he had devoted a lifetime to. As expected, he was captured and interned in the Manila area. U.S. troops returned to Luzon with top orders to rescue Dad Clelland. When located, he was provided the best that medics and dietitians could give him, so he could resume his operations: our Naval and Army small craft desperately required his expertise.

"When our Floating Detachment limped into Clelland's, Dad was 74, still a tremendous physical specimen operating his business with zest. While QS-6 was being made less unseaworthy, McCarthy stayed with Sam Schneidman's CIC unit in nearby Cebu City. "Seacat" Les Harrison was also there.

"As the senior agent on the QS-6, each morning McCarthy hitched a barge to Mactan to check on repairs. Dad would take time out to talk, explaining in detail what was necessary to keep afloat. And—he got CIC's Floating Detachment going again on its trip.

"One memorable event involved Bert Osmeña, a son of the P.I. president. One afternoon while QS-6 was docked in Manila preparing for a run through the Islands that evening, a truck rolled up and pulled close to the fantail. Stevedores began hauling cases of liquor aboard; it was a shipment of brandy, a product of Chile destined to Bert's home in Cebu City.

"Upon departure from Manila, there were 28 cases of 12 bottles each; on arrival at Cebu City there were only 27 cases. It seems one case was lost either in heavy seas or in combat! It was rumored that a number of CIC detachments at Cebu, Panay, Negros, Bohol, Mindoro,

Samar, Leyte and points east, west, north and south, were able to slake their thirsts with a certain, potent amber fluid. A visit from the Floating CIC was always welcomed."

* * *

The Forgotten Ship of the CIC Fleet

Agent James F. Conway, former Chicago attorney, felt that the Floating CIC Detachment's boat was not the only one in CIC's Fleet. This account of the vessel his unit acquired and used provides yet another picture of the life of a CIC agent in a lonely, isolated part of the Philippine Islands:

"One of the Floating CIC Detachment stops was at the Negros 487th detachment commanded by Dudley Skinker, leader of the 130 Skinker's Stinkers. Besides myself,[28] on the 487th team were: Leon Ashmore, James Bailey, Bernard Bergreen, Conrad Deslauriers, Louis Farley, Joseph Krys, Irving Levine, Rowland Quisenberry, Frank Seiter and Robert Schell. Levine was CO after Skinker was recalled to Manila.

"Disappointedly, the 487th's vessel was not mentioned by McCarthy. Also in 'Ann Bray's' CIC history, I find no mention of the magnificent boat that served our isolated unit so faithfully.

"Picture it: a 30-foot inboard Higgins boat, with rain-proof cabin midship with a machine gun turret in the center of the roof. We lacked the fixed machine gun, but if needed we could fire through the turret opening with a tommy gun ... the *Chicago Typewriter* lads from the 6th Service Command considered their personal weapon.

"The boat was a great platform from which to toss grenades into the water. This improved our food supplies: concussion from one grenade usually stunned a fine mess of fish to the surface, providing a nice fish fry.

"We acquired this dandy addition to the CIC Fleet in order to get our supplies from the Navy base at Iloilo, Panay, twenty miles across the strait from Negros. We boated over, high in the water, and after visiting the Panay CIC team as well as the Navy base, returned almost awash; our decks were invariably overloaded with crates of supplies, our biggest fear being the cases of beer would be washed overboard.

"Also, fresh water was not available at our 'marinas' (usually a bamboo pier or jetty); hauling it from the island's fresh water sources in buckets and jerrycans was a chore. The Army engineer inherited with our boat found it a bother, so he improvised. To save fresh water that was being used in the engine's cooling system, the engineer converted to salt water.

"One of our most valued informants on Negros was Judge Pablo Rivera, graduate of Cornell Law School, USA. Interrogated and tor-

---

[28] *Contributed by James F Conway*

tured many times by the Japanese, he did not waiver in his loyalty to P.I. and the U.S. When the war ended, CIC invited him and his family to take a ride with us on 'our' boat. One of the Rivera girls, Aiada, later took her Master's degree at U. of Michigan and married an American working in P.I. for Voice of America.

"I recall McCarthy's visit because I actually stepped onto the 'flagship' of the CIC fleet. Sitting at the jetty adjacent to our little thirty footer, QS-6 looked to us like the Queen Mary!

"McCarthy failed to mention one of the most popular members of his crew—known as Ape. Ape was great for morale on the QS-6. Possessing only a limited capacity for beer, Ape reacted to drinking same by reeling and stumbling like a human—which Ape wasn't. Normally Ape could fly across the deck from a stanchion to a guy wire, but with a little beer intake the results were disastrous, in fact very messy as he made a monkey of himself. But all personnel as well as natives assembled on the dock roared with laughter at Ape's antics.

"QS-6, the flagship, was warmly welcomed by all out-of-way island detachments. We knew there was an efficient refrigerator on board to keep medicines fresh. And we knew the QS-6 team would share its ample larder of cold beer, as well as its torpedo juice *iced martinis.*"

* * *

There are recorded instances (probably unrecorded ones as well) of CIC agents elsewhere making use of boats in their missions, but none involved the deliberate placement of a CIC detachment aboard ship for any extended time period, to-wit:

On 21 April 1943, the South Pacific CIC Detachment, Island Command # 3, Espiritu Santo Island, had acquired a fifty-foot fishing vessel for island patrol work. The vessel was manned for CIC by a Navy Warrant Officer and two Ensigns. And our agents protecting the Panama Canal definitely had two schooners—one in the Atlantic, one in the Pacific—for security work by November 1942. Agents stationed in a spy hot spot like Iceland, surrounded by the sea, undoubtedly had authority to summon boats when needed.

"MacLand" 24 April 1944: the CO of CIC Combat Det. "C," 1st Cavalry Division, recommended a boat be made available for CIC. This request was followed 9 May 1944 by 201st CIC commanded by Victor Cook, with I Corps then at Hollandia, New Guinea, urging that CIC be authorized an 18-foot inboard motor boat for amphibious operations. Records do not reveal if such requests were honored.

* * *

The floating CIC sub-office of Region 2 moved from island to island, speeding the process of screening collaborators. Smaller boats which the Region CIC already possessed enabled it to accomplish a number of purposes: they could transfer agents on short notice, deliver supplies, control unauthorized shipping, carry important written messages, and make contact with guerrillas in remote areas.

CHAPTER XXX

Incident at Burauen, Leyte[29]

Shots rang out across the plaza. Chips of stone flew from the pillars in front of the Municipal Building. The ricocheting bullets were flying in the direction of the 66th General Hospital, a U.S. Army unit with 1,500 bed patients. The idea of bullets flying off in the direction of those men lying on cots in a tent hospital roused the hair on the back of agent Arthur Hurlburt's neck. It took only a fraction of a second to decide to intervene.

In the early days of 1945 the 11th Airborne Division had swept through a city called Burauen, in central Leyte. The 11th followed the Japanese north and their CIC detachment went with them, leaving their house and files in care of a young agent until the area CIC could relieve him.

CIC in the Southwest Pacific Area was organized with a little over half its people in Area Detachments, the rest with combat Divisions, Corps and Army. As the combat agents moved forward with the troops, they were followed by the area teams, who were set up to work in a geographical area as long as needed, or at least longer than the combat troops. In Burauen this "as long as needed" turned out to be about five months, until a greater need for area CIC services was seen on the nearby island of Negros.

It was apparent on arrival at Burauen, a city of 35,000, that a huge challenge faced agent Hurlburt. While the upper crust of its society, school teachers, mayor, priest and a smattering of others, spoke English, Hurlburt was at sea in communicating with the rest of the population. How could he best carry out CIC's mission in this, his assigned area? The Japanese having just been driven out, the city and surrounding barrios were in total disarray. People were dying like flies from dysentery and other tropical diseases. For them there was no hospital and no regular system for distribution of food. A municipal government, mayor and police chief, had been set up by the 11th Airborne CIC, along with a makeshift relief system since PCAU had never shown up here.

The first incident on Hurlburt's first morning in Burauen was the stopping of a funeral procession in front of the house. They stood there, patiently waiting; they expected him to come out and open the

---

coffin to ensure there were no weapons inside. Eleventh Airborne CIC had found a pushcart holding a coffin turned over on the street spilling weapons of war—rifles, hand grenades, tommy guns. To be sure there was no more of that, the 11th decreed that each and every funeral procession would stop by CIC headquarters for inspection. With the center of combat miles away, Hurlburt told them such inspections would no longer be required.

On the day the shots rang out, a man was dodging the bullets, running zigzag, trying to make it into the front door of the Municipal Building. Four men with rifles were coming along behind, taking pot shots at him. They were all Filipinos. And CIC had no business, rather, no duty, to interfere in local affairs, let alone shoot-ups. CIC was in no way to involve itself in criminal matters, especially criminality among foreign nationals. But bullets were flying in the direction of wounded American soldiers. This bothered him and there seemed no one else around to do anything about it.

How do you approach four men, armed with rifles when you are carrying only a revolver? Very gingerly. Hurlburt sauntered across the plaza, not making any threatening gestures, watching the first man surrender his weapon to another, then all go into the Municipal Building. By that time he speeded up and arrived at the front door just as they were going out the back. Running through, he saw a large crowd gathered at the rear of the building, standing around an open area containing three of the four shooters. They were still armed. Standing at the edge of the crowd was a Captain, the commanding officer of the Sanitation Company of the 66th. Hurlburt approached him to ask if there was any way he could assist. But the Captain spoke first, volunteering to assist the agent! Half a dozen of the Captain's men were beside him. Something had to be done, and fast. Without further discussion Hurlburt said, "Grab him," pointing to one of the men. "Put him in a cell on the second floor of the Municipal Building." The man made no resistance. The second man also gave up with no fight. The third was going amok, ripping his shirt off, frothing at the mouth and swinging his rifle around him like a club. He was quickly overpowered and jailed also.

Where was the fourth man? The crowd pointed and the Captain with two of his men and the agent went off in that direction. Bystanders from the vantage point of second story windows directed the search party, and after four blocks their quarry jumped out from behind a house, standing in the middle of the street, with his rifle held at the ready.

Agent Hurlburt was not about to pull a weapon or make threatening gestures to a man armed with a better weapon. And the Captain and his men had no weapons at all. Hurlburt gestured, with a downward waving motion, for the Filipino to lay his rifle down. He understood and complied. Hurlburt then gestured for him to step back, which he also did. Then the agent told the sergeant with the Captain to step forward carefully and pick up the rifle. Which ended the incident, at least the hairy part.

* * *

CIC now had in custody four men who turned out to be Filipino soldiers. Earlier, at least one of them had been drinking and a policeman came in and decided to have fun chasing him. The chase had turned into a shooting match, when Hurlburt entered the scene.

The Captain and the agent thanked each other and the officer went on his way, leaving CIC with the problem of what to do with these men. But not for long. A Filipino corporal, resident of Burauen, whom the agent knew, came and pleaded to let the men go. "Filipino soldiers could not stand being in jail, it would mean their utter destruction." They must be released before night. He would be responsible for their conduct and would get them out of town immediately. Hurlburt relented on the three who had given up peacefully and released them into the corporal's custody. But the fourth man was sent off in a truck from CIC headquarters in Dulag and taken to an MP enclosure. He was released a couple of days later as no one showed up to press charges.

But the agent kept their rifles and told the corporal that their commander could pick them up the next day. He then sat down and typed up a receipt for them and relaxed until morning. Sure enough, after breakfast, along came a weapons carrier carrying eight men armed to the teeth. They looked like a group of Mexican bandits, with belts of rifle ammo strung across their shoulders, hand grenades hanging from their belts, one carrying a Browning automatic rifle, two with tommy guns, the others with an assortment of weapons. Their leader, who called himself Captain Cinco, leaped up the front steps, came in and politely asked for the rifles. Hurlburt invited him to sit and sign the receipt, which he did graciously and departed with his guns. Captain Cinco, labeled in a Colliers magazine article around 1946 as "The Firebrand of the Philippines," is a whole other story.

The next day agent Hurlburt was visited by a delegation of local citizens, heaping praises on CIC for doing something for Burauen that no one had done before. Apparently under Philippine law, civil police had no jurisdiction over soldiers. Sometimes when soldiers got drunk and boisterous they really raised Cain with the locals with no fear of reprisal from any authority. The delegation included the local priest, the mayor, the school principal, teachers and others. A couple of them had found a miniature bolo about 8 inches long, which they gave the agent as a token of appreciation.

Anticipating repercussions from superiors for getting into a scrape CIC had absolutely no jurisdiction over, Hurlburt wrote up a report—which no one ever asked him for.

* * *

One important job of Hurlburt's was to identify and arrest collaborators, take them to the stockade at Tacloban, the Provincial capital, get a receipt, and write a report on returning to his base. There was no judge or jury, no attorneys, no habeas corpus, no arguments, no consultations with superiors. Just arrest them, put them in, and write it up; there was no appeal. Once in, the prisoner stayed for the duration plus—until a review of the evidence by a higher army authority or a civil trial by the Philippine Government.

It was an awesome responsibility. This one American, with a badge and a gun and the authority to reach out and touch a man, could arrest and throw him behind barbed wire with no questions asked. There was never a question even from the agent's own superiors.

Besides the responsibility involved, how to accomplish it? Even during hostilities there is a good deal of movement of local people. They find ways to get around the combat, and go from here to there as their interests may dictate. When MacArthur returned, people who had gone from Leyte to Manila and done their collaborating there, found it a good choice to move out of that area and return to their homes, where their shenanigans were unknown—they hoped.

But they had not counted on CIC, which would send leads from Manila to the suspects' home area and have them picked up there. Some of Hurlburt's leads came this way. Other leads had been left behind by the 11th CIC on investigations they had started but had no time to complete before moving on. Other leads were dug up locally from investigations conducted in the area of Burauen. Hurlburt puts it this way:[30]

"Leads from detachment HQ at Dulag, on the coast, would take my local guide and interpreter and me out to the barrios in one direction, two, three or four miles one day. We would make our arrest, bring the man back to Burauen, then transport him to the stockade at Tacloban, go back and write up the case. In the next few days we might be a similar distance out in the other direction, looking for another collaborator.

---

[30] *Written by Arthur S Hurlburt*

"This activity had several drawbacks. It was hot and wet wading through rivers and swamps, and potentially dangerous from two sides. We never knew just who we were up against. Was the suspect smart enough to have built defenses, armed his neighbors, set up an ambush awaiting me? Or would the danger come from Japanese stragglers? There were many of the latter in the area, having left the hot battle zone to seek their way in another area. They traveled alone, or in groups of two or three, looking for a chance to steal chickens or rice from local farmers. They were out there because I had the heads of more than a dozen brought to me. I was lucky they did not get mine.

"After each such trip through the swamps to make an arrest, I kept trying to come up with a better way! Was there a way to get the local population involved in helping with this roundup of collaborators?

* * *

"One day on my weekly visit to HQ at Dulag an order was handed to me to pick up and intern Jose Allegro (not his real name). He was charged with collaborating with the Japanese near Manila. Foolishly, I did not ask for further details about what he had done. The next morning Sosing and I started out for Jose. Sosing knew about where he lived and we saw no difficulty, having done this same thing dozens of times before. Jose's house was about half a mile off the main road, about a twenty minute walk. The bamboo house, up on stilts, was at least six feet above the ground.

"We called out to Jose to come out; we wanted to see him. He willingly obliged and as soon as he hit the ground I put him under arrest and ordered Sosing to go through the house, just to be sure there were no arms there or anyone in a position to pick us off as we walked away. He found a disassembled .45 pistol and the man's wife and children. Taking the pistol along, I congratulated myself on arriving at the moment Jose was cleaning his gun!

"The way back to the main road took about 45 minutes of being out in the tropical sun and Jose asked for a drink of water as we approached a house by the roadside. I leniently agreed. We climbed up into the house and Jose had his dipper of water from the householder. As we were about to leave he asked for another. Again, I agreed. As soon as his hands were on the dipper he dove, headfirst, out the window into a bamboo thicket. I fired two rounds at him as he hit the ground and lost him. You can't see a man in a bamboo thicket more than six feet. After that he is gone, gone, gone.

"I sent Sosing back to town in the jeep, telling him to bring the

MPs back. I stood guard on the side of the thicket away from the road, knowing that Jose could easily have gone out the other side, crossed the road and been on his way in two minutes. It seemed like half an hour but was probably only fifteen minutes when Sosing returned with MPs. They asked, 'How bad do you want him?'

"Dead or alive," whereupon they pulled the slides on their .45s and we all headed into the thicket. Of course, Jose was long gone. I had lost a prisoner. It is difficult to describe the sense of despair and self-blame that came over me. Here I was, a Special Agent of CIC, trained to the hilt, equipped with handcuffs, supposedly with the intelligence to avoid this sort of calamity. Yet I lost my prisoner! He jumped out a window! He beat me at my own game! What a failure! I hadn't even been sharp enough to ask what he was wanted for. What did he do? He had murdered at least 97 of his own people on behalf of the Japanese!

* * *

"On the drive back to town my mind was working overtime, looking for a solution. I knew I must report the loss, but I'd give myself 24 hours and do some praying in between times. I wanted that man back so badly I could taste it. That was when I fully realized I needed the whole population of this city on my side. How to get it? Then, it struck me that whatever grapevine existed might be the answer. Where to find that? A crowd of people would be in the City Hall. A long line of supplicants was always there, looking for one thing or another from the mayor. Mr. Mayor, that was it.

"Within minutes I was banging on the mayor's desk with the palm of my hand, saying as loudly as I could, 'Mr. Mayor, I just lost a prisoner, Jose Allegro. And I want him back.'

"Of course, Mr. Hurlburt, I'll do anything I can, but just what do you want me to do?'

"I want you to get word to Jose through your own grapevine that I want him back. Tomorrow morning at sunrise I am declaring open season on Jose. And do you know what that means? It means that any American soldier, any Filipino soldier, any Filipino civilian, will have the right to shoot Jose on sight, no questions asked! That's what it means.'

"I was speaking loudly for everyone within hearing. Someone in that crowd might hate what Jose represented and would be pleased to help me. Then I went home to relax and pray a little.

"Next morning I went to breakfast at the 66th General Hospital nearby and returned home around 8 a.m. In the kitchen was a small boy with a message from Jose. He was hiding in the bushes, within 200 yards of his house, beside the river. The boy, in passing along the path had heard, 'Psst.' It was Jose. His message, 'Go to the CIC house and tell them to come and get me.' Some unknown person, a kind friend whom I will never know, had just fired a shot over Jose's head and he was in fear of his life. I gave Sosing a carbine and sent him with the boy to bring in Jose, alive.

"One more bad guy bit the dust—and I had my answer. I never again went into the boondocks to make an arrest or bring a man in. I didn't have to—I simply sent out a typed note, 'Mario Gonzales, you will come to the CIC office in Burauen at 8 a.m. next Monday. Signed, Arthur S. Hurlburt, Special Agent, CIC.' And it worked. I would send out three notes and, sure enough, on Monday morning, there would be three men, standing beside their suitcases, in front of my house, holding those notes in their hands. The truck I had called for would arrive soon from Dulag and take them off to prison, with no fanfare. Mission accomplished."

CHAPTER XXXI

Manila Rescued

First Cavalry and 37th Division troops with their CIC entered Manila almost simultaneously on 3 February 1945. The 11th Airborne was not far behind, coming up from the south. CIC agents were in the thick of the action. Elements of the 306th, as well as the 214th CIC, were on the heels of the division CICs; in fact, it seemed to be a race as to which team would arrive first. The last night before the entry, agents from three CIC teams held a very liquid reunion on the outskirts of the city in the San Miguel brewery. The vats had been opened, and beer flowed foot deep across the floor; thirsty agents fresh from hotter climates dipped helmet liners and even helmets into green beer for hours on end, or so it seemed—and with predictable results to long deprived stomachs.

Early next morning, with a vital bridge to downtown Manila destroyed, entrance to Manila was gained by driving jeeps and vehicles across a still-standing railroad bridge. CIC was finally in the heart of Tagalog country, and soon learned words that few forgot as beautiful maidens greeted them along the streets with flowers while serving cups of hot coffee, free of charge: "Maganda dalaga; mabuhay ang Philippines; salamat po."[31]

Fighting raged fiercely in Manila for another month, as the enemy clung suicidally to its well-fortified position. The Japanese defenders had dug in behind the enormous walls of old Manila, on the banks of the Pasig river. Gunfire was being exchanged across this natural barrier, with the enemy well entrenched behind the ancient, massive walls. CIC agents arrested collaborators, and picked up enemy (including Filipino) saboteurs within two blocks of this front-line!

While the Japanese clung to positions of strength, Manila itself was in shambles. Japanese fire and dynamite brigades and bitter house-to-house fighting reduced the once proud "Pearl of the Orient" to rubble. Elements of the 306th and 214th CIC, which had arrived on the heels of the combat troops and attached CIC teams (some claim the 306th got there first!), along with the 37th agents spent the first couple of nights in old Bilibid, where the Japanese had imprisoned a number of captured American GI's, including at least one of the survivors from the ill-fated Manila CIP detachment. Occasional rounds

---

[31] *Pretty girl; long life to Philippines; thanks.*

from enemy artillery caused the COs to move the units back a few blocks. Working out of 214th's new HQ, agent Frank Holeman found that on many of his jeep trips following Goff's orders he was driving down narrow streets and alleys that still had live land mines set by the enemy.

* * *

Manila was in chaos in the early few days. The leaders of all the CIC detachments met and divided the city and their duties in an effort to bring order. Guerrilla bands, some legitimate, others just bandits, were picking up and holding those they accused of collaboration; the bandits were trying to feather their own nests by getting rid of rivals. CIC issued orders for all prisoners to be turned over to the U.S., and CIC took sole charge of all suspects, with the Military Police providing the prisons.

The majority of the early cases investigated by the 214th involved sabotage, since the Japanese had used persons of both sexes and all ages to wreak destruction upon the city. Agents even picked up and questioned a seven-year-old boy who admitted being one of a gang of youthful fire bugs to whom the Japanese had paid 350 pesos to toss grenades into buildings occupied by American troops and headquarters.

CIC teams with combat troops concentrated on two phases of activities while the battle for Manila raged: searches and seizures and screening countless displaced civilians. When immediate evidence could not establish any degree of collaboration of suspects, they were left until the 493rd Regional CIC Detachment came in to conduct thorough investigations after fighting in Manila ended the first week in March 1945.

* * *

Agent Joseph Whitlow, now Lt. Whitlow, landed on Luzon by the end of January '45, straight from OCS in Australia. He joined Bradford's 493rd while the guns were still booming in the suburbs, dead bodies still lay in the streets and the old walled Intramuros section was in rubble. The agents were quartered in the San Miguel Brewery, owned by a rich, influential Filipino merchant named Soriano; detachment officers were a few blocks away in the palatial house of Hilario Mocado, Filipino politician. This was one of the largest CIC detachments—with a large mission: identify, investigate, imprison Filipino and American collaborators.

The investigations unit occupied the second floor of the brewery office. Four or five investigations officers were there, surrounded by a locally recruited force of Filipino secretaries pounding out typed copies of statements taken by the agents and their dictated reports. The 493rd had jeeps on the basis of one for each four agents who had to share as they drove around the ruined city in sultry heat, looking for elusive witnesses—many of whom could speak little or no English, and many seemed afraid to talk. Even as the agents conducted their investigations, they began to have a feeling of futility, thinking that after they left many who had collaborated minimally throughout the Japanese occupation would be let out of jail on the defense of having to do so just to exist.

Thirty or more of the agents were assigned mostly to investigate collaborators. Citizens brought in many complaints each day; they all had to be checked out. And the detachment needed some guidelines on the term "collaboration." MacArthur defined it for them as "one who committed treason" which in turn required two independent witnesses to the same act of treason. Once a CIC agent acquired at least two sworn statements to the same act of treason, the subject was sent to Palawan Island with no trial or delay. The trial would be after the war was over, and by the Philippine government.

Many of the complaints amounted to the magnitude of chicken-stealing—"buy-and-sell merchants." Others ranged from informing the Kempei Tai on loyal people, to torture and worse. The need-to-know principle was in effect, so it could require recollections of many agents to put together a complete picture of the activities of the 493rd.

It set up a "raid squad" which dropped in on suspects in the middle of the night. On one pre-dawn raid Whitlow conducted, they routed a group of trouble-making young gunmen out of bed. In another raid the suspected white men in uniform turned out to be American airmen from CBI; temporarily embarrassed, Bradford laughed it off as an inevitable incident of following up on all reported clues made to the detachment.

Its agents interviewed American escapees from Bataan who had not surrendered but had survived in the hills and mountains during the Japanese occupation. All the prisoners freed from Japanese captivity in Bilibid Prison and Santo Tomas were interviewed; many of the civilians among them were of many nationalities, and were passed on through to their countries after the interview. These interviews were to obtain all information possible on those who had collaborated, to separate the good ones from the evil.

One of the real heroes of the occupation was Ernest Tupas, whose cigarette burns all over his face were still vivid when interviewed while dining with us. A controversial interviewee, Manuel Rojas, a skilled fence-sitter who had remained behind when President Quezon left with MacArthur, was brought in from Albert Franco's Baguio detachment; Bradford interviewed him personally. He survived both the occupation and the CIC suspicions to later become president of his country. Benigno Aquino was another famous person who was jailed.

The success of the 493rd is evident from the numbers: some 500 very important Philippine politicians and businessmen, some of whom were prewar friends of MacArthur's, were sent to prison on Palawan Island, charged with collaboration. To Mac's credit, he let the word come down that if CIC had the goods, he would not interfere. But there was one notable exception; the agents sincerely thought they had the evidence to imprison Colonel Soriano, a prewar friend of MacArthur and the San Miguel brewery owner. Mac said "No!"—and that was the end of that.

But, the overall manner in which Colonel Bradford and his right-hand-man Tom Smith handled the 493rd's mission and its large contingent of agents was greatly admired by his men. It was a tribute to Lokey to be so respected by these agents, all professionals and business people in civilian life, most of whom had been promised early commissions for joining CIC!

* * *

New problems cropped up daily as agents set about the tremendous task of implementing an adequate counter-intelligence control. An early problem that reached serious proportions was to find among the ruins some buildings sufficiently intact to serve as offices. Also, operational controls became exceedingly difficult, largely because of the almost unbelievable mixture of varied races and nationalities in this city which had now attained an all time high 1,400,000 inhabitants.

The Chinese colony alone numbered 18,000 and large numbers of citizens of India, Formosa, East Indies, Soviet Union, and practically every European country, were found in the city. The security problem was further complicated by the presence of many German, Italian, and Spanish nationals; sorting out which of these may have been active as agents and party members was a formidable task.

CIC interned more than 200 Germans in special compounds at Holy Ghost College and Bilibid prison. Many Japanese agents were present, often in the guise of Filipino or Chinese citizens, and scores of disloyal Filipinos had been employed by Japanese agencies.

The resemblance of Japanese to Chinese resulted in many embarrassing situations until CIC issued special identification cards to the Chinese, and persuaded the numerous Filipino guerrillas to honor them. Another problem was the screening of 8,500 civilians, mostly

Americans, who became bitterly critical of CIC because they had to be cleared before being sent home. CIC was powerless to do otherwise, however, since the newly arrived American Consul refused to issue visas to these people until they had been cleared.

CIC was often asked to assist in the hiring of native personnel who were needed to assist Army engineers repair the bridges and buildings destroyed by retreating Japanese.

* * *

When fighting ceased in Manila, one interesting and exciting job assigned to 801st CIC agents was a treasure hunt! During the early days of the war before the Philippines fell, General MacArthur ordered money on hand to pay American soldiers placed in bags and sunk in Manila Bay. Certain GIs who reentered Manila on its liberation knew the approximate location of the sunken silver, and secretly planned to recover it. The plot was discovered by an 801st agent in a Manila bar, when he overheard a conversation about the treasure. The agent managed to talk his way into joining the group of soldiers, who had secured the aid of some Navy divers for the search.

When the divers recovered the money, the agent removed his shirt—a prearranged signal to other agents waiting nearby. They closed in at once, took command of the proceedings and recovered the entire treasure. The coins were silver pesos, and filled a box six feet long, two feet high and four feet wide!

From the first American landings on Luzon, and entry into Manila, loyal guerrillas proved invaluable to CIC as sources of information, as well as data, on various problems encountered in other areas. This help was necessary, but since some guerrilla groups had actually operated more for personal gain than for opposing the Japanese, their search for plunder led them to black market activities, and in the case of a few to extortion of wealthy Chinese.

In general, the guerrillas in Luzon divided into two principal camps. On one side were those known as the USAFFE guerrillas, who organized into various geographical commands, generally supported by General MacArthur who was in radio contact with them in a limited way. Sharing these groups' hatred for the Japanese, but diametrically opposed to them politically, was a rival guerrilla camp known as the Hukbalahap, more commonly known as the Huks. Led by Moscow-trained communist Luis Taruc, and Luis Alejandrino, this group was determined to accomplish communistic reforms by armed revolution if necessary.

Adding to the general aura of confusion was the trouble CIC faced in differentiating between the bonafide members of legitimate groups, and those bands of opportunists who found it expedient to become guerrillas. Particularly in Manila, the guerrilla situation approached farcical proportions as expressed in a report of the 306th CIC commander, Blair Labatt: "It appeared that anyone who could scrape up an army shirt was, ipso facto, a guerrilla captain. If he also had shoes he became a major." One report stated that a group of pickpockets organized a "guerrilla" unit because it proved to be more lucrative than their own trade.

With power as their one aim, the Huks were a grave security threat to both American and Philippine interests, often forcing legitimate appointees out of office—at gun point if necessary, with a fatal bullet if resisted. They were known to have committed atrocities that included rape and kidnappings. Law, order and justice meant to them what they deemed to be in the interest of securing their goal. When evidence was clear of out-and-out murder, and who the murderer was, CIC did not hesitate to arrest and imprison the suspect until the Philippine Government could prosecute. Order had to be gained and maintained.

Agents Leslie R. Harrison and Charles D. Lindsay of the 40th CIC were sent to San Fernando in Pampanga Province, to assist the 485th area team in working out some answers to the immediate Huk situation. At a dinner meeting attended by the agents were the Huk leaders, Taruc and Alejandrino plus several priests. The Huks bitterly criticized the U.S. Army for recognizing the USAFFE guerrillas instead of the Huks. Taruc boasted he had over 7,000 followers, and insisted the United States should commission him a General!

As the evening progressed, the anti-American comments became so pronounced that Harrison voiced a threat that he would arrest the leaders, at which time Taruc and Alejandrino stalked out.

Later that night CIC agents, accompanied by 40 American soldiers, raided Huk headquarters. A gun fight erupted, during which two Huk followers were killed. The raid netted a number of documents, one of which revealed that Pablo Angeles David, a local judge who was CIC's main contact in the town, was actually an informant for the Huks.

Even more interesting to CIC was a Huk list of 11 "wanted persons," on which agents Lindsay and Harrison were numbers two and three! CIC interned both Taruc and Alejandrino, as a result of the mounting evidence against them.

Throughout the Luzon campaign, members of the 2nd Filipino Battalion contributed greatly to the fulfillment of the CIC missions. They helped in many different ways, acting as linguists when they knew the local dialect, going on dangerous patrols with CIC agents, and on many occasions investigating causes of civilian unrest.

* * *

Cavite and Santa Rosa Sub-offices

The 214th set up a one-man office at the Cavite Naval Base because of reports of chaotic conditions there, involving guerrilla and bandit bands. Roger W. Mullin, a lawyer before the war, was selected for the job, and performed magnificently.

Viewing his accomplishments in our detachment headquarters in Manila, the boredom of remaining inside an office while the agents were encountering action daily finally got to me. When Mullin reported mission-completed to headquarters, I cornered Goff and requested to be allowed a little of this outside-the-office action.

At just that time, the 11th CIC was moving forward, leaving cases unfinished, and prisoners awaiting incarceration, in Santa Rosa Laguna de Bay. This was a small town some 30 miles south of Manila. It was time the 214th took over from the 11th. Goff assigned agents Charles Michod, an Illinois lawyer, and Clyde Keaton, a New Jersey highway patrolman, to accompany me; Mullin replaced me at detachment HQ as SAC.

The 11th CIC had occupied the best home in Santa Rosa, which of course had previously housed the Kempei Tai. The local guerrillas greeted the new CIC team with assurances they would continue to provide 24-hour guard service around the building, in the absence of any combat U.S. troops in the town. The two-storied house possessed that marvelous bathroom device, a commode, in addition to a bath tub. Water didn't come out of the tap but it didn't take long to remedy that situation.

CIC agents were allowed a certain amount of funds essentially to pay informants. In New Guinea most natives didn't really operate on a money system. Luzon was different, and seeing how the 11th CIC had managed to live and work on their own, I realized there were more possibilities to confidential funds to make our own lives bearable. With the help of the guerrillas, who had been cleared by the 11th CIC, our new team started hiring a staff of civilians. One of the first was a young lad given the task of keeping the upstairs bath tub and commode filled with water. Besides keeping the house clean, he also wielded a huge fan that kept the flies at bay during our meals.

We inherited the cook left behind by the 11th, and hired an assistant to help convert K-rations into more palatable fresh fish, eggs and meat. A wash lady was lined up to take care of clothes and bedding. Before it was all over, I hired a majordomo to manage the staff, so I only had to give instructions daily to one household staff.

Sleeping quarters were upstairs as was the largest room for our work area. With the closing of the Cavite sub-office, Santa Rosa was getting a stream of guerrillas from there as well as elsewhere who wanted to divulge the names of more collaborators. To assist in taking their statements, the next step in completing "headquarters" was to hire three secretaries from the town, one for each agent. Cozy? But it being the Philippines, all secretaries were male.

Anyone approaching the front door was halted by the guards, one of whom would come upstairs and announce the name and business of the caller. Santa Rosa was ready to do business, and we did so. A report of the case volume and pertinent data went daily to Goff at 214th. Knowing that one day he would drop in, I began to wonder what Goff would say about our arrangements.

* * *

We were extremely occupied at first with the unfinished cases of the 11th CIC. And informants were announced by the guerrilla guards on a daily basis, some coming from as far away as the naval base on the bay. Michod suggested that as many of these guerrillas were calling themselves majors and up, perhaps the team had better match them in rank in order to keep them coming. Had they known we were enlisted, they might have demanded to speak only to officers; in this, they were like many of our own army officers (especially in Washington, D.C.). Hence I took the highest rank I had yet assumed, colonel, in order to keep the informants talking; Michod and Keaton I addressed as major and captain.

Anyone of Japanese descent automatically came on our list of suspects, until cleared. This included the mestizos of half-Japanese blood. One case I decided to investigate personally was that of a mestiza who lived in an outlying barrio of Santa Rosa, married to a Filipino. When I found the typical bamboo house, the mestiza was home, as were several children. She was in her thirties, and I could discern distinctive Japanese features, though as we found this is not always a definite test. But she was frank with me, and my halting Tagalog seemed to put her at ease. After a half-hour talk, during which she offered me liquid refreshment that I refused, I decided she was not a security risk, and was definitely needed at home to care for the children. I got confirming opinions from the guerrillas later, who knew everybody in the barrios. Her husband could well have been a Makapili or Ganap, but in my opinion that possibility did not warrant this mother to be imprisoned, despite her bloodline.

* * *

One day one of the guards ran upstairs to report Japanese soldiers were seen in a barrio in broad daylight outside the town limits, and the guerrillas needed help from the CIC as they had only a few ancient guns between them, and of course each CIC agent was well armed, as I still carried my tommy gun with several clips. The number of the enemy sighted was two, though others could be nearby.

I quickly considered the situation and decided I would alone answer the call for help for several reasons. With my weapon I had greater fire power and more basic infantry training, and I was not a family man as my two agents were. I did not want to put their lives in danger, as this incident did not at first glance fall within the purview of CIC's mission—to catch spies. Yet, as I followed the guerrilla patrol toward the suspected hiding place of the Japanese, I wondered if they were only stragglers, or whether they had friendly contacts in Santa Rosa they were trying to reach. For instance, the mestiza I had interviewed a few days earlier?

I never had an opportunity to find the answer, because as we neared the spot I discerned the now recognizable sound of "bees buzzing around" my head. I was a target, and also I suddenly discovered I was now at the head of the patrol! Reacting as taught, I fired a burst from the tommy gun—and to my surprise heard shouts from the guerrillas. I had hit both, killing one instantly; the other was quickly dispatched by a guerrilla. I was relieved somewhat when we placed their ages at no more than 21, though I regretted they could not have been captured.

Walking slowly back to the office I began to dread what my CO, Marvin Goff, would say. I didn't have to wait long. Goff was visiting the office, and when he spotted the dead Japanese being carried by the guerrillas and me accompanying them with my weapon, he figured out what had happened—and jumped all over me for risking my life on such a non-CIC mission. Had there been evidence of an effort to contact a Ganap or Makapili in Santa Rosa, it would have been different.

* * *

Following this incident, the people of this small community now warmed up as never before to this tiny American unit that occupied the best *malaking tahanan*—mansion—in town. The mayor dropped by and said it was time for a victory celebration. To cement our relationship, I agreed—and then found out we occupied the expected location for a private victory party.

The mayor and staff invited key people and provided some of the food, but it fell upon us to provide the liquid refreshments. We located some empty bottles of Four Roses, and filled them with *tuba,* the strong native brew made from coconuts. We also shared some of our canned Spam, a rare treat for the Filipinos.

Juan Pambuan, the *piskal* (judge) of the province and our most reliable informant, took great pride in writing a short speech for me to deliver in Tagalog. Others rendered some of the native folk songs (*kondimun*) as well as Spanish songs with Tagalog words; my favorites that I still sing on occasions are *Tayuna sa Antipolo* (Let's All Go to Antipolo), and *La Paloma Mahal* (my favorite Mexican song, The Dove). The folks appeared to enjoy the evening and there was much toasting and drinking. In fact, the mayor and I tried to out-toast the other, resulting in the first time in my life that I ended up drunk. At least I was "home" and had only to ascend the stairs to fall in bed.

Next day a number of local citizens who had heard about the party started coming by to invite me to have lunch the next day at their homes. In each instance, I used one of the several hundred Tagalog words I thought I knew: "*Marahil*," which translates as "Perhaps" or "Maybe." The next day I painfully learned that these *Pilipinos* (there was no "f" in the Tagalog alphabet) felt I had given an unqualified "yes!"

I lunched at three different homes, and heard singing from three different, delightful children whose mothers were sure would be great entertainers some day. The singing was enchanting, but by the third meal I was stuffed, and could finish only with great difficulty the prime delicacy of meal, the freshest egg one can have: one still in the sac taken directly from the innards of the chicken and hard-boiled in a clear soup. My memory may be faulty, but I seem to recall it was named *inahin*—at least that's where it came from. I never used *marahil* thereafter, nor ever tackled the freshest egg again.

One day a high ranking officer from the XIVth Corps G-2 office visited the sub-office. He was halted by a guerrilla guarding the entrance, who sent a messenger up to the second floor to ask permission for the officer to be admitted. I, a SAC master sergeant, with agents Clyde Keaton and Charles Michod, each with a male amanuensis, were interviewing suspects—including a couple of high-ranking Filipino guerrillas (they had shoes). Invited to stay for lunch, the G-2 officer did so, feasting on freshly caught fish supplied by local natives, cooked by the civilian chef. All the while, the utility boy was fanning the ever-present flies away. The majordomo stood at my elbow and helped serve the food.

As the officer got up to leave, he made a request, followed by a promise. The request was to see if our team could arrange for enough fresh fish to supply the officers' mess at Corps HQ; I turned to my majordomo and asked in Tagalog if he would arrange this, and it was agreed. The promise was made as this colonel turned to leave. He shook my hand and said, and I quote, "Mr. Edwards, I will never call you Sergeant again!" And he didn't!

A few weeks later, Goff brought Mullin and me to XIVth Corps HQ and pinned second lieutenant's bars on us. Under the rules operating at that time, such an event meant the new officers could not remain with the 214th. Mullin went to a CIC team at Baguio, while I answered a specific request from the 306th to become its new officer in charge of investigations.

* * *

Sixth Army's 306th CIC HQ

Now a 2nd Lt. agent, I arrived at the 306th CIC, located in San Fernando, Pampanga province, across the street from Sixth Army HQ, by the end of April 1945. My friends Mike Horwitz, James English and Bill Owens (also brand new second lieutenants) were practically running the detachment. Harold Fredericks, who replaced Blair Labatt as CO, was on leave in the States; temporarily in charge was Captain Starbuck who was new to the theater and relied entirely on his four new officers.

Owens was scheduled to return to the States, though slated to spend a few weeks first at the 441st HQ now located in Manila. But he remained at the 306th long enough to bring me up to date on what had happened to him. The last time I had seen him was in Bilibid as we tried to sleep despite the noise of enemy shells exploding against the thick walls. Thereafter, Owens was assigned the specific task of inventorying all the treasures puppet president Laurel had left at his official residence, Malacañan Palace.

* * *

The biggest coup pulled off by a CIC agent in SWPA may well have been by this modest Texan[32], a staff sergeant agent until his commission.

In the fighting on Luzon, when the Americans had cleared Clark Field and pushed on to Manila, most of their supplies were reaching them from the landing site in the Lingayen Gulf, at least for the first few weeks. This meant supplies, food, ammunition, fuel, etc. had to be trucked right through the heart of the Hukbalahap stronghold. As Ann Bray points out, this was a rebellious group intent on staking out a claim in Central Luzon, at the very least, as its own.

As a matter of fact, overturned trucks, pilferage, outright thievery and even murder were occurring along this route. Bridges were being dynamited, stopping and slowing down the replenishment of

---

[32] *Encountering former A & M students in New Guinea, he refused offers of officer's rank to serve with them.*

supplies needed to sustain the American offensive. All fingers of suspicion pointed directly at the Huks. But troops from the fighting front could not be readily spared. Owens had a better solution, anyway. He made friends with the commander of a Huk regiment. For some reason, perhaps encouraged, the Huk CO and men called him "Cap'n Bilowens" or it may actually have come out "Blowens." Being an astute agent, Owens did not correct them.

He actually persuaded the Huk regiment to come over to the American side for the specific purpose of guarding the vital bridges and control points against the recurring incidents becoming harmful to the war effort. A deal was made, bringing them in as Filipino Scouts, and the big day arrived for an official ceremony at the Sixth Army HQ, where Bill was stationed with the 306th CIC. But a sad thing had occurred: someone in the War Department finally came awake, and realized that for the most part CIC was comprised of talented enlisted men who were performing miracles. So they finally brought out a more equitable Table of Organization about six months before VJ day, permitting the direct commissioning of a large number of the longtime CIC agents as second lieutenants. And "Cap'n Blowens," a university professor with three degrees, the author of scholarly books, with an extra high IQ, suddenly found himself required to fasten on a little gold bar to signify his new army rank of 2nd Lt.!

Feeling a little trepidation, Cap'n Blowens went to the parade ground in his second looey rank, and stood with Colonel White, Sixth Army's G-2, as the entire Hukbalahap regiment passed by, dipping its colors and saluting. But he had nothing to fear; the Huks respected this professor too much and continued to address him as "Cap'n Blowens" even if they did glimpse that flash of gold under a lapel.

* * *

My new duties meant not only responsibility for investigations in the immediate territory of the 306th, but also coordination and oversight responsibility for investigations by corps and division CIC teams in Sixth Army's jurisdiction. As combat actually diminished, the number of teams dwindled and then picked up later as plans to invade Japan were being formulated.

Memories of the landing at Lingayen Gulf on 9 January came alive when I read one of the first reports from a unit under 306th's command. It was a report from Ralph Sims, CO of the 211th CIC, that a certain Filipino should be added to the Wanted List, based on information he had betrayed a downed American flyer to the Kempei Tai. Sims had used phonetics to imitate the Japanese pronunciation of the Filipino's name, but I recognized it as the name of the Filipino whose confession I had taken on the beach at Dagupan—and I endorsed the report back to Sims with thanks, but "Subject was already imprisoned."

One of the saddest cases I faced concerned a Japanese soldier dressed in civilian clothes, who was captured by agent Albert Franco's unit in the Baguio area. The captive's misfortune was to have been in the Kempei Tai; otherwise it was doubtful he would have faced the same punishment. He was brought to Sixth Army which held a trial to determine his fate. I testified as an expert witness, telling the officers of the court what I knew about the mission and training of Kempei Tai agents. Had the soldier been captured in uniform, or if he truthfully spilled all he knew to our ATIS Nisei, it might have saved his life. I still have memories of agent Frank Holeman fixing the traditional hangman's knot on the rope actually used to hang the enemy. I could not bear to witness the execution.

* * *

Another agent arrested a 76-year old for collaboration on the affidavits of two witnesses. In custody at the 306th he denied the charge, claiming he belonged to a guerrilla band (MacArthur's Guerrillas) that had actively fought the Japanese on a number of occasions, and he specified those occasions. He also claimed he was too old to stand incarceration. The caution flag ran up at his statement that MacArthur was the godfather of a son born before the war. I ordered him examined immediately by a Sixth Army doctor who pronounced him fully able to spend time behind bars. This diagnosis was enhanced as continuing investigation revealed that he had fathered a son (in his 70s yet!) during the occupation, and named him after the commanding general of the Japanese troops in the Philippines. And no confirmation of his being a guerrilla could be obtained.

The expected call came in from higher headquarters inquiring about this friend of MacArthur's. I felt lucky the 306th was able to set out the foregoing, and was not instructed to release the subject but to continue the investigation.

* * *

San Fernando was about thirty minutes north of Manila, and as the investigation activity died down somewhat I made a couple of trips to that city to visit the 441st HQ and the 493rd (now a huge metropolitan detachment completing many of the most complex collaboration, the "buy-and-sell," cases still unresolved).

On one such trip I stayed over night to visit my friend, Dana S. Creel, who had completed OCS in Australia and was now a 2nd Lt. assigned to the 441st HQ. There was a dance on that evening, and I felt like it was finally time to celebrate my last promotion, the one to 2nd

Lt. that was so long in coming. So I arranged a date with a charming girl from Visaya, who in keeping with tradition brought along her chaperon.

I was taking turns dancing with my date and alternating with the chaperon. During a dance with my date, I saw a soldier aggressively demanding that our chaperon dance with him. I stopped and walked over to the soldier and said, "She doesn't want to dance with you." He turned on me and replied, "But you have two girls! That's not fair." Then suddenly he swung at me, knocking me down to the floor, and disappeared into the crowd of officers and soldiers.

A captain sitting at a nearby table jumped up and helped me to my feet, asking, "Lieutenant, do you want me to have that soldier arrested?"

The soldier must have been pretty drunk because I was not really hurt, just surprised at the suddenness of his action. Rubbing my jaw a bit, I replied to the captain, "No, thank you, sir. A month ago under the same circumstances I might have done exactly what he did."

The captain smiled knowingly, shook my hand and walked away.

* * *

Another incident that I cannot forget also occurred at that dance. My date's chaperon was an attorney. (There were probably more female attorneys at that time in the Philippines than in the States.) She and I conversed at times during the evening on the fate of the imprisoned Filipinos. I was curious as to the legal procedures she was employing to free those who were her clients, and she was curious as to CIC's procedures in acquiring information and developing evidence that ended in the arrest and imprisonment of our suspects.

I had no reason not to level with her. After all, there was that Armed Services radio that filled the air waves with information about the U.S. Army's CIC, what we did, what we wanted the loyal Filipinos to do to help us, and how to recognize our offices. It was a far cry from our concealed offices and hidden connections back in the States where even top army generals were still unaware of us.

A young American soldier stood nearby with his mouth hanging open at this revelation of CIC "secrets." After a few minutes of intense listening, he strode over, pushed me firmly and not too gently into a seat and whispered, "Listen, lieutenant. If you *are* in intelligence, you'd better stop spreading the news around, I'll have to report you for loose talking, see?" He strolled away before I could ask how things were back in the States when he left a very short time ago.

There could not be a Filipino over six years of age who didn't know more about the CIC, and the names of many its agents, than this average American and others like him back home.

Combat was definitely declining in the Philippines, with remnants of the enemy's forces hiding out in the mountains. The invasion of Japan loomed on the horizon. Sixth Army's General Krueger ordered the planning for landing on Kyushu, whereupon the 306th CIC in preparation undertook a security sweep of the civilian area immediately surrounding Sixth Army HQ. Then I took off for a special course put on by the 441st in Manila on the Japanese language, intended for those to be involved in the invasion. Owens stated years later he had urged this before he departed for home.

Before the course was completed, advance word was received of the efforts by the Emperor to end the war. Anticipating the best, the school was closed and each agent returned to his proper unit.

I arrived at the 306th in time to learn that General Krueger had ordered plans made for the occupation of Japan, with the Sixth Army responsible for the southern half of Japan, with Kyoto on Honshu being its headquarters, and Tokyo for the Eighth Army which would be responsible for the northern half.

Colonel White, the G-2, called the 306th's second lieutenants over to his office, to tell us that the occupation would be a counter-intelligence operation, hence the planning for Sixth Army's part was now up to our CIC detachment. Mike Horwitz led our the efforts, with input from the entire team.

About this time an engaging young officer by the name of John H. Norton had joined the 306th. He needed more experience with CIC operations, though he had been through the school at Hollandia. We felt that CIC had arrived when it was joined by this first known West Point graduate. And Norton got his big chance, which few envied: with the announcement of the end of the war, he was assigned to lead the first CIC team into Japan.

En route to Okinawa to prepare the initial occupation of Japan, the plane with Norton and part of his team plus ten Nisei interpreters crashed near Naha airstrip. Cause of the crash was attributed to an air alert then in progress. Highly regarded CIC agents also killed were his SAC, Oscar W. Keys, Jr., Roy C. Allmond, Donald R. Soper, and Gail N. Gaines. The interpreters attached to his team were Joseph T. Kuwada, M. Nakamura, Haruyuki Ikem, Kazuyoshi Inouye, (FNU) Kadoyama, Satoshi Kurokawa, Shunichi B. Imoto, M. Sogi, Wilfred M. Otokane, George T. Yamaguchi.

Headquarters for the 441st CIC in Tokyo for years was named the John H. Norton Hall in honor of this officer-agent.

CHAPTER XXXII

Okinawa

Weeks before the guns were silenced in the Philippines, CIC agents were aboard ships steaming north toward the Ryukus Islands, the main one of which was Okinawa, to participate in the landings almost in the shadow of the Japanese mainland.

What lay ahead they could only guess. There were no loyal guerrillas sending us information, such as we had in the Philippines. But of one thing CIC was very certain: that the remaining Japanese would fight bitterly. The big question mark was the civilian attitude toward the Japanese who had occupied these islands since 1916.

On Easter Sunday, 1 April 1945, Lt. General Simon Bolivar Buckner's Tenth Army launched the assault on Okinawa. In the initial landings were the 310th, 224th, 7th and 96th CIC Detachments. In addition, agents from the 310th (Tenth Army) were placed on detached duty with the 1st and 6th Divisions for the operation. On 9 April, the 27th CIC landed with its division, bringing to the operation a total of 69 special agents, including officers.

It soon became apparent CIC detachments would not function entirely as counter-intelligence units; "captured" enemy documents had been proven to be of immense value in fighting the Japanese, so even the 310th worked with corps and division units for more than a week, searching around captured airfields, command posts, and other enemy positions for this valuable source of information.

Could the long years of indoctrination by the Japanese have created an attitude of hostility in the native Okinawans to the Americans? CIC agents had feared the worst. But the Japanese had treated the natives as inferiors, so CIC was delighted to find that by first winning over the village chief or Hancho, it was then easy to recruit much needed "CIC aides." This applied at first to the more prominent and better educated natives, but even the ordinary citizens were eventually won over.

The next step was to direct all residents of the particular village to report to a central location. Here they were screened during which the aides interrogated their neighbors, using questionnaires prepared for them by CIC. Word soon passed from village to village that it was a "good thing" to be thus screened and thus available to work for the

Americans. Often after that CIC agents on entering a new village or town for the first time found the natives eagerly awaiting them.

Historically, enemy espionage and sabotage agents infiltrate the enemy territory in the guise of refugees and natives. To prevent this from happening in Okinawa, controlling the movements of the natives was considered highly important. CIC set up a system of identifying and controlling their movements by securing metal identification tags similar to those worn by our own troops. Each native was instructed to wear his tag or "bongo" at all times. In deference to the Oriental concept of masculine superiority, the metal tags were issued to men only; the women received paper or linen tags!

Use of natives as "CIC aides" during the screening process proved remarkably successful. Never before in the Pacific war had CIC relied so heavily on native help; a severe shortage of loyal and competent linguists demanded that Okinawans be used whenever possible.

One of the greatest challenges CIC faced was apprehending Japanese soldiers and Boei Tai labor battalion personnel, who donned civilian apparel and wandered about behind the American lines. Some of these were deserters; some were members of Japanese Army units that had been bypassed by American troops and were, in a sense, hiding in disguise. But there were others who were specifically detailed to slip through our lines to commit acts of sabotage. CIC had its work cut out.

* * *

Late in April agents confirmed the danger when they discovered a large quantity of discarded enemy uniforms hidden in a cave; collaborative evidence came from a captured lieutenant. He stated that soldiers in civilian clothing had been ordered into our lines as suicide squads, a kind of ground "kamikaze," with the objective of destroying equipment and personnel. The same tale was elicited from an Okinawan woman who added that anyone destroying American stores and troops would be rewarded by the Japanese.

The Japanese, apparently in their desperation, were using all the tricks. CIC picked up a small group of "civilians" and got the story from them that they had been ordered by the Japanese to surrender as civilian refugees, and then were to offer to persuade their fellow soldiers to surrender to the Americans. But in reality, the plan then was for them to return to their units with information on American strongpoints and location of ammo dumps!

And at one compound, a CIC interrogation team learned that some Okinawans were giving their identification tags to Japanese soldiers disguised as civilians. Similar reports came in from other sources, as CIC tried to tighten security. There were also numerous reports of unexplained incidents—such as, on 17 May an explosion wrecked a Naval construction fuel dump. A bridge behind American lines was badly damaged by explosives. The attempt was made to destroy a Seabee power shovel with dynamite. Obviously, enemy agents were at least partially successful.

On 13 June CIC officers Raymond L. Cobean of the 310th and Glenn S. Dunbar of the 27th Detachments, were driving across the Motobu peninsula in northern Okinawa for a meeting with natives. They were both killed in an ambush. Investigation revealed that enemy infiltrators were likely responsible, as bullet holes in their jeep were made by Japanese 7.6 mm ammunition, and several clips were found 15 feet from the road at the point of the ambush.

Another problem was caused by small bands of enemy troops who continued to fight as guerrillas. While the damage they inflicted was not great per se, they nevertheless terrorized the native population in an effort to intimidate them to act against the Americans. It became one of CIC's biggest jobs on entering a native village to try to counter this anti-American propaganda.

In a night raid in one village, Japanese guerrillas beheaded the Hancho who had cooperated with CIC and other American officials. The Japanese leader then ordered the remaining villagers to flee to the south. When they declared they wished to stay in their home village, the Japanese lined 50 of them against a wall and hurled grenades at them; 35 were killed outright, the rest badly wounded.

During the last three weeks of the Okinawan campaign, the Japanese frantically increased their attempts to infiltrate the American lines. To cope with the problem, the 7th CIC, augmented by agents from the 224th, operated with battalions, regiments, and even down to companies, while maintaining teams at all civilian collection points. This intense vigilance paid off!

CIC arrested 10 Kempei Tai agents who had made their way to the peninsula in civilian clothing. One of them led CIC to two others in hiding; they also confessed and gave information which led to the capture of the organization's executive officer. Convinced that Japan was losing the war, this officer then led CIC to a cave occupied by the Kempei Tai Unit Commander who committed suicide moments before the CIC could reach him.

CIC agents picked up many Okinawans who had been pressed into service with the Japanese Boei Tai labor battalions and had deserted to get out of the dangerous combat zones for safer northern areas. The Japanese had warned them that the Americans cut off ears and punched out eyes of all natives, so many of these Boei Tai deserters carried bamboo spears or grenades for their self destruction, rather than be captured alive.

In meetings with village leaders, CIC made efforts to counter such propaganda, but unfortunately these efforts were often hampered by our own troops, who in several instances had "molested" the native women.

CIC organized an informant network of volunteer Japanese prisoners to help locate large numbers of their comrades who in their desperation took to hiding out in caves; as the end of the fighting neared, many in this network revealed the location of the cave housing enemy headquarters. CIC raided the cave in an effort to capture General Ushiyima, the Commander, and General Cho, Chief of Staff; both however had taken the traditional way out for Japanese of their ranks. They had committed "seppuku," more commonly known to Americans as "hara-kiri"—that is, an honorable ritual of suicide.

But CIC had not been idle: they had captured a total of 900 prisoners during the campaign, including many on espionage-sabotage missions; by 15 June, six days before the official end, one CIC detachment had captured more prisoners through its security methods than any single infantry regiment taking POWs on Okinawa!

CIC's civilian informants could hardly be considered "confidential informants." In order to satisfy the informants' desire for authority and prestige, CIC issued them arm brassards inscribed with Japanese characters meaning "Advisor to U.S. Forces" accompanied by preferential treatment, including clothing, cigarettes, and PX items. One such informant was permitted to visit his family in another area twice each week, as a reward for his help. Knowing that these visits would be stopped when his usefulness was exhausted, the informant supplied CIC with valuable information for more than a month.

Near the end of June, counter-intelligence jurisdiction of the captured Islands in the Ryuku group passed to a newly created Island Command. This Command functioned under the 963rd and 496th CIC Area Detachments, assisted by the combat CIC team that had worked under the Tenth Army and remained on the Island until after the end of the war.

In the meantime practically all the combat CIC teams in the Pacific area were gearing up for the final invasion of Japan, which never came because Japan surrendered after two atomic bombs were dropped. All of our troops, including CIC, were dreading the thought of invading the Japanese homeland, because of the fanatical fighting they had learned to expect from Japanese soldiers and civilians alike. Pure speculation would have it that while much blood would be shed, not so much of it would be American but Japanese, as they were short on every essential item to carry on warfare.

* * *

Interestingly, while Ann Bray was teaching in the Far East Intelligence School in 1948 in Tokyo, one of the guest lecturers was a very well-educated and charming Japanese gentleman; before the war he had served as a naval attaché in Hawaii, and also in England. He had retired before the outbreak of war, and he volunteered to assist in the war effort. But the warlords had no assignment for him; he later learned that his prior connections in Hawaii and elsewhere caused them to distrust him.

As he explained it, he sat out the war up in the mountains raising food for himself and friends. Immediately on the ending of the war, he was sought out to act as interpreter, and was appointed as interpreter for the surrender party. This party was to fly from Tokyo to Okinawa to be picked up by a plane which General MacArthur would send there from the Philippines.

He related that it was very difficult to find enough fuel to fly the plane to Okinawa. They also suspected that one Japanese Air Force which had refused to surrender might be able to accumulate enough fuel to fly an intercepting plane, so they prevented this from happening by flying directly east for a period, and then swung around and headed for Okinawa. From there they went on as planned to the Philippines.

During the conference with General MacArthur who outlined the surrender terms, they were told that when our first troops came into Haneda airport, the Japanese must have a number of trucks in good working condition, fully provisioned with gasoline. When the emissaries explained they did not have sufficient fuel for this, General MacArthur curtly said, "You will have the trucks there." So when the first planeload of Americans was starting to land at Haneda, they were alarmed when they saw the airport surrounded by trucks with smoke pouring furiously from the rear of each. The explanation, the Japanese said, was "Those were charcoal-burning vehicles, the only fuel they were able to locate."

This tale was vouched for also by an American, then a member of CIC, who acted as interpreter for the American side of the party. He had lived in Japan for a number of years before the war, and explained, as did the Japanese gentlemen, that these were indeed charcoal-burning trucks. The lecturer also said that had the Japanese not been told by the Emperor that they must cooperate, they would have continued the war by fighting with clubs and anything else they could have found, because they were out of ammunition. Even the food supply in Tokyo would not have lasted for another week. Our troops, including CIC, were relieved at not having to make that final assault landing on Kyushu and Honshu.

* * *

Eyewitness Account of CIC on Okinawa

CIC's mission was usually well defined, as was combat intelligence's. But in actual combat the line of demarcation becomes blurred and functions overlap. That was the experience of the 7th CIC detachment during the Okinawa campaign, as revealed by agent Fred Gloe's eyewitness account:

"Each U.S. Army division in the Okinawa campaign had a 4 to 10 man CIC detachment. Since the U.S. Navy had overall jurisdiction of this campaign, there were a few ONI agents on the island; they kept busy in the civilian compounds tending to the housing, feeding, medical care, etc., of the displaced civilians.

"So it fell upon CIC to perform tasks loosely described as `counter-intelligence.' We searched caves recently occupied by enemy troops, looking for documents, weapons, and military information; we searched what was left of enemy corpses for Order of Battle Information—insignia, photos, maps, letters from home, photos, *etc.*; we facilitated the movement of civilians from battle areas to rear navy-maintained compounds while ferreting out enemy soldiers crossing our lines disguised as civilians; and in addition to a variety of similar functions, we acted as bodyguards for our language personnel. These interpreters needed protection from our own troops because, while true-blue Americans, they were ethnically Japanese.

* * *

"Okinawa was honeycombed with caves, some natural, some man-made, some a combination. Japanese made extensive use of them for everything from hospitals to command posts, concealment of troops, storage, weapons emplacements, and more.

"As our advancing troops bypassed many caves, they were anxious to seal them with explosive charges, to prevent hidden enemy from later attacking from the rear. But as caves were often a source of intelligence information, permission to seal was not granted until CIC first cleared them.

"A cave-searching procedure was quickly adopted. Since most man-made caves had more than one opening and several air vents, we would station one man at a high point in the terrain. Another agent would toss into the entrance a white phosphorus grenade which emitted dense clouds of smoke revealing to the high terrain observer any other outlets. After allowing the smoke to dissipate, two agents searched the cave while a third agent stood guard to make sure the cave was not 'sealed' with the others inside.

"With pistol in one hand and flashlight in the other, the agents gathered up all items of intelligence value, and as a by-product ushered out many coughing civilians. On one such detail, our CO Bill Attwood with agents Merritt and McCarthy, came across a pile of Japanese blankets. On impulse, Attwood started throwing off several layers, uncovering to their great surprise a Japanese officer plus a Japanese nurse! These captives ended up at XXIV Corps HQ.

"But that is not the end of the story: the two asked permission to marry. Some officer who perhaps saw good PR (pictures did appear in *Look*) arranged their wedding ceremony. Imagine how our front-line GIs reacted to this Japanese machine gun commander being permitted connubial bliss, when they hadn't enjoyed such privileges for a long, long time!

"Captors Attwood, Merritt and McCarthy were invited, so they dutifully jeeped on dusty roads to the rear XXIV Corps HQ wearing dusty, dirty combat fatigues. They were greeted at the wedding site by white-gloved, starched and cleanly attired MPs, who refused them admittance for being 'too dirty.'

"This was a bit too much for Attwood, not known as a retiring personality. A journalist himself, he located a few war correspondents and unburdened himself to them. Much of what he said was "blue penciled," and he was called on the carpet by Lt General Hodges, XXIV Corps CG, given an official reprimand and a freeze on any imminent promotion for 'mouthing off' to the press.

"From bits and pieces of what Attwood told later, he wrote a personal letter to an old family friend, Lt.General Richardson, stationed in Hawaii. This could explain why the reprimand was rescinded and Bill did not accompany the 7th Division to occupation duty in Korea. (In later civilian life, Bill was ambassador to an African nation, then was a news bureau chief in Paris, was associated with GEO magazine, authored magazine articles and at least one book. A direct quote from him is printed before the introduction in *America's Secret Army*.)

* * *

CIC Handling of Civilians

"Civilians were a problem which infantrymen were not expected to deal with. The Japanese military had thoroughly indoctrinated them with fear of Americans. They fled from our troops, lived under miserable conditions in caves, foraged for food at night with many dying by setting off tripwires that brought down perimeter fire. On many mornings, first light revealed civilian bodies just outside our defense lines.

"Our agents responded to company commanders' calls for help with a 'civilian problem' in forward areas. We established collection points for transporting civilians to compounds or to Navy medical facilities, to get them out of harm's way. But as the campaign wound down, an increasing number of Japanese soldiers were infiltrating our lines disguised as civilians. With limitations of personnel, time and space, it became impossible to interrogate all suspects—particularly with the language barrier.

"Our interpreters then suggested, and helped devise, a wholesale method of interrogation; we temporarily abandoned all the rules in the interests of military expedience. From groups of 25 to 100 civilians, our interpreters formed all 16- to 65-year-old males into a line. Our Nisei, with their innate ability, ferreted out enemy soldiers just by looking; they then asked one question: *"Nani Butai desuka?"* (What is your unit?) A denial was met with a wallop alongside the head with a sturdy stick. A second, harder wallop followed a second denial. After a few wallops, the suspect meekly gave unit number and affiliation.

"As this procedure was repeated down the line, many readily volunteered rather than take the punishment. Thus we could screen 100 in less than an hour, and move to another group. We were motivated to use this method also by the knowledge that fellow agents Glenn Dunbar and Cobean had died in an ambush behind our lines by probable enemy infiltrators.

"We had limited success, as we learned later that one Japanese officer had in error been cleared by CIC as a civilian.

* * *

Surrender of 250 Japanese Soldiers

"After Hiroshima and Nagasaki and the surrender by the Emperor, Japanese soldiers continued to resist in the hills of Southern Okinawa. With no communications to the outside, they didn't know of the surrender.

"It was at this point that Tim Ohta, a Nisei interpreter born and raised in California, volunteered to carry the surrender message to the Japanese under a flag of truce. I was assigned as Tim's bodyguard and accompanied him to the point where he ventured alone into Japanese-held territory and disappeared in the rocks. Would I ever see him again?

"After about an hour, Tim returned with two Japanese officers, one of whom was from the Navy. At Division HQ, they listened to a recording of the Emperor's surrender talk, and were allowed a private interview with a captured Japanese colonel. I watched the two snap to rigid attention on meeting the POW colonel whom they evidently recognized. We returned the two to their stronghold, carrying a message from the colonel.

"The next day a note was delivered that the Japanese would surrender in two days. On that day Tim and I arrived at the agreed surrender site. We had our own jeep but accompanying us were only two trucks and Marine drivers and one Marine officer.

"It was dawn, with mist still in the valley. I expected we'd be early and that the Japanese soldiers would wander down from the hills during the day. The scene which greeted us was unforgettable: the Japanese stood at attention in battalion formation, headed by a colonel. They were grouped in five companies, fairly well dressed, their weapons neatly stacked, and silent as we approached.

"Our Marine officer was clearly taken aback at this scene; after a brief conversation with the Japanese colonel, and having no radio to contact his command, he left with one truck to get more transportation. So for the next hour or so, Ohta and I and the remaining truck driver sat in the presence of about 250 Japanese soldiers who were permitted to sit in place, while their colonel remained standing. The colonel seemed uncomfortable, but so was I. Tim tried a few words with him but got only terse replies. Fortunately there were four cartons of cigarettes aboard our truck; Tim offered these to the colonel who instructed his noncoms to distribute them among the men. Each soldier stepped forward, saluted, took his cigarette and returned to the ranks—an amazing display of discipline in a defeated army.

"Finally the additional transportation arrived and the POWs were transferred to the rear. Later, a more formal surrender was conducted, with all the proper brass and dignitaries present and representing surrenders in other than our sector. But I was especially pleased that Tim Ohta later was awarded the silver star for his performance.

* * *

"The two Japanese officers who carried back the surrender message were not among the POWs. I don't know why, though I suspect; earlier, I had watched two Japanese soldiers commit suicide rather than submit to capture."

CHAPTER XXXIII

From Fighting to Occupying

In the summer of 1945 when the last Japanese guns were being silenced in the Philippines, American troops remained—fulfilling General MacArthur's promise to the Filipinos. The activity of the leaders of all our troops was to prepare for the final operations in Okinawa and Japan, while acting as a protective force against possible counterattacks.

Then on 14 August 1945, the war in the Pacific came to an abrupt halt with the capitulation of the Japanese Empire. At that time the Philippines was "home" to 74 CIC units, all operating under the Theater's 441st Headquarters in the first weeks following the surrender. On 14 November 1945, the 441st CIC relinquished all counter-intelligence in the Philippines to be coordinated under its First CIC Region; the 441st moved on into Japan itself.

Under a memorandum of 27 August 1945, CIC was to cease its investigation of wartime collaborators in the Philippines and turn over all records, together with some 5,000-plus interned Filipinos charged with treason, collaboration and subversive activities, to the Department of Justice of the Philippine Commonwealth Government.

From that time on, with their power to arrest Filipinos gone, all CIC agents could do relative to their hosts was to observe and report. While still charged with the mission of counter-espionage and sabotage, etc., against our own troops and installations, they had no authority to take any further action whatsoever against Filipino citizens. Very soon after VJ day, Pedro Castro, the General Secretary of the Communist Party, sent a letter to U.S. High Commissioner Paul V. McNutt in which he made basic demands upon the U.S. that actually amounted to "get out of the Philippines!" Nine days later the U.S. Communist Party outlined a similar policy, in a 1500 word article in the Daily Worker.

But action speaks louder than words. The Communist Party leaders had at their disposal a healthy guerrilla force that could act in a highly positive manner: the Huks. The Huks had been organized as a communist guerrilla band in 1942 to fight the Japanese, but their wartime record showed that most of their attention was directed toward their own survival. With the liberation of the Philippines, the

Huks seized effective control of the government in Central Luzon, and totally ignored the existence of the Commonwealth.

Huk leaders were all staunch Communists; Luis Taruc, the chief Huk, was on the directorate of the Communist Party. It was estimated that from 80,000 to 100,000 Huks possessed a total of 40,000 firearms, making them a force to be reckoned with.

The responsibility for quelling the Huk rebellion went to the Philippine Army's military police, who began their campaign in January 1946. CIC agents were dispatched to witness and report this attempt to subdue the rebels.

* * *

During their postwar stay in the Philippines, CIC could do nothing officially except observe, but memories and respect for what CIC had accomplished up to the end of the war exerted much influence on the training of CIC's Philippine counterpart; after all, this territory had been a part of the United States since the Spanish-American war. And the U.S. continued its efforts to groom, train and help the Philippines get through the birth pangs of its emergence as a full-fledged nation soon after the end of WW2. But CIC's always diminishing role in the Philippines finally became nonexistent, so on 15 December 1949, its activities were officially terminated there with the deactivation of the only detachment remaining—the 229th.

CHAPTER XXXIV

Assignment in Japan

Ralph "Ruffy" Silverstein was CO of the 32nd CIC attached to the 32nd Division, which was assigned a region on southern Honshu, the largest island in the chain that makes up Japan. With him was Joseph Whitlow who recalls that they were quartered in the dormitory of a school at Yamaguchi, and had very little contact with the division except to draw rations and supplies. The team latched onto a cook, houseboy, maid, and an interpreter, and until their mission was clarified had no official duties other than making contacts with the local police chief and assistants, and even with the governor of the province who dropped by to meet them.

One assignment came in to intercept a high official of the Japanese occupation government of Korea. He was reputed to be carrying a lot of money back to Japan, now that Korea was freed from the Japanese. With agent Al Ingalls and an interpreter, Whitlow went to the designated spot on the beach and found there were hundreds of people wading ashore in the absence of a dock; there was no organization of any kind to handle the flood of people, so the assignment was a blank, though they continued with interviewing local officials in nearby towns.

When MacArthur decreed that all Japanese were to turn in every weapon they possessed, CIC was swamped, even in the small town of Yamaguchi; thousands brought in pistols, guns, swords, old blunderbusses from ancient China (some real collector items). Agents hired local carpenters to make wooden boxes to ship the weapons out. Many of the swords found their way to the States. Years later, the Japanese government made an effort to recover as many as possible, as they possessed historic value to the former owners.

* * *

Whitlow describes a visit to Hiroshima: "I took a train to look at it. This was a sight I shall never forget. There was nothing higher than chest height, except the steel-framed buildings. Everything had been burned out; molten glass was everywhere. The only life was around the railroad station with people passing through."

He still has vivid memories of other cities he passed on the way to embark to return home in December. "There was absolute devastation: locomotives and cars turned upside down from the bombing, rails ripped out, factories all burned, with little sign of life around. My impression was that Japan had been knocked out before the Hiroshima bomb was dropped. Through our interpreter in Yamaguchi, we got the impression from people we interviewed that they all knew the jig was up when Iwo Jima fell. This feeling was universal and is reported in publications in recent years that argue Japan would have surrendered, given more time, with either the atom bombs or the planned invasion of our forces."

* * *

Prior to the surrender of the Japanese Empire on 14 August 1945, two alternate plans were being made to guide CIC operations in an occupied Japanese homeland. "Olympic" was the code name if a full scale military invasion were required, but if the enemy were to surrender its homeland without combat, the alternate CIC plan was "Black List."

"Black List" was of course the plan used. Under it the very first CIC agents entering Japan plunged into a number of tasks not too closely related to their normally recognized mission. CIC was charged with keeping an eye on how well the Japanese were complying with terms of the surrender, as well as the published orders of SCAP, the Supreme Commander of the Allied Powers. In addition, investigating certain foreign nationals, including the Chinese and Koreans, was necessary to determine their involvement if any in the war.

A primary task also was the dismantling of the Japanese intelligence framework, especially the Tokko Ko (thought police) as well as the Japanese counterpart of CIC—the Kempei Tai. Other tasks included locating and arresting Nazi agents in Japan, and apprehending suspected war criminals for trial was high on the list.

Other jobs for CIC were locating caches of weapons and ammunition, turning same over to Allied powers; scanning many thousands of documents for historical material relating to Axis connections, as this could provide vital information to the authorities in ETO; uncovering deposits of money and precious metals; and ferreting out U.S. citizens suspected of treason while prisoners of war or residents of Japan during the war.

As it turned out, CIC had physically arrested only two of the top Japanese war criminals before the Supreme Commander of Allied Powers (SCAP) ordered the now cooperating Japanese Government to apprehend a list of war-crimes suspects.

One SCAP directive ordered the release of all prisoners held by the Japanese under the broad category of political offenses. CIC interviewed large numbers of these political prisoners, and reaped a harvest of valuable information, especially from those who had suffered tortures at the hands of their guards, whom they were able to identify in subsequent war crime trials. A few of these prisoners became confidential informants, providing valuable information later on.

Another directive forbade former members of the Tokko Ko and other intelligence agencies from being hired by other government departments; CIC uncovered a number of violations of this order.

As to hordes of precious metals, CIC agents located over 13 tons of silver in Osaka and uncovered an attempt by the Japanese Navy to conceal silver bullion with private firms. At Nunazu, in Shizuoka Prefecture, they discovered half a ton of gold, silver, platinum and copper. During investigations at Shimonoseki, agents recovered 7.5 million yen that two former workers of the Bureau of Communications of the Korean government were attempting to make off with. In the German Consulate in Kobe was a half million dollars worth of radium, and in Nagoya Naval Base were 4 tons of nickel coins, 800 tons of copper coins and 1500 tons of Chinese copper coins. The network of informants routinely established in the beginning of the occupation was definitely paying off!

Pursuant to express orders from SCAP, CIC conducted a special investigation of the large German colony located in Kobe. Agents confiscated pictorial records, documents, photo-films, as well as monetary and other negotiable assets of the Nazi party that were in the possession of German nationals.

The CIC assigned to the Sixth Army's part of Japan (about one-half, the southernmost portion) seized one war criminal in its area accused of mistreating foreign nationals arrested by the Japanese in Kobe. He was Gerhard Kahner, an admitted agent of the Gestapo; questioning him developed useful information on war crimes involving others, and included testimony on the beheading of some American flyers in captivity.

* * *

The organization of the Kempei Tai was of special interest to CIC, as the handiwork of this intelligence and counter-intelligence unit had been viewed wherever American troops had recovered territory from the enemy. Usually in the Philippines when a CIC unit first entered a liberated town, village or city, they found the Kempei Tai headquartered in the best house or building; so CIC moved into these superior dwellings and buildings.

CIC survey of Kempei Tai revealed the duties, personnel and key personnel of the membership in each location. Would the Kempei Tai go underground and continue a cloak-and-dagger conflict with the Allies? CIC sought to answer this question by a very thorough investigation of its former members, their reserve status, the possibility of its members filtering into civil police units, and any connection of its members with an organization of discharged Kempei Tai members known as the Keisatsukan.

The past, present and potential future actions of other Japanese political, civil and military organizations were likewise thoroughly screened, in order to insure the safety of Allied troops. Included in this screening were, among others, former members of the Kokuyu Kai (Black Dragon Society), the Tokumu Kikan (a spy agency of the Japanese armed forces), and the Dai Nippon Seiji Kai (Greater Japan Political Society). The leaders of all such organizations were put on a "watch list" for any sign of subversive activity.

At a number of seaports, there began to occur a series of clashes between large groups of Chinese and Koreans. These grew out of demands for better conditions and wages at labor camps, charges that Chinese former prisoners of war were still being used as coolies, and demands by Koreans for immediate repatriation as well as more food. The Japanese agency responsible for preventing such disturbances was the Tokko Gakari, and the Dai Niki section of the Osaka Prefectural police. The CIC had to step in to determine the extent of these clashes, and whether there were hidden causes that were directed against the security of the Allied occupation forces.

* * *

The following story of gaining the friendship of local Japanese is an example of the ingenuity used by our postwar detachments to perform their mission:

* * *

CIC Saved A Historic Moat in Matsuyama, Japan

From the Iwakuni/Hiroshima area along the southern coast of Japan's main island of Honshu, it is 90 minutes by ferry boat across the Seto Inland Sea to the island of Shikoku, in the prefecture of Ehime. One lands in Matsuyama, a unique, historic city which is also the gateway to beautiful scenery and a mild climate. Ehime Prefecture faces the Seto Inland Sea, called the "World's Park" for its scenery and scattered islands and water, and has the Ishisuchi range, the highest in western Japan, for its background.

Included among unbelievable sights is Dogo Hot Springs, famous as the oldest in Japan, an ideal spot for tourists for its foods, restaurants, folk craft—and above all, for the kindness and friendliness of the people. Japanese tourists have been flocking there for some 3,000 years!

In the center of Matsuyama is 400 year old Matsuyama Castle, surrounded by a magnificent moat. Magnificent to the citizens, but a breeding spot for mosquitoes! Thus opined the occupying American forces: it must be covered over, and put out of the business of breeding disease-carrying insects.

But, local citizens cried out against the plan, "The moat must be preserved! The moat belongs with the castle. Seen from nearby spots, the castle with its moat are observed to change from season to season. The water in the moat is especially enjoyable and looks quite different, depending on the weather, the time of day, and the angles from which one views it."

How could these citizens be helped in their campaign to preserve a *moat*?

* * *

In 1949, 441st CIC Headquarters in Tokyo had a detachment covering Ehime Prefecture. Its office was in Matsuyama, with personnel billeted in Bansuiso, which translates as French Chateau.

In charge of the detachment was George S. Rea of Jackson, Tennessee. He had fallen in love with the people, the town—and the buildings, not only the Bansuiso lodgings for the detachment but the other buildings, and especially Matsuyama Castle—and its moat.

When the Allied military administration suggested that the moat of Matsuyama Castle be filled in to prevent the breeding of mosquitoes, Rea declared himself against doing so, allying himself with a local citizen's group that was fighting this suggestion. He began using every contact and argument he knew of. After all, waters could be sprayed to kill mosquito larvae, he pointed out. He finally succeeded in persuading the Army to withdraw its plan. When asked why he did so, he said, "I hated to see the beautiful appearance of Matsuyama city defiled."

Rea served as CO of the Ehime detachment from 1949 through 1952. When the local citizens got the word that Rea's tour of duty in their city was drawing to a close, a petition was initiated and sent to Lawrence G. Smith, CO, 441 CIC HQ. It was signed by the Governor of the Prefecture and many others, and it contained this statement:

"We are proud to say that George Rea has really rendered great services in his job and is loved and respected by the people of Ehime Ken for his lofty character and excellent ability. He is the pride of this prefecture and it is our strong desire to have him in his office for even a day longer." It was hand delivered personally by Ehime Prefectural officials!

While this quite properly impressed Rea's superiors and was entered in his personnel records, the inevitable had to occur and in a few months he was shifted elsewhere. But as he was departing he was recorded as stating, "Matsuyama is my second home town, and I wish to visit there again." And he did: in 1974, 1976, and again in 1980.

In Rea's own words, uttered on this return there in 1974, "The Matsuyama Castle in the center of the city and its surrounding moat cannot be separated because it is a whole thing together. It is one great view, the figure of nature. I couldn't bear to fill in the moat." If and when he makes yet another visit, the banners will fly in his honor for saving the moat around historic Matsuyama Castle.

* * *

The mission of the CIC detachment in Ehime Prefecture undoubtedly was accomplished more smoothly because of this one thoughtful act by the unit's CO. There was nothing lost, and much gained, by participating in the rescue effort.

CHAPTER XXXV

Korea

By mid-1946, the bulk of CIC investigations had shifted from Japanese jingoistic activities, which had generally proven to be harmless, to a growing concern with an increase in the activities of the Japanese Communist Party (JCP). CIC's operations in Japan multiplied many times in magnitude and importance, when on 25 June 1950 reinforced communist forces invaded the Republic of Korea—and the United States once again was at war, despite its being labeled a "police action."

No one had known what to expect of Korea when the sudden collapse of the Japanese opened it up as yet another territory for U.S. troops to occupy. The only "comprehensive" plan for Korea was contained in a single sentence from the Cairo Declaration of 1942: "The aforesaid three great powers (Great Britain, Russia, and the United States), mindful of the enslavement of the people of Korea, are determined that in due course Korea shall become free and independent."

* * *

The XXIV Corps, part of the Tenth U.S. Army then in Okinawa, was designated the Occupation Force for Korea, less than a month before they were to move in. There were no directives, no plans, no trained Military Government personnel. In short, Korea had for all practical purposes been completely forgotten, if not simply put at the bottom of a list of things to do!

Shortly before embarkation for Korea the XXIV Corps Military Government officers did receive instructions, but these proved to be more confusing than helpful. They placed the XXIV Corps in the same position as the Sixth and Eighth Armies in Japan, by instructing the XXIVth to "supervise the functioning of those agencies of the Japanese Imperial Government in the areas of their commands." These instructions proved to be meaningless; on arriving in Korea, the XXIVth found few if any functioning Japanese agencies.

The American Army was charged with liberating the area of Korea south of the renowned 38th parallel, an operation which began in September 1945 about two weeks after the Soviet Union moved forces into the area north of this parallel. Since this geographical line had been established "merely" to facilitate the original liberation of the peninsula from the Japanese, the Americans tended to take it for granted that the 38th parallel line would disappear in favor of a unified military government. In spite of all incidents and experiences throughout the world in dealings with Russia, high-ranking U.S. Government officials were still naive enough to believe the Russians meant this.

During the first two months of the occupation, CIC agents along with the remainder of the occupation forces were busily engaged in disarming the Japanese soldiers, assembling all Japanese nationals preparatory to repatriation, while trying to maintain a semblance of law and order. Soon a directive from Washington outlined the basic mission of the Military Government (MG) in Korea: Korea was to be completely separated from all ties with Japan, and MG was to pave the way for the earliest possible establishment of an independent Korean government.

* * *

The Japanese were moved out of Korea without incident. No sooner had they left than the first big obstacle to Korean independence became painfully obvious. During the years of their occupation, the Japanese without exception had held all positions of responsibility in government and industry. On being liberated, Koreans' hatred of all Japanese prevented keeping the able Japanese ones in responsible positions.

When the last of the Japanese left Korea, the last Oriental with any administrative background had also departed. As an example of the degree to which the Japanese held all positions of responsibility: there was not a single Korean capable of even operating a locomotive!

The 38th parallel had solidified quickly into a permanent border as the Russians set up a communist-dominated state in North Korea. That the North Koreans and their Russian masters intended to settle for nothing less than communist control of all Korea may not have been apparent to most MG officials, but the evidence was certainly there. CIC, however, based on its experiences in other areas, was aware of the indications, and was fully prepared for this situation, but just as fully unable to do anything about it other than report the observations and opinions of its agents.

CIC agents in Korea during this period led an exciting, adventurous existence, probably more so than in any other occupied zone; they never knew from one day to the next what to expect, except that almost always it would be connected with communist subversion of some sort. They uncovered one gimmick which had not been used as widely anywhere else: counterfeiting became a huge enterprise carried out in the Chicasawa Building right in the middle of the U.S.-oc-cupied territory. After losing many sympathizers when CIC caught them red-handed, the Communists stopped this activity in South Korea, and were forced to import counterfeit notes printed in North Korea.

The American occupation in Korea officially ended on 15 August 1948 when the Republic of Korea with Syngman Rhee as President became recognized as the government of South Korea.

* * *

American officials did not wish to remove troops from Korea immediately, as it would leave the new government and its small army facing stronger forces from the North. But Russia's announce-ment they would leave North Korea by 1 January 1949 forced America's hand. Russia pulled its forces back to the Manchurian bor-der, stated it was out of North Korea, and demanded that America get out of South Korea also. By 29 June 1949 the last U.S. forces were out of Korea—at least for a while.

CIC agents in Korea and all those to whom they reported knew that our withdrawal from Korea represented only a brief interlude which the Communists intended to use to solidify their position. A comprehensive positive intelligence report dated 8 August 1947 pre-pared by Donald F. Whitaker, officer in charge of CIC Information Section for General Albert C. Wedemeyer (on an important trip to the Far East to report on communist activities and intentions) stated: "The aim of the Soviet Forces in North Korea is to establish a communist government for the whole of Korea; they will not agree to any govern-ment for all of Korea that will not result in the establishment of a com-munist state; and there will be no united, free democratic—in the Western sense—government for the whole of Korea until such time as the present Communist Soviet Government in the USSR is destroyed, either by internal revolution, or through the action of outside, liberat-ing forces."

The report went on to summarize concisely the events in North Korea since the Russians had taken over, and to quote from the writ-ings and speeches of North Korean Communists and by Soviet au-thorities. And so, on 25 June 1950, the North Koreans moved into South Korea and a few days later United States troops, joined by rep-resentatives of other United Nation members, moved in, and another war was on.

And CIC was there also.

* * *

While the Korean conflict was going on, CIC in Japan had its hands full dealing with communist influence. The following story sheds light on this, as well as demonstrates the contribution to CIC by our Nisei. They were a highly talented, gifted group of individuals about whom less is known than even the CIC. *Also, little is known about the outstanding work performed in postwar Japan by the CIC. One of the ATIS heroes of WW2, and of CIC in Japan, enlightens us somewhat with this* Case of the Seven Dwarfs, aka Ni Ichi Ni Jiken:[33]

Seven members of the Japan Communist Party (JCP) were holding a meeting in a Tokyo area house on 2 December 1951. Acting on a tip from a confidential informant, Tokyo police swooped down and arrested them on the charge of espionage against the Allied Forces. The war in Korea was still on, with Americans as well as their Allies deploying troops to South Korea to combat invading communist Koreans backed by communist China and Russia.

Incriminating evidence found at the scene included maps showing the location of key U.S. bases in Japan. Moreover, information supplied Tokyo police was that a communist bigwig would join the seven at the house.

Under the rules then in effect, such cases had to be completed within a specified time frame. The Japanese authorities were unable to finish their interrogation and investigation of the seven within the allotted time; therefore, they hurriedly consulted with local U.S. officials of the Allied Occupation Forces in Japan. Result: the responsibility to continue the case was transferred to the Americans.

The 441st CIC Detachment, Tokyo Office, received the actual assignment. It selected its CIC linguists to form a team with Japanese counterparts who had been involved in the case since the 2 December arrest. The CIC linguists included these agents with extensive interrogation experience in the Pacific Theater during World War II: Mac Okumura, Noby Yoshimura, and Spady Koyama.

Yoshimura and Koyama had served together in General MacArthur's GHQ in Australia in 1943-4, and Yoshimura was among the selected linguists on Battleship *Missouri* in Tokyo Bay for the surrender ceremony in 1945. In addition, Oliver Burton provided outstanding support. Koyama had recruited Burton in 1948 for language training at Presidio of Monterey; Burton vindicated Koyama's judgment by graduating at the top of his class. Burton had preceded Koyama's next assignment in Tokyo and welcomed Koyama's support in transferring him into CIC assignments as a fluent linguist in Japanese.

American born Spady was among the first Nisei to serve in SWPA, where his valuable knowledge of Japanese placed him as an

---

[33] *Contributed by Spady Koyama*

ATIS interrogator in Australia, then in Dutch New Guinea. During the liberation of Leyte on 25 October 1944 he was wounded by a kamikaze dive bomber, and after a year in hospitals was discharged with 40% disability. Recalled to active duty Jan '47, his disability was waived for a direct commission for ultimate duty in Japan as an intelligence officer, where he performed the type of work illustrated by this article. He later served in Korea. He retired in 1970 as a full colonel while on the staff and faculty of Army Intelligence School. His final disability adjudication was 100%.

His immediate boss was Lester Dalrymple, commanding this section loaded with competent linguists. After weeks of intensive investigation by the combined teams, the case was ready for presentation in a court of law. The single charge was espionage, tried in the U.S. Provost Court in what turned out to be the last major case before the Peace Treaty that ended WW2 for Japan.

The trial began on 18 February 1952, with the daily events noted in detail and forwarded by CIC linguist Tom Momii to Ann Bray (then stationed in Tokyo) for processing up through the chain of command.

As the prosecution summoned each CIC linguist to take the stand, a reporter from *Akahata* (Red Flag), official newspaper of the JCP, was observed not just taking notes but also making sketches of, and describing, the CIC linguists. As the trial continued, Koyama received a threatening telephone call in Japanese at his home; and he was authorized to draw a weapon to protect his family and himself. Fortunately, the threat was not followed up.

* * *

The trial continued with five defense attorneys concentrating on technicalities as their main hope: challenging members of the court on bias grounds, questioning the binding on the court of the Potsdam Agreement, attacking the validity of the search warrant that unearthed the damaging evidence, questioning whether the actual search was proper and legal under existing SCAP regulations, and maintaining that the search itself was a violation of the Japanese constitution that provided "the right of persons to be secure in their homes against arrest and seizure shall not be impaired." All such defense motions and challenges were overruled by the court.

The trial ended with the convictions of defendants with varying prison terms. Ironically, the Peace Treaty became effective shortly thereafter, and all seven were freed in a blanket release of political prisoners. To all intents and purposes, this wrapped up the case.

The Japanese authorities, however, felt the case was a classic showcase of successful cooperation between Japanese and Americans that led to the verdict against the defendants. They held an informal reception for personnel involved in the case, inviting Yoshimura and Koyama. They toasted the Americans and presented them with a small sake drinking cup with the Imperial chrysanthemum inside each, plus a pack of cigarettes with the Imperial crest on each cigarette. The Japanese authorities then introduced the entire case into their Police Academy training program!

* * *

The working relationship with Japanese counterparts continued to flourish. The successful rapport established during the Case of the Seven Dwarfs definitely contributed to the outstanding rapport existing still between the U.S. and counterparts in Japan.

Addendum

Some of the material accumulated in the search for records is general in nature and does not fit the "yearly" pattern used up to this point. The following chapters fall into that category and are presented in this Addendum for a more complete background on anti-American Filipinos and of CIC's total history and demise as a separate entity:

Japanese Fifth Column in the Philippines,
A Pocket History of the CIC,
and Ann Bray's Final Curtain

Omitted from this account for lack of space were three complete chapters that would shed more light on the battle we waged to gain recognition from our own Army that CIC existed, and why. A synopsis of their contents:

A) Major F. C. Brennecke wrote a comprehensive analysis[34] dated 26 September 1942 in which he spelled out the need for CIC to be a *separate* corps, on a level with the Corps of Military Police, citing excellent reasons: one was the low grades and ranks that caused many exceptional prospects to avoid entering CIC; another was that it caused many in CIC to find means of exiting into other parts of the Army that offered appropriate ranks for the type of work done.

B) In 1946, John Schwarzwalder wrote *We Caught Spies*, the first book published about the CIC. It covered action in North Africa, Italy and Europe, where CIC was responsible for capturing literally thousands of enemy agents. He believed he had permission from the Army as long as he did not divulge the identities of CIC agents involved, which he faithfully observed. While the book was not censored technically, after its publication our Army moved in to stop further printing,[35] actually removing books from the printers and taking steps to prevent further distribution—which seems to me a form of censorship.

C) In the early 1950s, a thoughtful general, then commanding CIC with HQ at Fort Holabird, ordered the compilation of the history of CIC to serve as a guide for the future. A committee was formed to pursue all records then available, supplemented with personal interviews with agents who remained in the Corps, and with others who could be located and contacted through the National CIC Association

---

[34] *Contributed by Allan F Hull*
[35] *Evidence gathered by postwar Agent David B Birt*

of the veterans. Officer-agent Ann Bray was second in command of this committee and devoted the rest of her life to fulfill its purpose.

* * *

After several years, the first draft of 30 volumes was distributed to CIC major centers around the world, to be proofread and for additions and corrections to be sent to Holabird for an expected revision. By then, the Army had put new leadership in command of CIC, which officially disbanded the committee and discontinued the project. Once again, CIC had hit a snag.[36]

---

[36] *From an article by Richard L Goodbar for the Golden Sphinx*

CHAPTER XXXVI

Japanese Fifth Column in the Philippines

When liberating Americans marched from Lingayen to Manila in January 1945, an estimated 5,000 fifth columnists burned towns, demolished buildings, and actually shouldered arms against us. Reports of this have been meager. The vast majority of Filipinos were either neutral or loyal to the U.S., and as Japan failed to develop an effective partnership with enough Filipino leaders, the majority of Filipinos bitterly turned more anti-Japanese the longer the war lasted.

There were Americans in the Philippines who resented lack of press reports of this anti-American activity. Our soldiers who fought against Filipinos in Japanese uniforms certainly did, as they cursed these enemies who could change into civilian clothes and pass through our lines as refugees with little effort.

The groups from which this fifth column was largely drawn were the Sakdals, Ganaps, and Makapilis. There were a few other small, scattered groups not large enough to do much harm. Who were these dissidents that caused us problems? They were the dregs of a troublesome prewar group.

* * *

The Sakdal Party

Before 1930 Benigno Ramos was a clerk in the Philippine Senate. Dismissed for insubordination, he organized illiterate peasants and laborers of Central and Southern Luzon against his political enemies. These people had begun to turn against oppressive landlords and politicians, and Ramos took advantage of this discontent and unrest in this platform against American rule:

1) complete independence, with no control nor American influence;
2) return of the Philippines to its oriental heritage, under Japan's guidance;
3) limiting powers of officials appointed or controlled by Americans;
4) agrarian reform by doing away with the feudal landlord system, and redistributing the wealth.

Such a platform appealed greatly to these poor Filipinos. Ramos added to the mystique of his movement by creating numerous secret societies and intensifying his anti-white propaganda. His followers soon blamed Americans and their appointments for all their misfortunes.

In 1930 Ramos started a paper called The Sakdal (meaning "to accuse" in Tagalog, today the national language), thus his followers became known as Sakdalistas. In 1933, he declared it a political party. That same year he went to Washington to speak against a commonwealth and for immediate, complete independence. He failed but his effort gained many new Filipino converts, so that in 1934 his party elected a governor, two representatives, plus minor officials.

In 1934 Ramos traveled to Japan reportedly to secure Japanese aid for a Sakdalista revolt to overthrow the Philippine Commonwealth government before it could become established. He sent printed propaganda from Japan that persuaded many of his party that Japan would help when the time came.

On 1 May 1935, an uprising took place in provinces surrounding Manila, but it didn't last and many of its leaders were arrested. Efforts to extradite Ramos from Japan for trial in connection with the revolt did not succeed. The revolt leaders testified some of them actually expected Japanese soldiers to help. And this was in 1935! Though some were found guilty of subversive activities, the majority were released with a pardon by the American governor-general. Those sentenced served less than a year. Those in authority were amused by the absurdity of a few thousand illiterates armed with bolos rising up against the might of American and Philippine armies. They banned Sakdal as a party, thinking that would end the matter.

* * *

The Ganap Party

The Sakdal Party was officially banned, but secret societies continued to operate with the same platform. Uprisings continued in Central and Southern Luzon. In 1938 a new political party, the Ganap (Tagalog for "perfection"), came into being with the same platform and with Ramos as titular head. And by 1939 Ramos returned from Japan to take up his program in person. Evidence indicates he was commissioned to set up an espionage system for the Japanese. He was interned in 1939 for subversion. When Pearl Harbor Day occurred, some two thousand of his known followers were quickly picked up and interned as security risks. Though no records exist, it is a safe bet that CIP's "Lost Manila Detachment" participated in this roundup, much as they did in Hawaii. The Japanese released them along with others when Manila fell to the invaders.

As the Japanese occupation began, there were an estimated 400,000 Ganaps, mostly in Luzon. Ramos offered them to the service of Japan. But the Japanese made a clean sweep by abolishing all existing parties and forming one national party called the Kalibapi, of which Ramos was made a director. He also began forming the former Ganaps into military and labor organizations for the Japanese, and used them as a network to report on guerrilla activities.

General Artemio Ricarte and Pio Duran joined forces with Ramos at about this time. Ricarte was a leader of the Insurrection against the Americans, a contemporary of Aguinaldo. He called himself "the Viper." In 1901 he had entered Manila to start an uprising and was captured. Refusing to take the oath of allegiance to the U.S., he was banished to Japan where he continued to write propaganda for distribution in the Philippines. He also managed to maintain contact with some of the secret societies; in fact he was the head of one called Tangulan, in Bulacan, formed in 1930 as the start of a new Philippine Republic. After the fall of Manila, Ricarte returned triumphantly with the Japanese.

Pio Duran was a political opportunist who perceived the Ganaps to be a quick way to power. His knowledge of what went on in Malacañan Palace proved valuable to Ricarte and Ramos.

In 1943 the Japanese began training Ramos' Ganaps in guerrilla tactics and intelligence methods. Some 10,000 Filipinos received basic military training in this way, and were then attached to various Japanese units. Some were selected for the military intelligence training school in Fort Santiago for espionage and sabotage.

Puppet President Jose P. Laurel declared war against the U.S. in September 1944, which was enthusiastically greeted by the Sakdal-Ganaps. When Laurel decreed against conscripting Filipinos to fight with the Japanese against Americans, he was accused of having made a hollow declaration. Japanese officials in Manila cooled on Laurel and openly courted Ramos, Ricarte and Duran, who offered the Ganaps under their command, and promised to recruit more. They wanted to form a Filipino Army to fight the Americans; this Army was to be called the Makapili.

* * *

Founding the Makapili
"Kalipunang Makabayan ng mga Filipino" (Tagalog for League of Patriotic Filipinos) was born in Manila on 8 December 1944 with fanfare. Its name was later shortened to Makapili. Its founders present at its inauguration were: General Yamashita, Laurel and other puppet

dignitaries, and the trio of Ramos, Ricarte, and Duran. Yamashita was present only to demonstrate the sanction of the Japanese army.

It was believed in political circles in Manila that Laurel attended because he feared its formation was a try to take his power away. Events proved his fears were warranted. The trio promised Yamashita an army of 60,000 Filipinos with a voluntary enlistment of 20,000 each month. By now they had 80,000 Ganaps with some training from which to build their army. Had the U.S. advance not been so rapid, it is quite likely that Laurel would have been replaced by the trio.

* * *

Makapili Objectives

Those who have minimized the problem of collaboration by Filipinos should take a closer look at the announced objectives of the Makapili. A significant one stated the Philippines was "bound to shed the blood and sacrifice the lives of her people in one crucible with the lives of the other East Asians in order to eradicate Anglo-Saxon influence in East Asia." Another was "to collaborate unreservedly and unstintingly with the Imperial Japanese Army and Navy in the Philippines."

These were straight from the propaganda machine in Tokyo. The concern of Americans, and especially CIC, were the numbers of Filipinos who believed them enough to fight for them, and to betray their fellow Filipinos loyal to the U.S. By VJ day, the CIC had incarcerated over 5,000 charged with everything from treason and betrayal of downed U.S. pilots to open and willful collaboration with the enemy against the interests of the Philippine Commonwealth and the U.S. Had the power and mission of the CIC not ceased on VJ day, who knows how many additional inmates there would have been?

* * *

Makapili Accomplishments

As announced on 8 December 1944, the Makapili was intended to be a Philippine Army, on an equal basis with the Japanese Army in the Philippines. The trio of leaders were made major generals, and other ranks were to equal those in the Japanese Army. Makapili soldiers were to be outfitted by the Japanese and trained both as regular soldiers and as espionage agents and saboteurs.

Many partially trained Ganaps were eager to become Makapili, but recruitment failed the expectations of the trio, partly because of lack of time and partly because the Japanese were unable to feed and equip them. Also retarding recruitment were conflicts between the three leaders. Estimates of the final Makapili strength were 10- to 20,000. In January 1945, 1,000 well-trained, well-equipped Makapili were stationed at Christ the King College in Quezon City. Detachments of similar strength were reported in other sections of Luzon. The numbers outside Luzon, if any, were negligible.

Japanese officers were unwilling to trust Makapili in combat as separate detachments. In most cases they were assigned to Japanese units. This was an affront to Makapili leaders, but they could do nothing about it because soon after the installation ceremonies of this new organization the retreat from Manila of the advance guard of military and political figures began. Americans landing on Luzon beginning 9 January 1945 aborted Makapili recruiting and nullified its command. Makapili soldiers were left depending on the Japanese units to which they were attached.

It is difficult to determine the actual aid Makapilis gave in defending Luzon. Makapili active resistance crumbled in Central Luzon before the Americans arrived, reducing them to sabotage and espionage. But elsewhere—Bulacan, Rizal, Laguna, and Tayabas—they fought alongside Japanese soldiers. Our troops could not tell if they were fired at by Japanese or by Makapilis. Many Makapilis were killed in combat; more surrendered with the Japanese, or deserted to surrender to Americans. Hundreds were still fully armed when surrendering.

Probably the Makapili were more valuable to the Japanese in espionage and sabotage. The large number of displaced civilians roaming the provinces, coupled with the small numbers of CIC agents, made screening almost impossible. As a result, Filipinos went between combat lines with comparative ease. As the Makapili were trained to infiltrate, they undoubtedly secured tactical intelligence; some were captured with maps of American positions or other incriminating evidence on their bodies. Some carried passes actually identifying them as spies! We were hampered in detecting some because we were forced to rely on other Filipinos for clues and information. And few Filipinos would betray close friends or members of extended families (which were large by our standards).

Proof of sabotage by Makapilis was less difficult. Captured ones confessed to the burning of Tarlac and Camp O'Donnell, as well as destroying buildings and key bridges. Makapilis were the cause of much of the demolition and burning in Manila, even though a great deal was toward civilian rather than military installations.

* * *

American Policy toward Makapilis and Ganaps

We had sufficient evidence to justify a policy declaring Makapilis enemies, so those captured would be prisoners of war. Instead, each case was judged individually, resulting in many who were guilty of the worst forms of subversion being released without punishment. It was impossible to investigate thoroughly all the many hundreds captured; there were too few CIC and too little time before the war was over. When Makapilis surrendered or were captured, they claimed they were forced by the Japanese as most all Filipinos charged with collaboration were saying. Too frequently this plea was accepted. Leniency toward Makapili soldiers gradually developed, so that toward the end of the Luzon campaign many were released as soon as they surrendered.

But as a rule, the Ganap and Makapili leaders were investigated more thoroughly. By VJ day a number of them awaited trial by the Philippine Commonwealth on charges of treason, though too many were cleared of subversion. Feeling was particularly strong among U.S. soldiers who were exposed to bullets fired by Filipinos. Loyal Filipinos were also dismayed at the soft treatment of Makapilis and Ganaps; they felt every Filipino caught wearing a Japanese uniform should have been executed.

* * *

The Ganap Relations with the Hukbalahap

Certain parallels existed between these two organizations: both drew their members from the peasants and laborers of central and southern Luzon; both favored agrarian reform; both wanted immediate complete independence for their country.

There the parallels ceased. The Hukbalahaps (contraction of Tagalog for "The People's anti-Japanese Army") were sincerely for agrarian reform and independence. On the other hand, the Ganaps were the tools of Benigno Ramos, who used agrarian reform and independence as bait to gain followers. Ganaps were strongly pro-Japanese; the "Huks" were just as strongly anti-Japanese.

In 1942 certain Ganap leaders approached the Huks to invite them to cooperate for agrarian reform and complete cooperation with the Greater East Asia Co-Prosperity Sphere. The Huks refused; they preferred to remain what their name spelled out—and they did so to the very end and beyond.

* * *

The Sakdal-Ganap-Makapili were crushed by the U.S. during the Luzon campaign. Ramos and Ricarte were reported dead and Duran interned on treason charges, as were many others. But the majority never stood trial; some 400,000 in all were the rough estimates, a small number in a 17,000,000 population. But they were concentrated in one area that was filled with trouble and social unrest for at least a generation.

The CIC lost its authority to arrest as of VJ day. The U.S. turned the task of trying and punishing the 5,000-plus charged with subversive activity over to the Philippine Commonwealth government on 2 September 1945. At the same time it placed all civilian control into the hands of the Commonwealth Government, even though that Government was not yet well established.

The U.S. was out of it completely on 4 July 1946 when the Philippines gained their complete independence. But CIC was around for a while longer, even as late as 1947, gathering loose ends and additional evidence in connection with the trials in Japan as well as those in Manila. This CIC unit designation was the 1135th, which we might say is the "Last CIC Manila Detachment"—putting a final ending to the "Lost CIP Manila Detachment," which lost all but three or four of its members in Japanese concentration camps or in combat action against the enemy.

* * *

(The source of the foregoing has not been determined. It was found in the accumulation of papers in the editor's possession. It may well have been written by an erudite CIC Special Agent named Walter Hauboldt, or it may have come from the typewriter of Special Agent William A. Owens or from his collection of CIC memorabilia which is now in a special William A. Owens section at Texas A & M University. I have made slight changes in a few places for cosmetic effect, and to update it as much as possible to the present time.)

CHAPTER XXXVII

A Pocket History of CIC

(Most of this was produced for Bray's manuscript by Dr. J. P. Finnegan, Army Historian, Arlington Hall, Virginia. Additional comes from B. J. Sweeney's A Brief History of U.S. Army Counter Intelligence.)

* * *

Between 1942 and 1961, a unique organization, the Army Counter Intelligence Corps (CIC), safeguarded the U.S. Army from sabotage, espionage, and subversion. Its heraldic symbol was the sphinx, a mythological beast associated with the combination of wisdom and strength. Although the Corps no longer exists, the counter-intelligence function it performed continues to be carried on by other elements of today's Army.

Roots of CIC went back to WW1. In August 1917, Colonel Dennis Nolan, G-2 of the AEF (American Expeditionary Force in France), requested the Adjutant General to supply him with fifty sergeants with a secret service background and a knowledge of foreign languages. The men were needed to protect the AEF from possible threats to its rear from spies in a foreign land.

Fifty French-speaking civilians were hastily recruited into CIP (Corps of Intelligence Police), given a month's infantry training, and sent over to France where many were weeded out as undesirables: Frenchmen who had evaded their country's military service, or common criminals. More suitable candidates were eventually found. By the end of the war, 400 CIP agents were on duty with AEF. In the U.S., another 250 supported the "Negative Intelligence" Branch of the General Staff's Military Intelligence Division.

The Army continued limited counter-intelligence efforts even after Armistice Day. CIP agents provided security for the American delegation at the Peace of Versailles, and furnished similar support to the American Army of Occupation in Germany until that force was withdrawn in 1923. A small group of CIP agents continued to serve in continental U.S. (CONUS) and overseas departments in the period between the wars, although Depression-era economies pared it to a force of about 16 agents by 1934—such "ludicrous proportions it can hardly be said to have existed at all."[37]

In 1937 or 1938 the FBI enlisted the assistance of six loyal Japanese-Americans to penetrate an espionage ring operated on our west

---

[37] *Seth, Secret Servants, pp 147-148*   274

coast by one Yamamoto. Though amateurs, the six supplied the general outline of Japan's plans for sabotage on the Pacific coast when war started. Yamamoto discovered the penetration but the FBI was able to reach only four in time to save their lives; the other two were murdered, with no legal evidence as to the murderers. The State Department refused to act against Yamamoto, so the FBI resorted to the "Al Capone" method: arrest and jail for income tax evasion.

In June 1939 there were reports of Japanese and Nazi spies in Panama, Hawaii and the Philippines. Takahiro Wakabayashi, a Japanese, helped by Guiseppe Sotanis, an Italian, obtained a concession to plant cotton in Costa Rica. He then brought in 21 laborers from a Japanese colony of 20,000 in Chimbota, Peru, ostensibly to start the cotton plantation—which was actually a camouflaged airfield.

This information resulted in the directors of the FBI, ONI, and the Army's Military Intelligence Division reaching an agreement in 1940 on the jurisdiction of each to investigate espionage and sabotage, with the agreement renewed early in 1942.

* * *

The approach of WW2 revived the Army's interest in counter-intelligence, as it appeared the country was confronted by a threat of unknown dimensions from an Axis Fifth Column. The CIP was allowed to expand; for the first time, officers were detailed to the force, and it acquired its own Chief and school. By Pearl Harbor there were 400 CIP agents; following Pearl Harbor, by the end of 1941 the strength had increased almost overnight to some 1,000.

As of 1 January 1942, the organization was redesignated the Army Counter Intelligence Corps, a name which more explicitly defined its real functions. At first, most CIC activity took place in the continental United States, where CIC agents operating in civilian clothes gave counter-intelligence support to the Army Service Commands. It was soon decided that Army tactical units needed CIC support as well. Accordingly, CIC detachments were organized on cellular lines and attached to each division and to higher headquarters. This caused a further authorized strength in CIC to 3,000, of whom 2,000 were assigned to overseas units.

At the end of 1943, however, CIC received a severe setback. The activities of its investigators had displeased some officers high in the Army hierarchy. CIC personnel had also apparently stepped on some political toes. As a result, CIC in CONUS was abolished. Agents in the United States (outside of those with Army Air Forces, Transportation Corps, and Manhattan Project) were merged with the criminal investigators of the Provost Marshal General's Office to form a new Security Intelligence Corps (SIC). Concurrently, the CIC's school and staging area, and the post of Chief, CIC, were eliminated. However, CIC personnel continued to serve overseas with tactical units in over 200 detachments. CIC personnel would see action in every theater of war, and a CIC team would drop with the first wave of 82d Airborne Division paratroopers in the invasion of Normandy.

Experience soon demonstrated the Army had acted prematurely in dissolving the CIC. With the collapse of Germany in May 1945, the focus of U.S. military effort shifted to the Pacific. It became clear that the Army would need additional CIC personnel to support any invasion and occupation of Japan. In order to secure these assets, it would have to reinstitute specialized CIC training and set up a CONUS rotation base to which CIC personnel in Europe might return. As a result of these considerations, the CIC at home was revived in June 1945, and the position of Chief, CIC, was restored shortly thereafter. The CIC School was reestablished and soon moved operations to Fort Holabird, Maryland, a small Army post in an industrial suburb of Baltimore which would become inextricably linked with the history of Army intelligence. The term "the Bird" was soon heard worldwide as graduates of the Holabird school were assigned to units. A technical laboratory and language training courses were added for selected individuals.

* * *

The initial CIC effort overseas after WW2 was directed toward rounding up war criminals and nipping in the bud any attempt to reestablish totalitarian organizations or resistance movements. However, the imperatives of the Cold War soon forced CIC to redirect its attention to dealing with the threat of communist subversion both at home and abroad. In the continental U.S., the principal mission of the CIC was performing personnel background investigations on individuals under consideration for sensitive military or civilian positions with the Department of the Army. The large CIC detachments in American occupation zones overseas, on the other hand, found themselves in the front lines of a silent war against communist subversives and hostile agents. This was after OSS had been dissolved, and the CIA (Central Intelligence Agency) had not yet been fully organized and functioning; until CIA was fully operational, CIC in Europe was performing its duties, and CIA used CIC's cover as well as informant nets until it could fully take over. A respectable number of former CIC agents went into CIA and continued doing what they had been trained to do and done well.

The Korean War once more found the CIC committed to a tactical role in support of U.S. combat troops. When the war broke out in June 1950, the divisions of the Eighth Army on occupation duty in Japan were without attached CIC detachments. Provisional detachments were quickly organized and accompanied the units as they went to Korea. CIC detachments assigned to each division and to higher headquarters performed an invaluable role in Korea mopping up the hordes of low-level North Korean agents sent across the battle line by the communist regime. Elements of CIC also performed additional specialized intelligence duties.

After the Korean War had been terminated by a cease-fire, there were a number of changes made which impacted on CIC. In 1955, the mandate of the Army Counter Intelligence School at Fort Holabird was broadened to include Field Operations Intelligence and Combat Intelligence, and the school was redesignated the Army Intelligence School. In 1957, the Army reorganized its tactical intelligence units. CIC personnel for the first time was integrated into units which contained other intelligence specialists. And on 1 January 1961, the CIC became the Army Intelligence Corps, with positive collection as well as counter-intelligence responsibilities.

In 1965, an even greater reorganization of Army counter-intelligence capabilities went into effect. In the past, CIC and its successor, the Intelligence Corps, had the mission of selecting, training, and administering a highly specialized and select body of Army personnel. The conduct of investigations was controlled by the G-2s of the various higher commands. However, as a result of an Army study entitled Project SECURITY SHIELD, it was decided to centralize the direction of counter-intelligence operations in CONUS under an operational major Army command.

* * *

The U.S. Army Intelligence Corps Command came into being on 1 January 1965, assuming control of the CIC groups which previously had been subordinated to the commanders of the six Zone of the Interior Armies and the Military District of Washington. The organization of the new command presented span-of-control problems, however, since its commander retained his position as Chief, Intelligence Corps, and simultaneously served as Commandant of the Army Intelligence School and Commander of Fort Holabird.

The difficulty was solved by breaking up the Command's integrated structure to allow its head to devote full time to his CONUS counter-intelligence mission. The U.S. Army Intelligence Command (USAINTC) was created in July 1965. Separate commanders were allotted to the post and the school, and the Intelligence Corps was disestablished in March 1966.

USAINTC had a short but turbulent existence. The Command was established just as the United States was caught up in a wave of domestic unrest. Riots in the inner cities and a sometimes violent anti-draft movement overwhelmed the resources of local authorities to keep the peace. Federal troops were repeatedly alerted and were sometimes deployed. USAINTC was called upon to provide domestic intelligence to support the Army commanders tasked with the civil disturbance mission. This led to charges that the Army was "spying on civilians." But on 2 March 1971 the Secretary of the Army testified before the Committee on the Judiciary of the U.S. Senate:

"The records clearly indicate that military resources were employed because civilian agencies, Federal, State and local, had demonstrated a lack of capability to provide the quantity and types of information believed to be necessary effectively to cope in a timely fashion with the emergency then prevailing."

Still, as a result of the political and press clamor, the Army counter-intelligence mission was severely curtailed. An independent civilian Defense Intelligence Service was created in 1971 and replaced by the U.S. Army Intelligence Agency, a field operating agency of the Assistant Chief of Staff for Intelligence.

* * *

In 1977, again there was a sweeping reorganization of the whole intelligence structure of the Army. USAINTC was merged with other Army intelligence assets into a new U.S. Army Intelligence and Security Command (INSCOM), which took over the responsibility for performing intelligence, security, and electronic warfare operations for the Army at the echelon above corps. As part of its mission, INSCOM now provides counter-intelligence support to theater commanders and to the Department of the Army in CONUS.

Under INSCOM, counter-intelligence functions have been fused with signal security capabilities to create a new unified intelligence discipline given the name Operational Security (OPSEC). Army counter-intelligence personnel operating in a tactical environment at the corps level and below have been integrated into multi-discipline combat electronic warfare and intelligence (CEWI) units.

It is doubtful the Army will ever again have a counter-intelligence organization of specialists as intelligent, mature and professional as it had in its CIC in WW2 and subsequent years—especially such an organization with such dismally low ranks. And it seems to have no desire to duplicate it with human beings, an attitude attacked as short-sighted as recently as 1991, when retired Major General Julius

Parker, Jr. (former commander, U.S. Army Intelligence Center and School) was reported as saying, even as he hailed the improvements in sophisticated military technology: *"I'm stressing the importance of all these disciplines. But when you have one missing, there is an inherent weakness in the system."* He was decrying the lack of human covert agents, which would apply to counter-intelligence agents as well.[38]

* * *

UPDATE: Fort Holabird moved to Fort Huachuca, Arizona, and in recent years Army intelligence now has an all-embracing Military Intelligence Corps (MIC), effective 1 July 1987, incorporating all of its elements under this title *even including CI agents retroactively.* So former CIC special agents, whenever and wherever, may now legally call themselves former "MIC Special Agents."

---

[38]   *Arizona Daily Star, 19 January 1991*

CHAPTER XXXVIII

Final Curtain

Ann Bray died 5 December 1976 at the age of 71. Otto E. Fiedler, then chairman of the National Counter Intelligence Corps Association, printed this in the association's newsletter, the *Golden Sphinx*: "There is no way for me to express the loss we all felt with the passing of Ann, our 'First Lady of Counter-intelligence.'... a charming lady, steadfast soldier, very *very* special agent, fine teacher and a loyal comrade in arms."

The Indianapolis Star published: "Ann Bray was a newspaper reporter, wartime Counter Intelligence Corps operative, Army major and journalism teacher whose wits and talent made her star shine in a man's world before the women's liberation movement became the fashion.

"One of the first women in the CIC and a graduate of the Corps' first training class, she served in Japan during the Korean War and later in Germany. Retiring from the Army in 1963 she taught journalism at Northwest and later at Mooresville High. Her life was (one) of service to her country and experiences and insights which she shared with others, adding to their lives."

Richard L. Goodbar who worked with Ann at Holabird on the history committee wrote this about her: "The marker for Ann Bray's grave should contain the words, *Custos Fidelitatis (guardians of loyalty)*, the motto of the Army Counter Intelligence Corps, because those two words sum up her view of the role of CIC personnel as the guardians of loyalty of Army personnel and the shield which would deny to all enemies of America any information that would give them help or the least bit of comfort. To Ann, wearying work and long hours in investigations and case analyses were of no consequence, so long as the mission was accomplished."

After years of laboring with others on the 30-volume history of the CIC, Ann condensed what she deemed the most interesting parts of the history into a manuscript of several hundred pages. This was a first draft of what she hoped would end in a book, but she passed away before being able to pursue this ambition. Into the final chapter of that first draft, she poured her soul and love for CIC and her bitter disappointment. Portions of that final chapter are worthy of being repeated here, as it exemplifies the constant battle of CIC against the Army for recognition and even survival:

"As this is being written, Army Counter-intelligence is in shambles, its organization destroyed, its ability to function less effective than at any time since the beginning of WW2.

"This destruction was brought about by complex maneuvers, the reasons for which are not always clear, but were bold and clearly drawn. The final death blow was dealt in 1971, by forces at the top echelons of our government, in a manner that leaves little doubt careful planning had preceded it.

"One previous attempt had been made in 1943—also at the top. But it was not completely successful because many CIC agents needed in our combat forces and base commands over the world were already with their outfits. But security for Armed Forces in the United States was severely handicapped, and the Corps was unable to send replacements and augmentation units to worldwide spots where and when they were critically needed. Many had to be recruited and trained overseas. Only the extremely high caliber of agents who had to take on this on-the-job training kept CIC from suffering severely.

* * *

"On hostilities ceasing, stateside CIC was taken from the Provost Marshal and reorganized; its training school was reestablished and enlarged. President Roosevelt was dead, his advisers had departed Washington as had his widow; and President Truman was his own man. The reconstitution of CIC was accomplished rapidly to provide Occupation areas with trained agents: danger was anticipated from underground Nazis, and from a more determined onslaught from communism in the U.S. as well as in Japan and Germany.

"Following its reorganization, the U.S. Army's CIC reached its finest hour. By 1968 it had gained unprecedented renown within the national intelligence community as well as federal and state law enforcement agencies. One important factor which brought the organization to a state of maturity was the centralization of CI operations under the Army Intelligence Command as of 1 January 1965 at Fort Holabird, Maryland. Its investigations met high professional standards. Its security services were thorough; its reporting on civil disturbances without peer among investigative bodies.

"In civil disturbance reporting, Army CI outperformed the FBI, primarily because Army had more agents, more extensive deployment, and a better communications system. At the height of the civil disturbance period, a CIC agent could get a report from the street to Fort Holabird HQ in 20 minutes, from practically any city in the U.S.;

seconds or brief minutes later, the report was in Operations Center in a lower basement of the Pentagon. (In fact, as long time loyal CIC officer Bernard Sweeney proudly told a group of visiting CIC veterans, this communication facility was at last worldwide, not hindered by Army red tape as in WW2.)

"Today CIC has been destroyed. Counter-intelligence in the Army is thus weaker and less effective than at any time since the beginning of WW2. There is no point in dwelling at length but a brief explanation belongs here.

"I admit a certain degree of prejudice. As an agent in CIC for 15 of my 20-year Army career, I served in a variety of assignments in the U.S., Japan, and Germany, investigating persons being considered for positions of trust with the Army, investigating espionage and sabotage cases, as well as conducting security surveys. I served as case officer, analyst, researcher, and staff officer.

"I had the opportunity to know intimately the deeds of CIC, the dedication and integrity of the overwhelming majority of its members, and the protection we were providing against the harm men who hate this country were trying to bring.

* * *

"What brought the organization to its present chaotic state? There is a kind of narrow-mindedness and jealousy found too often in those who are too little for the positions in which they are placed. This jealousy for the acclaim which CI was receiving in its mature role no doubt had a part, as did power politics, both partisan and departmental. This strangely will lead many to take certain stands because they think they can reap attention and advantage.

"And then there is ignorance. The beginning of the death knell was an article by a former Army captain, who had served for a time as a law instructor at the Army Intelligence School at Fort Holabird. He was a law school graduate, a Ph.D. candidate in political science, aspiring to be a professor of American Government. He had never spent one day as a CIC agent, had never taken part in any investigation or served in a staff or operational position in any intelligence unit; but his 'conclusion' (was) 'Army surveillance was not only improper from a constitutional perspective, but wrong and unnecessary and dangerous for the Army.'

"The article was filled with inaccuracies. For that reason it was not initially taken seriously by Army counter-intelligence officials or by the Pentagon.

"Soon after it appeared Senators spoke out in shocked tones. Senator Fulbright had it read into the *Congressional Record* as if it were

Gospel. Some of the news media accepted the article without any attempt to check its facts. Little was said about the Army's constitutional obligation to protect the United States and restore domestic order when so directed by the President.

"Some members of the Senate continually praised the author for 'his fearless patriotism' and expressed doubt, sometimes insultingly, of Defense Department representatives. The lone voice who continually tried to place the case in perspective was Senator Hruska, generally ignored by the news media.

"The report of the hearings published in the *Indiana Law Journal* deals with 'horrors' of having civilians investigated by Army personnel, who are citizens too with a stake in their country's future. Not surprisingly, (the writer) avoids any mention of what the civilians were doing that triggered these investigations. One quotation will show the mental attitude of this man and presumably reflects the attitude of the majority of the committee: 'Perhaps no other activity of government poses such a threat to individual liberties as the use of the military for domestic programs. The country can no longer afford to permit any governmental agency to conduct domestic intelligence in a secret and uncontrolled fashion.'

* * *

"This domestic intelligence was not being conducted in a "secret and uncontrolled fashion," but with full constitutional authority, with the knowledge and approval of the President, the Secretaries of Defense, Army, Navy, and Air Force; plus the Joint Chiefs of Staff, the Directors of the FBI and the CIA, and most of the national, state and local law enforcement agencies.

"Army CI used no subterfuge in informing its superiors and the FBI and CIA regarding its observations of dissident civilians involved in civil disorders. Army CI kept all the officials and organizations mentioned above fully informed of its work, and from them received high praise and a rating of 'inestimable value in protecting the security of the United States.' And let us remember this was at a period when NO ONE knew when certain areas of our country might have to be placed under military law to protect lives and property.

"Many at the Department of Army and the Defense Department fought as long as they could but finally gave in, possibly through fear for the retribution that might come to them for standing up against a situation under control of men whose every attitude seemed to be 'Don't confuse us with facts; we've already made up our minds.'

"And so, unfortunately for our Armed Forces' security, Army CIC and its operational parent the Army Intelligence Command, which had performed so effectively on a mission approved by all the governmental agencies mentioned above, were stripped of most of their CI functions because of a political climate within the U.S. made passionate by radicals and fanned by the media.

"To please them a new organization was set up, called the Defense Investigative Service, with the mission of performing the background investigative mission of the whole Defense Department. This mission the Army Intelligence Command could have performed without additional personnel and less money. It had the deployment, communications network, and operational experience. With civil disturbances winding down, the Command could easily have absorbed the total defense mission.

"Even if the decision were carefully made that Army investigators should stick to Army business, there seems no logical explanation for dismantling an organization that was serving in a proven, highly effective manner, and against which no valid criticism of integrity, efficiency, loyalty and need could be leveled.

* * *

"The Defense Investigative Service has now been in being for nearly five years. Its effectiveness can be judged by the fact that it takes 60 to 90 days, often longer, to run the type of simple background investigation the Intelligence Command completed in 30 days. Worse still, investigative techniques which employ lower standards than the Army used have led many professional observers to fear that counterintelligence security provided by this service would not protect Armed Forces from penetration by any foreign agents that half tried.

"In fact, one technique not generally known until recently is alarming as it permits personnel access to SECRET information *without any verification that the enlistee is the person he or she claims to be*, according to an AP story in *The Baltimore Sun* on August 8, 1976. Under this system an enlistee must pass an Entrance National Agency check to be accepted into the service, which means that the *name he or she gives* is not found listed as a danger to security in the files of the national agencies checked. If enlistee is assigned to a job requiring a SECRET clearance, clearance is granted on the strength of that flimsy check.[39]

"Pentagon officials, the *Sun* relates, claim the problem of false identity is 'not serious enough to warrant the cost of a beefed-up security check.' The Pentagon added *only about 15 individuals* were discovered as having enlisted under false identities during the preceding year!

"But W. Donald Stewart, former inspector general for the De-

---

[39]   *Remember, Ann wrote this shortly before her death in 1976.*

fense Investigative Service, a severe critic of the system, says 'the 15 are only the tip of the iceberg.' Stewart, headquarters supervisor in the FBI espionage section from 1956 through 1965, moved to the office of the Secretary of Defense.

"According to the AP story, Stewart has stated, `The Pentagon has no idea how many may have enlisted under assumed identities....at no time is the identity of the enlistee proved by one who has known him,' or even by comparison of fingerprints taken after his enlistment with those on file with any agency.

"At this point anyone who has ever had any experience with Army Intelligence must have cold chills.

* * *

"The only CI activity still permitted the Army for its own protection is controlled by a 'shocking' document, put out by the Army, known as the 1 June letter, too long to discuss at length here. It has been superseded by an Army regulation.

"Among unbelievable provisions of this letter is one that prohibits Army from collecting civil disturbance information on civilians within the U.S. until a disturbance has begun, meaning that Army units being sent into such a disturbance at the order of the President would have no background on the nature of the disturbance, the identity, *modus operandi,* or possible lines of action of its leaders; in other words going in blind! Furthermore, information collected during such a disturbance must be destroyed within 60 days after the disturbance!

"This provision alone permits less extensive files than those kept by any newspaper or library! It appears that the powers that be desire that Intelligence personnel work in a bell jar, with no memory of the past, no knowledge of the present, and no clue to the future. These rulings make it simple, and much more satisfying to rioters, snipers, America-haters, revolutionaries, lovers of foreign ideologies—don't they?

"The forces, whatever they may be, that were behind the dismantling of Army counter-intelligence, are probably the same ones who now are using every possible means to destroy the FBI and the CIA, and as this is being written, they have begun their attacks on the National Security Agency (NSA), whose work is the breaking of secret codes of foreign nations working feverishly to break ours.

"Shall we join with Henry L. Stimson who, upon becoming Secretary of State in 1929, abolished the small code-breaking machine, saying `Gentlemen do not read each other's mail.' We can be quite sure they are reading ours, or will be soon if vultures are successful in destroying the last vestige of U.S. intelligence protection!"[40]

---

[40] *No doubt things are better now, but these last words in Ann's manuscript shows her bitterness at how the situation looked when she wrote it.*

* * *

If you have read this book carefully, you will have the answers to the questions on the back cover. To clarify, these factors played a part: high ranking Army officers' jealousy of the highly talented men reporting to our G-2s; fear of intelligence agents looking over their shoulders; ignorance of how to use this unique organization. The general on MacArthur's staff who ordered records destroyed was a noted strict infantry officer, which may account for his action. My question to those who destroyed the separate organization is: When the FBI goes astray, that entity is not abolished—its head man is simply replaced with Congress laying down guidelines for his successor; why wasn't that done with CIC instead of dismantling an organization that served so well for so many years?

CIC IN SWPA

The following list of agents in the Southwest Pacific Theater represents the various units as of 28 February 1945. Shifting of personnel from one unit to another was almost continuous, due to the rapidly changing military situation. Many more agents began pouring in from the Central Pacific and elsewhere from this date on.

6th CIC Detachment (6th Inf Division)—Webster, James R.

Shepard, Grant E	Davies, Davis	Nichelson, Geo J
McGarraugh, Eston A	Nugent, John H 3rd	Radeloff, Walter A
Weinstein, Benjamin J	Mohr, Leon	Hogg, Roy J
Hartnett, William C	Krieger, William D	Holm, Leo S

11th CIC Detachment (11th Airborne Division)—Caziarc, Dean H; Barbee, Frank L

Nye, Harry F	Guillet, Fernand P	Charon, George
Francis, Walter G	MacDonald, Robert A	Wright, Turbutt M L
Herrmann, Louis G	Finn, David	Fagan, Frank C
Powell, Irving L	McGrath, James H	DuBois, Rene E

24th CIC Detachment (24th Inf Division)—Connelly, David I; Hanan, Albert

Muscolina, Frank A	Pate, William E	Slocum, Albert I
Lambrick, Jos T Jr	Knapp, Lealand M	Terry, Ben
Mathews, Elijah R	McQuaid, John G	Claxton, Robert L Jr
Thume, Jack G	Cassel, Robert D	Guthoehrlein, Oscar

25th CIC Detachment (25th Inf Division)—Holman, Natt B

Helmken, John C Jr	McDermott, Jos R	Mallor, Norman M
Perko, Kenneth A	Prout, William C	Townsend, Paul B
Corliss, John C	Moses, Henry A	Dickie, Roland B
Schwartz, Lee	Martin, Walter F	Woodman, Richard S

31st CIC Detachment (31st Inf Division)—Trout, Clarence W

Ardis, Carlton V	Bonelli, Rocco J	Braun, George P
Deckinger, Harold	Gunn, William A	Lamb, William L
Redmon, William H	Conrad, Albert H	White, John D
Gardner, Hubert C	Ragsdale, Curtis W	Perkins, John W

32nd CIC Detachment (32nd Inf Division)—Lynch, Mark J.

Parker, Henry C	Miller, John H	Schneider, John B
Lebano, Ernest	Ryken, Peter S	Singer, Jerome L
Calevas, Harry A	Canady, Kenneth M	Hulnick, Robert B
Weeks, Clarence A	Baker, Charles D	Griner, Ellsworth
	Naver, Emil M	

33rd CIC Detachment (33rd Inf Division)—Donahoe, Bernard M

Horgan, William P	Kimball, Hiter J	Lindquist, James J
Hudson, William O	Kroll, George L	Petty, Estil P
Brady, John J Jr	Rosa, Oreste R	Cavan, John J
Sandercock, Vincent R	Daly, John R	Gerow, William L

37th CIC Detachment (37th Inf Division)—Stilwell, James E

Goggan, Walter H	Boggy, Dale H	Ferguson, George T
Rosenthal, Robert	Luchetti, Lucas R	McGraw, Edward F
Jones, Tilford A	Spalt, Harry L	Harkins, James I
Duven, Edward J	Franco, Albert M	Woods, Rudolph A

38th CIC Detachment (38th Inf Division—Baldwin, George A

Binford, John R	Murray, John R	Murray, John J
Larkin, Joseph C	Locke, Victor	Simard, Albert F
Batsakis, Nathan	Henderson, Marshall	Carmody, Frank E
Schwartz, Murray	Rebeck, Henry M	Kozak, Alexander
	Sheridan, Francis	

40th CIC Detachment (40th Inf Division)—Klein, Earl A

Fusselman, Wm J	Houser, Paul W Jr	Lynam, Patrick J
King, James C	Lindsay, Charles D	Menchine, William A
Smith, Theodore B	Angle, Rosy S F	Tauger, Bernard
King, Allyn P	Ward, Alfred W	Chandler, Robert W

41st CIC Detachment (41st Inf Division)—Gluckin, Lawrence

Vodden, Herbert C	Hedge, Harry C	Fee, Orville H
Carlisle, James L	Cramer, Robt L	Hogan, Joseph J
Jansen, Harold L	Bertholet, Frank	Lawless, John J
Lowry, Clarence W	Charves, James M	Scranage, Wm C
	Jones, Geo R	

43rd CIC Detachment (43rd Inf Division)—Hodgson, Ray W

Holland, Keith E	Schoepflin, Merle	Alajajian, Jerry
Macomber, Robt C	Fleisig, Philip F	Guiterman, Herbert
O'Brien, Edward M	Housh, Lawrence J	Fabian, Max
Hager, Eric H	Jackson, Raymond E	

93rd CIC Detachment (93rd Inf. Division)—Townsend, Caspar Jr

Robinson, Ernest C	Bivins, Horace	Johnson, William A

182d CIC Detachment (Americal Division)—Keenan, Albert J

Weber, Eugene F	Foster, Edw J	Jones, M B Jr
Brown, Walter C	Houda, Eugene W	Lucht, George R
Kraft, Clarence A	O'Rear, Cecil G	Breor, Paul J
Stibal, Frank E	Hoene, Howard F	Bowen, Phillip F

201st CIC Detachment (I Corps)—Cook, Victor I

Malbuisson, Paul	Brown, Ralph J	Korta, Armand
Smith, Paul F	O'Shaughnessy, William	Goff, Charles D
Robinson, George M	Wagner, Walter	Montgomery, Fleet
Rubin, Lawrence A	Miller, George W	Jewett, Albert
Mayfield, Charles	Clark, Jos P	

210th CIC Detachment (X Corps)—Hurley, Joseph P

Reed, Sumner C	Strachan, Henry	Lovell, Walter J
Dillman, Francis	Kaps, Charles T	Nerenberg, James W
Hurley, James W	Wilson, Gerald M	Nern, William F Jr
McLaughlin, Edw F	Collucci, Lucian J	Bradford, Philander S
	Kaar, Joseph W	

211th CIC Detachment (XI Corps)—Sims, Ralph

Johnson, Wm H	Caston, Homer R	Heaton, Henry O
Aldecoa, Fermin J	Majewski, Henry F	Beltz, Donald G
Brechler, Kenneth S	Kennon, Clement R	Horne, Archie A
Starbuck, Wm H	Dreyer, Wm J	Hanley, Martin V
Myer, John D	Edwards, Paul M	

214th CIC Detachment (XIV Corps)—Goff, Marvin C Jr

Edwards, Duval A	Holeman, Benjamin F	McMinn, Robert S
Mullin, Roger W	Lee, Otto C	Schneider, Edward J
Cole, Dan M	Keaton, Clyde H	Salomon, Jason
Hill, Warren R	Kingsley, John E	Nicholas, Thomas A
	Michod, Charles L	

306th CIC Det (Sixth Army)—Labatt, Blair P; Frederick, Harold F

Norton, John H	English, James W.	Kamerick, Stanley E
Hoss, Robert L	Park, Woonha	Tuthill, David R
Leong, Wm. B S	Cordova, Arthur	Horwitz, Milton G
Ackerman, Thomas R	Hosinski, Edmund J	Devenow, Chester
Owens, William A	Ripley, James J Jr	Tredway, Paul W
Bowman, Walter W	Towne, Maurice H	Jennings, Edmund A

308th CIC Detachment (Eighth Army)—Turner, Chapman

Wright, Arthur W
Roberts, Cyrus D
Feener, Ulysses G
Alter, David E
Fair, Fisher A
Smith, Willard R

Krell, James R
Wilpers, John J
Heydorn, Howard M
Stedler, Richard J
Page, Merritt G
Elsing, William T

Kaag, Robert L
Zimmerman, Chas F
Notaro, Frank R
Fenimore, William R
Lyons, Robert B
Hourston, Edward M
Reuter, Frederick K

440th CIC Detachment (USAF NORSOLS)

Lynch, James J
Cook, Richmond

McCarthy, Robert J
Barry, David R

Little, Allison L

441st CIC Detachment (Theater Headquarters)—Galloway, Jennis R

Carlson, Russell
Wilkins, Lloyd H
Stewart, Roger S
Earle, Richard G
Colbach, Roman H
Wilson, Alton A
Blackley, Horace A
Bellatti, Walter R
Johnson, Arthur W

Warren, Edmund A
Corkery, Gerard J
Major, Thomas H
McCloskey, John D
Brooks, Walter
Hogg, Calvin R
Cartwright, Peter C
Maloney, Peter J
McNally, Robert W

Malapit, Mariano S
Evans, William D
Bank, Vernon C
Reyes, Edward
Murphy, Francis J
Wickson, Edward J
Born, Harry E

442nd CIC Detachment—Geiss, Ermal P

Nicholas, Woodrow
Spring, John C
Wendt, Charles

Boyd, Edgar E
Genovese, Ernest R
Weitzel, Walter M

Strouse, Lynn
Hennessy, Charles C
McKenna, James A

443rd CIC Detachment

Scoville, Joseph
Hout, Ernest G
Trapp, Robert L

Andrews, James J
Breckenridge, James W
McKee, James B

Krizan, Joseph F
Thrift, Edgar M
Pennink, Karel

444th CIC Detachment—Spencer, George B

Lincoln, David W
Kelly, John M
Komori, Arthur S

Casey, William P
Ryan, Lewis H
Shaw, Ormand B

Casey, Charles J
Wolf, Charles H

445th CIC Detachment—Platt, John O

Keniston, Walter
Bley, Robert W

Mulligan, Regan F
Hale, Frank C

Venable, John D

446th CIC Detachment

Slaughter, Archie B

Horaitis, George L

447th CIC Detachment—Applegate, Thomas W

Wright, Edwin W
Hayes, Emery L
Hedtke, Reuel E
Salevouris, Emmanuel
Carlson, Robert R
Herzog, Robert E

Cougill, Vernon E
O'Hearn, William G
Koss, Raymond F
Hicks, William J
Lede, Alfred E
Beasley, Everard J
Walters, David W

Katis, Bruno B
Hackney, Eugene O
L'Ecluse, William F
Ruttkay, Louis K

448th CIC Detachment—Roach, Philip O

Riley, Harold L
Messenger, Marshall
Turner, Morris
Ward, John O
Akers, Lloyd D

Zimmerman, William
Freshwater, Roy L
Timmons, William H
DeVlaming, Daniel
Turnblazer, Wm J

Wilson, Benjamin O
McNee, Wesley D Jr
Johnson, Andrew

449th CIC Detachment

Bledsoe, James A
Anderson, Robt E
Leynse, Waldo H
Jones, Thomas L
Guthrie, Wayne L
Labberton, Helios

Morrison, Wm. S
Eidam, Louis C
Lee, Powell A
Oloans, John M
Sherry, Orville M
Smith, Eldon K

Bertin, LeRoy V
Savino, Carl F
Sherwood, Wm O
Green, Martin L
Solomon, Paul J
Walsh, Charles E

Swanson, Kenneth L
Bloss, Edward G
McCabe, James V
Clemons, Willis J

Floyd, William N
McGowan, James P

Hoffstein, Geo R
MacNabb, Malcolm L

Chenery, Charles E
Mikaitis, Daniel
Schutt, Paul M
Claytos, Don D

Holloway, James L
Tokos, George M

Emmert, Leonard J
Gibson, Luke M
Everett, Junius A
Screthchings, Homer B

Tarpley, Harburd
Thompson, Horace S
Vaughn, Cleatis L
Schmidtchen, Paul D
Taylor, James E
Wilson, Joseph P
Zink, Joseph M
Conaty, Francis S
Trinidad, Arsenio
Winchester, Geo A
Cross, James S
Swenson, George W P
Castor, Russel E
Petersen, Henry
D'Arcy, Stephen J
Wagner, Charles W
Hansen, Jarvis B
Barratt, Peter T
Elledge, Fred Jr
Metcalf, Richard
Newville, Donald F
O'Brien, George M
Barton, Thomas G
Erickson, Oscar J
Redding, William J
On, Lewis O
Garrity, Hubert M
Ferguson, Prescott

Hower, Alfred
Tse, Sum F
Gray, Eldon A
Olbes, M Z
Almiranez, Irineo

450th CIC Detachment
Guysi, George S
Davis, Marlin H
Mathis, Robert W
Fowle, Eliot R

451st CIC Detachment—Geismer, Alan S
Larson, Paul E
Brown, Albert A

452nd CIC Detachment—DeLuca, Andrew A
McIsaac, Neil K
Adamo, Frank

453rd CIC Detachment
Marcum, Carles P
Pittman, Paul E
Small, Keppel O
Scheper, Henry E

454th CIC Detachment—Wood, Eugene H
Thompson, John B
Abraham, George J

455th CIC Detachment
Hance, Young D
McCann, John C
Manyo, Peter A
Curry, James R

456th CIC Detachment—Canon, Jack Y
Fletcher, Lindsay Z
Kendall, Cliford
Brown, Charles A
Gray, Harry C
Mignola, Joseph Jr
Levitan, Irving A
Buck, Harold D
Phillips, Thomas W
Carlino, Alexander
Maliaman, Dalmacio
Durkin, James H
Redus, James W Jr
Conway, Carl F
Mikol, Edward G
Hopkins, James F
Thomason, Karl W
Tomlin, John G
Murphy, Edwin A
Hunt, Thomas R
Bauguss, Oran C
Burns, Eugene J
Russell, Robert F
Kornfeld, Jerome M
Brown, William T
Cook, Roy L
Schulze, Milton J
Lester, Thomas C
Caulfield, John D

457th CIC Detachment—Goodrick, Carl H
Adricula, Julian D
Thomson, Robert B
Balintong, Flaviano
Drye, Richard L
Beaton, Harold D

McQuillan, John J
Rust, Gordon D
Allmond, Roy C

Gravlee, George M
Coats, Frederick F

Pignatelli, John C
Motley, Herman H

Jones, Jack M
Rath, Paul F
Spencer, Geo D
Wallace, Thomas L

Barnes, Stanley L
Bean, Truett E

Timpone, Joseph P
Westendorf, John R
Bogert, Regis Z

Kraft, Lloyd
Seyler, James A
Malden, Henry M
Cline, Franklin A
McCarthy, David H
Sloan, William W
Martin, Arthur R
Combs, LeRoy
Schein, Ellis
Spurgeon, James
ERudicel, Rex S
Seckel, William C
Hall, Charles A
Jasmine, Harold A
Sampson, Donald M
Stanford, Lee R
Jackson, Everett
Kohlman, Jack L
Shannon, Robert L
Strong, Vinton L
Keller, Geo A C
McConnell, Wilmer
Small, Loren E
Vandersluis, Francis
Ortega, Fernando
Milner, Keith A
Winetsky, Morris

Girard, George K
Kaeser, William H
Carey, John H
Shoon, Goon Wah
Keys, Oscar W Jr

458th CIC Detachment—Sayers, William H

Hurlburt, Arthur	McLeod, William J	Hert, James B
McKeown, Robert J	Beath, Andrew B	Hannaford, James J
Riffel, Carlyle H	Nichols, Paul R	Kortas, Francis J

459th CIC Detachment—McColl, James W

Lee, Randall P	Park, Chauncey C.	Walker, Dow E.
Peel, Robert	Davis, Earl H.	Kapourelos, Anthony
Murphy, John E	Minet, Edward E.	Murray, John W.
Myles, Thomas F	Cappuccilli, Edmund	Johnson, Harrison H.

473rd CIC Detachment—Smith, Thomas D

Griffith, Jack C	Anderson, Harry A	Willis, Cecil A
Simpson, William B	Victor, Robert C	Jackson, Thomas
Segrest, Ralph W	Merrick, Richard L	Strobel, Charles E
Babcox, Reid B	McCauley, William H	Reed, Jefferson L Jr

474th CIC Detachment

Chilton, Walter C	Bowler, Michael S	Ellerd, Arthur A
Ouelette, Orie D	Anderson, Raymond	Scantlebury, John R
Mason, Walter A	Massey, Walter B	Hendricks, Fred A
Deininger, Eugene H	Looney, Jack M	

479th CIC Detachment—Camp, Charles S

Schroeder, Wm E	Tate, Albert, Jr	Cawthon, Harold C
Gillette, Hubert J	Stern, Charles H	Phifer, Nelson L
O'Connell, Daniel J	Conners, Eugene M	Price, Lindsay E
Duncan, Alexander S	Hamilton, William B	

480th CIC Detachment—Gilmore, Gerald E

Kimmel, George J	Powell, William S	Burress, Chas R
Shanahan, Timothy	Streetman, Harold	Vine, William A
Collins, Benjamin I	Morledge, John W	Debold, Frank P
Wilson, Robert E	Tomlinson, Frank J	Canning, Stephen

481st CIC Detachment—Bingham, Charles M

Zinsmaster, Arthur	Bihy, Clarence F	Hahn, Edmund J
Johnson, Louis W	Smith, Harry	Sonnichsen, Alex C
Robb, Fred	Long, Robert C	Zimmerman, Charles F
Moddemeyer, Wm O	Kane, John D	

482nd CIC Detachment—Stapleton, John T

Lounibus, Edwin C	Monroe, Richard S	Morris, Owen M
Barnes, Richard R	Janasov, Edward C	Walker, Aubrey W
Henderson, Derrious	Morrison, Henderson W	Turner, Francis E
Palmer, Dorwin L		

483rd CIC Detachment—Cook, Denver F

Taylor, Merton R	Moore, Thomas E	Aneda, Joseph R
Schneidman, Samuel	Caudill, Julian E	Humphrey, Don G
Scott, Harlan	Reichert, George F	Yeaman, William R

484th CIC Detachment—Claflin, Beecher N

Noell, Robert M	Hoenstine, Garland	Moss, Julius O
Lisy, Clayton J	Day, James D	Holloway, John L
Anderson, Leland R	Borgman, John H	Peterson, Eldon A
Wittig, Lawrence M	Polk, James W	Matthews, John P

485th CIC Detachment—Hanna, George R

Cannon, Samuel S	Furey, Robert J	Combs, Howard G
Ivers, John P	Laird, Norman W	Wishart, John W
McCourt, James E	Curtis, Arthur H	Yenser, Herbert K
Hicks, Charles D	Duncan, Louis C	

486th CIC Detachment—Cuddeback, Howard L

Palmer, Cleddie A	Spilman, Wm. R	Cronan, Frank X
Cochran, Doyce E	Getzov, Morton J	Smith, James A Sr
Meyers, Howard	Dangler, Frank J	Wilson, Milo D
Oakes, John C	Long, Robert E	

487th CIC Detachment—Skinker, Dudley G

Bailey, James M
Bergreen, Bernard
Seiter, Francis J
Levine, Irving L

Farley, Louis W
Deslauriers, Conrad
Krys, Joseph F
Ashmore, Leon E

Conway, James F
Quisenberry, Rowland
Schell, Robert M

488th CIC Detachment—McGillicuddy, Daniel

Simons, Leo E.
McCrary, Walter L
Harrison, Leslie R., Jr
Nichols, Harry C.

Campbell, Wm E, Jr
Cohen, David H
Blair, Charles E
Gibbons, Edward F

Ketchum, Neal O
Greenwald, Willard
O'Grady, William J.

489th CIC Detachment—Wathen, Frank J

James, Edwin S
Cullen, John P M
Brown, Francis T
Waering, Peter K

McGrath, Edw J
Hemphill, Roderick
Bushey, Mitchell
Cook, Robert W

Furey, Francis S
Starr, John L
Wood, Glenn

490th CIC Detachment—Douglass, Arthur R

Ulrich, George W
Desmond, Robert
Levesque, Joseph R
Markley, Charles W

Koury, Louis G
Smithy, Walter S
Barendsen, Robert D
Foley, William J

Myhan, William P
Sorkin, Bernard R

491st CIC Detachment—Friedrich, Robert E

Thrasher, Wm H
Lemoine, Everett C
Shields, James S
Essiambre, Frank F

Weiss, Albert L
Millard, Gerald
Golden, Philip A
Rutkowski, Stanley E

Belinkle, Milton
Owen, Claude M

492nd CIC Detachment—Hurst, Paul A

Nelson, Perry A
Wellspring, Thomas
Coakley, Daniel J
Brewster, Carl N
Burkhardt, Elmo L
Parks, Philip F

Kunsler, Albert M
Hiraoka, Wm. T
Engel, Regis F
Sullivan, Homer
Mina, Moises O
McDevitt, Frank D

Bauler, Edgar C
Gridley, Frederick
Cavalierre, Angelo J
Kruger, Norman R

493rd CIC Detachment—Bradford, Lowell J "Lokey"

Barnhouse, Wilmer
Huckaba, Donald L
Chin, Ching Y
Gleason, Roland E
Chu, Kenneth K

McVay, Fredrick D
Rosa, Jose D
Ingojo, Jose B
Hague, Alfred E
Phillips, Gene K

Shingleton, Everett
Wing, Ernest H
Urban, Richard L
Harrison, Herbert C
Best, Vernon A

613th CIC Detachment—Lander, William T

Reilly, James W
Ward, James A
Kelley, Joseph S
Sandalls, Wm T

Yakobian, Geo J
Gengher, Edward L
Kalischer, Murray
Gorrie, Robert T

Broz, James L
Klerlein, Edw T
Pridgen, Samuel R
LaCosta, Thomas

801st CIC Detachment (1st Cavalry Division)—Inwood, Jerome A

Reifer, Harold
Connelly, John F
Matasavage, Vincent P
Youker, Malcolm P

Rollen, Walter R
Kopcho, Clarence B
Leynse, Humphrey
Deubel, Charles C

Bradshaw, Horace
Walker, Albert E
Peterson, George W
Brock, Ruebin C

904th CIC Detachment—Recor, Loren E

Grybos, Anthony
Wood, Alvin R
Garza, Ray B

Creeth, John H Jr
Storey, William E

Smith, Robert B
Westrell, Harlan A

962rd CIC Detachment—Richards, Jack A

Burgess, Marvin R
Taylor, Tom H

Searight, Richard
Wehrle, Henry L

Dunlea, Thomas A
Katzin, Marshall P

IN SWPA but at OCS: Creel, Dana S
Others were coming into SWPA via the Hollandia training school;
included among these was Gilbert Gonzalez, San Antonio TX, who went to
the Manila 493rd and on to Japan.

HAWAII

Many agents were not long in Hawaii, but went through there to their assigned destination. The following list is believed to be complete, not only for those simply passing through but for those who stayed long enough to participate in training and/or CIC missions:

Robert C Adair, Everett J Afook, William F Aimone, Malcolm D Aitken, Robert T Aitken, Victor M Aitken, Joseph F Allocca, Edward K Aldworth, Nano Aluli, Ernest E Anderson, Frederick S Anderson, Robert G Anderson, Clifford M Andrew, Robert M Ansteth, Harry G Anthony, Thomas E Armstrong, Judson H Atchison, William Attwood, Dean M Aungst, Eugene C Auryansen.

Edward S Babcox Jr, Reid S Babcox, Morton Bach, Mintel A Bailey, Edward M Baker, Alexander M Bakewell, John J Baldi, George A Baldwin, Richard W C Baldwin, Nathan F Banfield III, Clayton Barker, Robert A Barker, Sandy L Basham, Nathan G Batsakis, Richard J Beckman, Franklin H Benecke, Direk Benson, George Bichnell, Virgil E Billow, Robert S Billstrom, Henry C Biscoe, Maurice R Black, John W Blair, Frank O Blake, Ward M Blake, Samuel H Bluthe, Clement W Bojar, Edward S Bolden, Charles A Bono, Emanuel F Bonvencin, Marlin V Bordner, James W Breckenridge, Milan C Brenkus, Nathan R Brown, Robert E Brown, Edwin H Bryan, James A Burke, Charles W Butler, Roger W Butner, Charles P Bufithis.

Asunction B Cacatian, George Callahan, Charles S Camp, Louis D Capocci, Roman R Cariaga, Marshall D Carnell Jr, James Cartwright, Charles Cassidy, Owen Cassidy, James C Castle, Aaron M Chaney, James E Chen, Ching Y Chin, Kim Fan Chong, Philip R Cibotti Jr, Kenneth A Clifton, Raymond E Colby, Albert J Connelly, Richard W Cooksey, Reagan P Coon, Benjamin R Coppolo, Phillip Correll, Roger H Coryell, William G Cosgrove, Harry L Costigan, Harry R Covington, Ralph J Cox, Ezra J Crane, Allor B Crouch, Robert G Curlee.

John R Daly, Joseph H Danis, Thomas H Davies, Bruce Davis, Thompson B Davis, Glenn M Deal, Robert Deviner, David O Dillon, David R Dingeman, Bernard M Donahoe, Bernard P Donohoe, Jacques S Dove, William F Doyle, Eugene Z Dubose, Eugene H Duffy.

William K Elliot, William E Elliott, William Elmore, Earlan J Erickson, Othello V Esposito, Auaman E Everson.

Donald F Fairbanks, Joseph J Fallon, Donald M Fenton, Everett Ray Ferris, James A Fitzpatrick, Marvin J Flam, Ian S Flannery, Thomas E Flinn, Francis J Foley, John Foley, Lon Foster Jr, Harold P Friis, William Fritz, Robert S Fuerth Jr, Ichiro Fujita.

Lorenzo S Galeno, Arthur H Gamache, John P Gavan, Edward O Geer, Louis T Genung, Scott T George, William F Gibson, Kirby M Gillette, Lee F Gledhill, Frederick H Gloe, John R Goetz, William R Gordon, Edward Gorman, Arthur M Gray, Paul H Green, Wayne D Gregg, Dana M Groff, Israel H Gross, Nicholas L Gustin, Arthur E Gutman, John E Guyant.

Richard G Haas, Ernest L Halford, Sam J Hall Jr, Kenneth R Harbridge, Robert K Hardesty, William F Harrington, Carl E Harry, David G Hayner, Sam C Helman, Gordon W Helton, Hubert H Henderson, Henry Hertner, Howard M Heydorn, Bernard L Hill, Benjamin O Hills, Wayne W Hills, Charles N Hiner, William T Hiraoka, Robert Hoffman, Charles L Holder, William A Hudson, Lloyd L Hughes.

Tadao Igeta, Jiro Ikemori, Gero Iwai.

William S Jackson Jr, Douglas Jaques, John D Jenkins, Frederick D Jensen, Edward P Johnson, Zebulon V Johnson.

John F Kallam, Kanemi Kanazawa, James H Kane, Warren B Kanne, Edwin I Kawahara, William M Kawato, Lawrence A Kearnes, Robert L Kelleher, George H Kendall, James E Kilgarriff, Herbert F Kimpton, Gordon M Kingsberry, Vincent S Klikna, Kanao Kobayashi, Arthur S Komori, Nicholas Konstantakos, Clarence K Krueger.

Kam Fook Lai, Kenneth K M Lau, James B Layman, Edward Y K Leong, Addison W Lewis, Vern V Long, Hubert D Ludwell, Samuel K Lyman, Patrick W Lynch, Burl G Lynn.

Harold A MacArthur, Michael S Machida, Charles W Markley, Morrill W Marston, John M Martin, Miles D Matsumoto, Frederick G Max, Manuel Maya, Ian L McGarr, Charles J McGuire, Robert L McKee, William C McKee, Archibald C McKillop, James H McKinney, James T McManaman, James L McMillan, Lewis E Menechino, Byron M Meurlott, Eliot D Michaelson, Robert C Miller, Dale V Moles, Paul L Montieth, Cecil I Moore, Alfred W Morse, Maurice Mungovan, Francis M Murphy, John J Murphy.

Carl P Nehren, Edwin P Neibauer, Frederick C Newman Jr, Paul F Nockels, Harold D Nolan.

Peter Obsencia, Joseph H O'Donnell, Warren S Ogata, Timothy T Ohta, John J O'Leary, Michael J O'Reilly, John H Ortner, Teruo Oshima, Kermit P Owens.

Roy C Packler, Charles P Paone, Pedro J Pardo, Horace E Pascal, Lyle M Peddicord, Aulis A Peterson, Herbert C Pittman, John R Porteus, Carl Potstada, Orville C Pratt, Clyde L Prestwood, James T Pritchett, Walter L Prock Jr, William Y Pryor, Francis J Pufahl, Anthony Puleo, Emmett H Pullman, John K Purcell.

William H Radloff, Robert L Radabaugh, Henry M Rebeck, Robert J Reiley, William J Rennert, Sheldon P Riley, Charles J Rinoldi, John H Robinson, Judge K Rowley.

Richard Sakakida, Roger I Sanford, Edward Y Sawamura, William C Sayre, Lawrence M Scanlon, John E Scholl, Robert D Schuck, Rudolph H Schwarz, Francis M Scoboria, Jackson D Scott Jr, Walter S Scott, Dave Shanks, Frank Sherrill, Max H Sheward, Goon Wah Shoon, Leo E Simmons, Albert G Simpson Jr, Roscoe P Simpson, Donald F Sinn, Kwong Yin Siu, Charles W Slabaugh, Golden Slusher, James C Smathers, Fred F Smith, Samuel H Snow, Philip B Souder, William S Sparks, George B Spencer, George S Spencer, John K Spencer, Wayne B Stanard, Howard V Stephens Jr, Cambell W Stevenson, John S Sullivan, George R Sutherland.

Robert N Tait, Homer G Tanner, William L Taylor, Basil A Thomas, Melvin W Thomas, Charles P Till, Paul E Tognetti, Harry F Tompkins, Richard L Tubman, Elbert Turner, Otis D Turner Jr, Joseph T Twitty.

Hisao Ueki.

Gerald M Van Dyke, John D Velie, William L Villone.

Oscar S Wagner, Wayne S Wallace, Monteith Weaver, James R Webster, Roman H Weide, James V Welch, John B West, Delbert S Westling, James J Wilcoxon, Alan G White, Albert G Willis Jr, Andrew S Wong, Albert D Woodle Jr.

E B Yale Jr, Kiyashio (Kiyoshi) Yamashiro, Charles F Young, Ralph D Young.

BIBLIOGRAPHY

Abaya, Hernando. *Betrayal in the Philippines*. New York: A. A. Wyn, 1946.

Aitchison, Ray. *Thanks to the Yanks?* Melbourne, Australia: Sun Books,1972

Arthur, Anthony. *Bushmasters, Jungle Warriors of World War II*. New York: St. Martin's Press, 1987.

_____. *Deliverance at Los Baños*. New York: St. Martin's Press, 1985.

Australian Military Forces. *Jungle Warfare with the Australian Army*. Sydney: Halstead Press, 1944.

Bidwell, Shelford. *The Chindit War*. New York: Macmillan, 1979.

Bosworth, Allan R. *America's Concentration Camps*. New York: Norton, 1967.

Botting, Douglas & Sayer, Ian. *America's Secret Army*. New York: Franklin Watts, 1989.

Boyd, Carl. *Hitler's Japanese Confidant*. Lawrence, KS: University Press of Kansas, 1993.

Bray, Ann. *The Spy Catchers, vol. 1*. Unpublished manuscript, 1985.

Cochran, Thomas C. *The Great Depression and World War II*. Glenview, IL: Scott, Foresman, 1968

Congdon, Don, ed. *Combat: The War with Japan*. New York: Dell, 1962.

Considine, Robert, ed. *General Wainwright's Story*. Garden City, NY: Doubleday, 1945.

Cortesi, Lawrence. *The Battle for Manila*. New York: Kensington, 1984.

_____.*Pacific Breakthrough*. New York: Kensington, 1981.

Craig, William. *The Fall of Japan*. New York: Dial Press, 1967.

Deacon, Richard. *Kempei Tai: History of Japanese Secret Service*. NewYork: Berkley, 1983.

Douglas, Keith. *A Portrait of Brisbane*. Bathurst, Australia: R. Brown & Associates, 1988.

Eichelberger, Robert L. *Our Jungle Road to Tokyo*. New York: Viking, 1949.

Falk, Stanley L. *Bataan, the March of Death*. New York: Berkley,1972.

Farago, Ladislas. *The Game of the Foxes*. New York: David McKay, 1971.

Farwell, Byron. *The Gurkhas*. New York: Norton, 1984.

Feldt, Eric A. *The Coast Watchers*. Garden City, NY: Doubleday, 1979.

Flanagan, E. M., Jr. *The Los Baños Raid*. New York: Berkeley, 1986.

Gow, Ian. *Okinawa 1945, Gateway to Japan*. Garden City, NY: Doubleday, 1985.

Groves, Leslie M. *Now It Can Be Told*. New York: Plenum, 1962.

Harrington, Joseph D. *Yankee Samurai*. Detroit, MI. Pettigrew, 1979.

Hosokawa, Bill. *Nisei, the Quiet Americans*. New York: William Morrow, 1969.

Hoyt, Edwin P. *Storm over the Gilberts*. New York: Van Nostrand Reinhold, 1978.

Hunt, Frazier. *The Untold Story of Douglas MacArthur*. New York: Devin-Adair, 1954,

Ichinokuchi, Tad. *John Aiso & the M.I.S.* Los Angeles: M.I.S. Club of Southern California, 1988.

Ienaga, Saburo. *The Pacific War 1931-1945*. New York: Pantheon, 1978.

Ind, Allison. *Allied Intelligence Bureau*. New York: Modern Literary Editions, 1958.

Irons, Peter. *Justice at War - Japanese American Interment Cases*. New York: Oxford University Press, 1983.

Johnson, Thomas *Our Secret War*. Indianapolis, IN: Bobbs-Merrill, 1929

Kenney, George C. *General Kenney Reports*. New York: Duell, Sloan & Pearce, 1949.

Kiko, Mang (Icasiano, F. B.). *Horizons from my Nipa Hut*. Manila: Nipa Hut,1941.

Krueger, Walter. *From Down Under to Nippon, Sixth Army in WWII*. Washington, DC: Combat Free Press, 1953.

Layton, Edwin T. *And I Was There*. New York: William Morrow, 1985.

Leahy, William D. *I Was There*. New York: McGraw-Hill, 1950.

Liston, Robert. *Spies & Spying*. New York: Platt & Munk, 1967.

Lord, Walter. *Day of Infamy*. New York: Henry Holt, 1957.

_____. *Lonely Vigil—Coastwatchers of the Solomons*. New York: Viking, 1977.

McCoy, Melvin H., Mellnik, S. M., & Kelley, Welbourn. *Ten Escape fromTojo*. New York: Farrer & Rinehart, 1944.

McDougald, Charles C. *The Marcos File*. San Francisco: San Francisco Pub., 1987.

McGee, John H. *Rice and Salt*. San Antonio, TX: The Naylor Co., 1962.

Mashbir, Sidney F. *I Was an American Spy*. New York: Vantage Press, 1953.

Mayo, Lida. *Bloody Buna*. Garden City, NY: Doubleday, 1974.

Miller, Francis T. *History of World War II*. Iowa Falls, IA: Riverside Book, 1945.

Morgenstern, George. *Pearl Harbor, Story of the Secret War*. New York: Devin-Adair, 1947.

Morison, Samuel E. *New Guinea and the Marianas*. Boston: Little, Brown 1953.

Nash, Boris T. *The Alsos Mission*. New York: Grosset & Dunlap, 1969

Owens, William A. *Eye-deep in Hell*. Dallas, TX: SMU Press, 1989.

Piccigallo, Philip R. *The Japanese on Trial*. Austin: U. of TX Press, 1979.

Porter, Betty Joan. *The US CIC, WWII*. Unpublished essay, 1994.

Prange, Gordon W. *At Dawn We Slept*. New York: Penguin, 1981.

_____. *Target Tokyo, the Sorge Spy Ring*. New York: McGraw-Hill, 1984.

Rachlis, Eugene. *They Came to Kill*. New York: Random House, 1961.

Riess, Curt. *Total Espionage*. New York: G. P. Putnam's Sons, 1941.

Reports of General MacArthur. General MacArthur's staff. DC: US Government Printing Office, 1966.

Romulo, Carlos P. *I Saw the Fall of the Philippines*. London: George G. Harrap & Co., 1942.

Russo, Nick, ed. & 41st Infantry Division Association. *41st Infantry Division, Fighting Jungleers*. Paducah, KY: Turner Publishing, 1992.

Scaff, Alvin H. *The Philippine Answer to Communism*. Stanford, CA: Stanford U. Press, 1955.

Schwarzwalder, John. *We Caught Spies*. New York: Duell, Sloan & Pearce, 1946.

Secrets and Spies. Pleasantville, NY: Reader's Digest Association, 1964.

Seth, Ronald. *Secret Servants*. New York: Farrar, Straus & Cudahy, 1957.

Singer, Kurt, ed. *Three Thousand Years of Espionage*. New York: Prentice-Hall, 1948.

Smith, R. H. *OSS—Secret History of America's First CIA*. Berkeley, CA: U of CA Press, 1972.

Spector, Ronald H. *Eagle Against The Sun*. New York: Free Press, 1985.

Spencer, Louise Reid. *Guerrilla Wife*. Chicago: People's Book Club, 1945.

Steinberg, David J. *Philippine Collaboration in World War II*. Ann Arbor: Univ. of MI Press, 1967.

Steinberg, Ralph. *Island Fighting*. Alexandria, VA: Time-Life Books, 1978

_____. *Return to the Philippines*. Alexandria, VA: Time-Life Books, 1980.

Talbot, Carol T. *Escape at Dawn*. Wheaton, IL: Tynedale House, 1988.

Tateishi, John. *And Justice for All*. New York: Random House, 1984.

Thorpe, Elliott R. *East Wind, Rain*. Boston: Gambit Inc., 1969.

Toledano, Ralph de. Spies, Dupes, and Diplomats. New York: Duell, Sloan and Pearce, 1952.

Utinski, Margaret. *"Miss U"*. San Antonio, TX: The Naylor Co., 1948.

Weckerling, John *Japanese Americans Play Vital Role in US Intelligence Service in WWII*. San Francisco: from *Hokubei Mainichi*, 1946.

Willoughby, Charles A. & Chamberlin, John. *MacArthur 1942-1951*. New York: McGraw-Hill, 1954.

Wolfert, Ira. *American Guerrilla in the Philippines*. New York: Simon & Schuster, 1945
_____.*Battle for the Solomons*. Boston: Houghton Mifflin, 1943.

Woodward, C. Vann. *The Battle for Leyte Gulf*. New York: Ballantine, 1947.

Yoshida, Jim, and Hosokawa, Bill. *The Two Worlds of Jim Yoshida*. New York: William Morrow, 1972.

GLOSSARY

A-2 .... Air force equivalent of Army Intelligence Officer
ATIS .... Allied Translators and Interpreters Section
AWOL .... Away Without Leave
Axis .... Alliance of Germany, Italy, Japan and others vs the Allies
CBI .... China-Burma-India Theater of Operations
CIC .... Counter Intelligence Corps
CID .... Counter Intelligence Division; also Criminal Investigation
    Division of Provost Marshal
C-in-C .... Commander in Chief
CIP .... Corps of Intelligence Police, first name of CIC
CIT .... Combat Interrogation Team, term used in CBI only
CG .... Commanding General
CO .... Commanding Officer
FBI .... Federal Bureau of Investigation, headed by J. Edgar Hoover
FCC .... Federal Communications Commission
FFC .... Foreign Funds Control
FNU .... First name unknown
FSS .... Field Security Service, Australian counterpart of CIC
G-2 .... Chief intelligence officer in division and higher units
HQ .... Headquarters
JCP .... Japanese Communist Party
MG .... Military Government
MI .... Military Intelligence
NCAC .... Northern Combat Area Command, used only in CBI
NCICA .... National Counter Intelligence Corps Association
NEI .... Netherlands East Indies
OCS .... Officers' Candidate School
ONI .... Office of Naval Intelligence
OPA .... Office of Price Administration
OSI .... Office of Special Investigations, today's Air Force CIC
OSS .... Office of Strategic Services, headed by "Wild Bill" Donovan
PIO .... Post Intelligence Officer
S-2 .... Intelligence officer in units smaller than division
SIC .... Security Intelligence Corps, headed by the Army's
    Provost Marshal
SWPA .... South Western Pacific Area, MacArthur's territory from
    Australia northwards
USAFFE .... U.S. Armed Forces in the Far East
ZI .... Zone of the Interior

CIC UNIT (DETACHMENT) NUMBERING SYSTEM IN WW2

Units with infantry and airborne divisions had the same number of the division they were attached to: 6th CIC = 6th Infantry Division; 11th CIC = 11th Airborne Division.

Those with armored divisions had 3 digits beginning with 5, ending with the division number (no armored divisions in Pacific).

Those with cavalry divisions, 3 digits beginning with 8, ending with the division number: 801st = 1st Cavalry Division. Also applies to other irregular units.

Units with corps had 3 digits beginning with 2, ending with the corps number: 214th = XIV Corps detachment; 211th = XI Corps.

Those with an army had 3 digits beginning with 3, ending with the army number: 306th = Sixth Army detachment; 308th = Eighth Army.

Units with 3 digits beginning with 4 = areas in Australia, Philippines, Island Commands in South Pacific, field offices in CBI, districts in Central Pacific area, in Advance Sections, Theater HQs, and army groups (but not with group number): 441st = Theater HQ.

Units with Army Air Forces, 3 digits beginning with 6, with Air Force number: 607th = Seventh Air Force.

Logistical and Air Force Special Commands: 3 digits beginning with 7.

Special status, not consistent: 3 digits beginning with 9: 901st.

PHOTOS

First School under its new name of Counter Intelligence Corps was held in January 1942 in Town Tower Club, Chicago; later that year the School moved to the Women's Club, 66 E 11th Street

1942: CIC officer-agents in Noumea, South Pacific
L-R: Wesley Baldwin, Marvin C Goff Jr, John Stapleton
(Photo courtesy of Marvin Goff)

Townsville, N Queensland, Australia, November 1942. First agents stationed in N Queensland, L-R: Arthur Jackson, Duane Williford, Ugo Ceccarelli, Leland Anderson. (Photo courtesy Arthur Jackson)

CBI: An early CIC agent, Leroy T Newland, by a sign in Maymyo, near Mandalay, Burma

Pt. Moresby NG, May 1943
L-R: Leland Anderson, John Choate

487th CIC's "war ship" off Negros Island P.I.
(Photo by James Conway)

SWPA: Officer-agent Blair Labatt
(Photo courtesy J Roy Galloway)

Base A CIC Office, New Quinea: L-R: Art Ziegler, Nichols
(Photo from Arthur Jackson)

1943: Eleanor Roosevelt Thanking CIC Officers for Guarding her on Visit to South Pacific. (Photo courtesy Marvin Goff)

Palma Rosa "Castle," Brisbane, Australia: CIC School, and Quarters for Agents Transferring Through to New Assignments. (Photo courtesy Galloway.)

306th Officer-agent Edwards, Luzon 1945
(Photo Courtesy Tom Ackerman)

441st CIC Agent Gilbert Gonzalez, Tokyo 1945

Downtown Manila P.I., 4 blocks from Pasig River: Special Agent Edwards (Photo courtesy of Robert McMinn, 214th CIC)

Pelelieu Island, Pacific, after Christmas 1944, L-R: Wm F Aimone, CO 81st CIC; Larry Gluckin, CO 41st CIC, on a visit to 81st.

475th CIC, Mindanao P.I.
L-R: R Castor, G Horaitis, Wm Foley, G B Spencer

"Asia," homeless Filipino boy who aided 306th on Leyte and Luzon

*Postwar Japan: Agent Spady Koyama Badly wounded
in the Leyte landing, this loyal ATIS Nisei later entered CIC, serving with
distinction in postwar Japan*

*Postwar Matsuyama, Japan: Ehime CIC HQ, Bansuiso where Emperors
once strolled (Photo courtesy George S Rea)*

Knickerbocker Hotel, Chicago 1992 National CIC Association's 46th Convention, L-R: Arthur S Hurlburt, Duval A Edwards (Photo courtesy Robert MacDonald)

RED APPLE PUBLISHING

Peggy J. Meyer, editor/publisher
PO Box 101, Gig Harbor, WA 98335
206-265-6595, 1-800-245-6595, Fax: 206-265-6596

ORDER FORM

Date _____ Order Nbr. _____

NAME _____

ADDRESS _____

CITY, STATE, ZIP _____

TELEPHONE _____

I would like to order the following books by Duval A. Edwards:

BOOKS	PRICE	QTY.	AMOUNT
SPY CATCHERS OF THE U.S. ARMY in the War With Japan	$17.00	_____	_____
THE GREAT DEPRESSION and A Teenager's Fight to Survive	$11.95	_____	_____
Sub-total			_____
Sales tax (Add 7.9% in WA only)			_____
Shipping & Handling			_____

1-2 books, add $2.00
3-4 books, add $2.50
5-6 books, add $3.00
7-9 books, add $3.50
10+ books, add $4.00

TOTAL _____

Send payment with order form to Red Apple Publishing